Jewish Cooking For Dummies®

D1245167

Ten Commandments of Jewish Cooking

Follow these guidelines, not as directives from the Bible, but as ideas to enhance your pleasure:

- ✔ **Enjoy the cycle of celebration:** Jewish festivals revolve around the table. There are many of them, and they give plenty of chances to celebrate. Shop for tasty foods and plan special treats for the holidays.

- ✔ **Feast with family and friends:** Share the fruits of your kitchen. You and your family will find the holidays more joyous and memorable. Plan potluck meals if you would like to share not just the eating, but the cooking, too.

- ✔ **Use both fresh ingredients and time-savers:** Fresh ingredients in season are the top choice. Shop the best produce markets, and you'll find fruits and vegetables at their peak. When you have no time to cook it all from scratch, enjoy a home-cooked meal anyway. Fit the preparation into your schedule by taking advantage of time-saving equipment and buying fine quality foods at a good deli or bakery.

- ✔ **Remember the healthful aspects of Jewish cooking:** Make wholesome choices when cooking traditional specialties. See how to make them leaner while keeping their character. Try the exuberant flavors of Sephardic cuisine. You'll love the invigorating seasonings of this Mediterranean branch of Jewish cuisine.

- ✔ **Find out how easy kosher menus are to devise:** Check the *Keeping kosher* line in each recipe to see whether a dish is dairy, meat, or pareve. You'll find the principles of keeping kosher easy to get used to.

- ✔ **Use marketing as a chance to expand your knowledge:** Exchange cooking ideas and insights with the vendors and the other shoppers. Make friends with the butcher, the produce person, the baker, and the lox expert at the deli — you'll find out how to get the best and freshest foods.

- ✔ **Discover the wonderful flavors and convenience of long-simmered dishes:** See why many Jewish cooks find that slow-cooked dishes are often the most suitable for busy schedules. You can simmer them unattended or make them ahead, and they'll be ready when you need them.

- ✔ **Be frugal:** Some of the best traditional dishes like cholent were created from the need to use ingredients at hand to their best advantage. Make good use of your foods. Don't forget how useful extra bread and cookie crumbs can be for making tasty treats. Be frugal with your time, too. Plan to have leftovers so that you have the basis of your next meals.

- ✔ **Cook to your taste and try new flavors:** No traditional food is set in time like a dictate from the scriptures. Throughout the ages, cooks have tried new ingredients when they could find them. Today, a much greater variety of foods is available. Be adventurous! If you come across an unfamiliar ingredient in a recipe, don't hesitate to try it. Add seasonings gradually and flavor your food to your own taste.

- ✔ **Have fun and be confident:** As you cook, enjoy the aromas and flavors. Taste as you go along, and, if you're new to cooking, you will gain familiarity with the ingredients. Always remember, if you cook it with love, it will be good!

Famous Jewish Foods

Blintzes: A crepe with a difference, a thin pancake wrapped around a cheese or other sweet or savory fillings.

Bourekas: Filo pastries with fillings of feta cheese, spinach, or potato, from the Mediterranean Jewish tradition.

Challah: Jewish egg bread, usually braided.

Knishes: Turnovers with meat or potato fillings in a pie pastry, from the eastern European Jewish tradition.

Mandelbrot: Twice-baked nut cookies resembling Italian biscotti.

Matzo ball soup: Full-flavored chicken soup with dumplings made of matzo meal.

Noodle kugel: Casserole of egg noodles, eggs, and savory or sweet flavors. A popular version combines the noodles with apples and cinnamon.

Rugelach: Filled cookies made of rich pastry dough rolled around sweet cinnamon-nut or fruit filling.

For Dummies: Bestselling Book Series for Beginners

Jewish Cooking For Dummies®

Celebrating the Jewish Holidays

Holidays are the highlight of the Jewish calendar. Planning them helps the family look forward even more to these happy occasions. Although I give you approximate times, check a current Jewish calendar to find the exact date of upcoming Jewish holidays for this year.

Rosh Hashanah: Jews celebrate Rosh Hashanah, the Jewish New Year, for two days. A variety of foods on the festive dinners symbolizes the hope for a good year. Honey, fruit, and sweet vegetables give the holiday meals their special character. Time of year: September–October.

Yom Kippur: This solemn day of fasting is preceded and followed by feasts. Time of year: September–October.

Sukkot: In early autumn, nature tells everyone that it's time for a party. Sukkot honors nature in several ways, including meals in a picnic-like setting. This harvest holiday celebrates the fresh produce of the season. Cooks make lavish use of vegetables and fruit to enliven the holiday meals. Time of year: September–October.

Hanukkah: This fun-filled festival of lights and latkes, or delectable holiday pancakes, is celebrated for eight days. Potato latkes have become one of the best known specialties of Jewish cooking. Partnered with an array of toppings and other treats, they are the heart of Hanukkah parties. Time of year: November–December.

Purim: This is a joyous festival of gaiety, games, costumes, and sweets. Filled three-corner cookies called hamantaschen are the most notable. Families, friends, and neighbors celebrate by enjoying these treats and sharing them in a cookie exchange, a popular custom of the holiday. Time of year: February–March.

Passover: For the springtime festival of Passover, cooks prepare a great variety of unique holiday foods. A dinner banquet called a Seder begins the celebration. Matzo replaces bread and is the basis for many Passover specialties, from appetizers to desserts. Time of year: March–April.

Shavuot: This two-day holiday is a dairy lover's dream. Cheesecakes and cheese blintzes hold a place of honor on the table. Time of year: May–June.

Shabbat: This holiday gives a chance to celebrate with family and friends every week. Cooks prepare the holiday foods in advance because Shabbat is a day of rest and relaxation. Of the many Shabbat favorites, cholent is one of the best known. This overnight meat and bean casserole appears on Jewish family tables around the world. Time of year: Every Saturday.

Tips on Kosher Cooking

- **Buy kosher meats and birds:** Purchase beef, veal, lamb, and poultry labeled kosher.
- **Choose kosher fish:** Select fish that have fins and scales. These include most fish commonly available in markets.
- **Serve dairy foods and meats separately:** Prepare recipes that include either dairy foods or meat. Check the *Keeping kosher* line in each recipe to remind you. Plan your menus so that they are based on either dairy or meat foods and supplement them with pareve foods.
- **Use pareve foods in all types of meals:** Match pareve foods with dairy or meat foods or serve them on their own. They include eggs, fish, vegetables, fruits, grains, legumes, and seasonings.

For Dummies: Bestselling Book Series for Beginners

Jewish Cooking

FOR

DUMMIES®

Jewish Cooking
FOR
DUMMIES®

by Faye Levy

Hungry Minds™

Best-Selling Books • Digital Downloads • e-Books • Answer Networks • e-Newsletters • Branded Web Sites • e-Learning

New York, NY ◆ Cleveland, OH ◆ Indianapolis, IN

Jewish Cooking For Dummies®

Published by
Hungry Minds, Inc.
909 Third Avenue
New York, NY 10022
www.hungryminds.com
www.dummies.com

Library of Congress Control Number: 00-111275

ISBN: 0-7645-6304-1

Printed in the United States of America

10 9 8 7 6 5 4 3 2

1B/TR/RS/QR/IN

Distributed in the United States by Hungry Minds, Inc.

Distributed by CDG Books Canada Inc. for Canada; by Transworld Publishers Limited in the United Kingdom; by IDG Norge Books for Norway; by IDG Sweden Books for Sweden; by IDG Books Australia Publishing Corporation Pty. Ltd. for Australia and New Zealand; by TransQuest Publishers Pte Ltd. for Singapore, Malaysia, Thailand, Indonesia, and Hong Kong; by Gotop Information Inc. for Taiwan; by ICG Muse, Inc. for Japan; by Intersoft for South Africa; by Eyrolles for France; by International Thomson Publishing for Germany, Austria and Switzerland; by Distribuidora Cuspide for Argentina; by LR International for Brazil; by Galileo Libros for Chile; by Ediciones ZETA S.C.R. Ltda. for Peru; by WS Computer Publishing Corporation, Inc., for the Philippines; by Contemporanea de Ediciones for Venezuela; by Express Computer Distributors for the Caribbean and West Indies; by Micronesia Media Distributor, Inc. for Micronesia; by Chips Computadoras S.A. de C.V. for Mexico; by Editorial Norma de Panama S.A. for Panama; by American Bookshops for Finland.

For general information on Hungry Minds' products and services please contact our Customer Care Department within the U.S. at 800-762-2974, outside the U.S. at 317-572-3993 or fax 317-572-4002.

For sales inquiries and reseller information, including discounts, premium and bulk quantity sales, and foreign-language translations, please contact our Customer Care Department at 800-434-3422, fax 317-572-4002, or write to Hungry Minds, Inc., Attn: Customer Care Department, 10475 Crosspoint Boulevard, Indianapolis, IN 46256.

For information on licensing foreign or domestic rights, please contact our Sub-Rights Customer Care Department at 212-884-5000.

For information on using Hungry Minds' products and services in the classroom or for ordering examination copies, please contact our Educational Sales Department at 800-434-2086 or fax 317-572-4005.

Please contact our Public Relations Department at 212-884-5163 for press review copies or 212-884-5000 for author interviews and other publicity information or fax 212-884-5400.

For authorization to photocopy items for corporate, personal, or educational use, please contact Copyright Clearance Center, 222 Rosewood Drive, Danvers, MA 01923, or fax 978-750-4470.

Hungry Mindsˉ is a trademark of Hungry Minds, Inc.

About the Author

Faye Levy has lived in the capitals of the United States, Israel, and France, the countries with the world's largest Jewish communities, and has written cookbooks in three languages — English, Hebrew, and French. In addition to *Jewish Cooking For Dummies,* Levy is the author of *1,000 Jewish Recipes* (Hungry Minds, Inc.), deemed by *The New York Times* "a culinary bible" and referred to by the *Los Angeles Times* as "the joy of Jewish cooking." She is also the author of *The Low-Fat Jewish Cookbook* (Potter), and *Faye Levy's International Jewish Cookbook* (Warner Books).

A four-time award winner, Levy won the James Beard Cookbook Award for *Faye Levy's International Vegetable Cookbook* and earned awards from the International Association of Culinary Professionals for *Vegetable Creations, Chocolate Sensations,* and *Classic Cooking Techniques.*

Growing up in a traditional Jewish family, Levy began her Jewish schooling at the Hebrew Academy of Washington, D.C., and continued at Hebrew University in Jerusalem and at Tel Aviv University, graduating magna cum laude in sociology and anthropology. Living in Israel and discovering the exciting Mediterranean Jewish cuisine was for young Levy a culinary awakening and a powerful inspiration for her career. Levy then trained as a professional chef at the Parisian cooking school La Varenne, where she spent six delicious years.

For over ten years, Levy has been a nationally syndicated cooking columnist for the *Los Angeles Times Syndicate.* Over the same period, Levy has also been the main cooking columnist for Israel's leading English newspaper, *The Jerusalem Post,* where she focuses on Jewish and kosher cooking. She has written articles on Jewish holiday cooking for many major U.S. newspapers and for *Gourmet* and *Bon Appétit* magazines and enjoys teaching Jewish cooking classes. Faye Levy loves cooking, eating, and celebrating with her husband, Yakir Levy, at their home in Woodland Hills, California.

Dedication

For the loving, inspiring cooks of the Kahn and the Levy Families, especially my mother, Pauline Kahn Luria, and in memory of my mother-in-law, Rachel Levy.

Acknowledgments

I would like to thank all the cooks who contributed so generously to my knowledge over the years. Meeting other food lovers to exchange tips on ingredients, shopping, and cooking has always been a source of pleasure to me. Thanks especially to all those Jewish mothers who shared their family favorites and joyfully explained to me how to prepare them, even when they didn't know how to give precise recipes and even at the time when I didn't know yet how to cook!

Thanks most of all to my mother, Pauline Kahn Luria, who has taught me so much about Jewish cooking and culture, and my mother-in-law, Rachel Levy, who introduced me to the Yemenite branch of Sephardic cooking. I have learned so much from my family as well as my in-laws and their extended families, with Jewish culinary backgrounds from places as diverse as Morocco and India. Special thanks to my sisters-in-law Mati Kahn, Hedva Cohen, Etti Levy, and Nirit Levy for so many delicious dishes. Warm thanks to my brother, Tzvi Kahn, and my brother-in-law Yahalom Levy for the family memories and food tips. Thanks also to my brothers-in-law Prachya Levy and Avi Levi; to my aunt Sylvia Saks, my late uncle Herman Saks, and my husband's aunt Mazal Cohen; to my neighbors Valerie and Hayim Alon; and to my Jerusalem friends Ronnie Venezia and her late mother Suzanne Elmaleh.

I spent enlightening years with Israel's leading cookbook author Ruth Sirkis in Tel Aviv and with world-renowned cookbook author Anne Willan in Paris. Throughout the time that I lived in France, I was also privileged to study with master chefs Fernand Chambrette, Albert Jorant, and Claude Vauguet at La Varenne Cooking School. I thank them wholeheartedly for teaching me the art of cooking.

Later I learned from students in my own cooking classes, too, as well as from fellow shoppers at the food markets. I appreciate their having given me insight into their specialties.

At Hungry Minds, Inc., I am grateful to Linda Ingroia for doing so much to get this book off the ground and to have it produced attractively. Thanks to Kelly Ewing for her valuable editing suggestions and for being flexible with my busy schedule. I also appreciate the helpful comments of recipe tester Emily Nolan. Thanks to photographer David Bishop and to food stylist Roscoe Betsill for the fine presentation of the food, to reviewer Elaine Khosrova, to Patty Santelli for the nutrition analyses, and to Elizabeth Kurtzman for the illustrations.

Finally, thanks to Yakir for helping me to find the right word, the best version of a dish, and for helping to make my 30 years of culinary exploration such a sumptuous feast.

Publisher's Acknowledgments

We're proud of this book; please register your comments through our Online Registration Form located at www.dummies.com.

Some of the people who helped bring this book to market include the following:

Acquisitions, Editorial, and Media Development

Project Editor: Kelly Ewing

Senior Acquisitions Editor: Linda Ingroia

Editorial Administrator: Michelle Hacker

Editorial Manager: Pamela Mourouzis

General Reviewer: Elaine Khosrova

Recipe Tester: Emily Nolan

Nutrition Analyst: Patty Santelli

Photography Design Director: Michele Laseau

Cover and Insert Photographer: David Bishop

Food Stylist: Roscoe Betsill

Prop Stylist: Randi Barritt

Cover Photos: David Bishop

Production

Project Coordinator: Maridee Ennis

Layout and Graphics: Amy Adrian, Jeremey Unger, Erin Zeltner

Proofreaders: Andy Hollandbeck, J. Mahern, Susan Moritz, Nancy Price, Linda Quigley

Indexer: York Production Services, Inc.

Hungry Minds Consumer Reference Group

   Business: Kathleen A. Welton, Vice President and Publisher; Kevin Thornton, Acquisitions Manager

   Cooking/Gardening: Jennifer Feldman, Associate Vice President and Publisher

   Education/Reference: Diane Graves Steele, Vice President and Publisher

   Lifestyles/Pets: Kathleen Nebenhaus, Vice President and Publisher; Tracy Boggier, Managing Editor

   Travel: Michael Spring, Vice President and Publisher; Suzanne Jannetta, Editorial Director; Brice Gosnell, Publishing Director

Hungry Minds Consumer Editorial Services: Kathleen Nebenhaus, Vice President and Publisher; Kristin A. Cocks, Editorial Director; Cindy Kitchel, Editorial Director

Hungry Minds Consumer Production: Debbie Stailey, Production Director

Contents at a Glance

Cartoons at a Glance

By Rich Tennant

"Walt took up baking just after retiring from the Navy. That's why all his blintzes look like submarines."

page 139

"Your latkes need work. The children are mistaking them for dreidels."

page 7

"Why don't you start with some falafel and I'll finish smoking the salmon."

page 293

"Today we celebrate Passover, which commemorates a long journey, and considering how far I had to travel for a good roast of veal, seems most appropriate."

page 41

"You don't have to tell me the kitchen's a spiritual center of the house. God knows I pray for a good matzah Kugel every Passover."

page 225

"I'm using a slow cooker and all you have out is kosher meat. Should my slow cooker also be kosher?"

page 169

"QUIT MOPING-YOU WON FIRST PLACE IN THE MEAT LOAF CATEGORY, AND THAT'S GOOD. I'M THE ONLY ONE WHO KNOWS IT WAS A CARROT CAKE YOU ENTERED"

page 265

Cartoon Information:
Fax: 978-546-7747
E-Mail: richtennant@the5thwave.com
World Wide Web: www.the5thwave.com

Recipes at a Glance

Chicken and Turkey

Cookies

Desserts

Fish

Soups

Vegetables

Table of Contents

Introduction

*J*ewish cooking is an ongoing celebration. Ever since I began learning how to cook, I have found cooking one of the most enjoyable things I can do. Whether it's a holiday dinner or an everyday supper, Jewish meals are an expression of joy. With the relaxed style of this cuisine, the food is a pleasure to prepare as well as to eat. This cuisine is simple to prepare because it's based on dishes created in homes over the ages, rather than inventions of restaurant chefs. Shopping is easy, too, because you don't need a lot of ingredients for each recipe.

When it came to cooking, I was definitely a dummy when I started out. Barely out of my teens, my very traditional prospective mother-in-law gave me immediate motivation to learn. "How can I let my son marry you," she said, eyeing me nervously, "when you don't even know how to cook?" Adding to her challenge, she said, "I knew how to bake pita bread when I was only six years old."

She was willing to teach me, but she cooked by feel and never measured anything. Yet I was determined to gain the skills needed for cooking as soon as possible. Following a cookbook and recipes from friends the best I could, I took my first hesitant steps in the kitchen. I slowly learned by trial and error.

An important discovery for me was that cooking turned out to be fun. When a dish came out good, what an exciting surprise for me! Even better, what a pleasure when my family and friends enjoyed it! I realized that my mother-in-law had done me a big favor.

As a beginner, I made plenty of mistakes, but I never forgot the lessons I learned. I've kept them in mind in writing this book.

About This Book

I have arranged *Jewish Cooking For Dummies* by Jewish holidays and also by soups, main courses, and other main parts of the meal. When you are looking for a traditional holiday dish, turn to the first part. In search of an easy, appealing chicken entree or a scrumptious dessert? Check out the parts devoted to these foods. Of course, you can read the book from cover to cover, to get a good idea of the scope of the Jewish kitchen. You can also see the book as a cooking course, to hone your skills of cooking in general. You also find tips from Jewish mothers throughout the book to make cooking easy.

Foolish Assumptions

You may wonder why this book is called *Jewish Cooking For Dummies*. My mother certainly wondered when I told her I was writing it! The title is not meant to be insulting. Rather, it reflects my approach to cooking. I assume that you are interested in cooking festive Jewish meals, but you may not know the difference between matzo meal and farfel. Or maybe no one has ever explained to you what Ashkenazic and Sephardic Jewish cooking styles are, or why cholent for Shabbat cooks all night.

Jewish Cooking For Dummies provides explanations to these questions and takes the mystery out of keeping kosher. Whether or not you have much experience in the kitchen, you'll find the recipes easy to follow. In this book, I guide you step by step through the preparation of the most famous specialties for celebrating the Jewish holidays. You also can find delicious, wholesome, simple-to-prepare weekday dishes that appear on Jewish tables around the world.

Conventions Used in This Book

In writing the recipes, I have made a few assumptions about the basic ingredients and equipment you will use:

- Butter and margarine are unsalted.
- Eggs are large.
- Salt and pepper are to taste.
- Pepper is freshly ground black pepper unless otherwise noted.
- Flour is all-purpose.
- Sugar is white granulated sugar unless otherwise noted.
- Dairy products, such as milk, sour cream, and butter, are "regular" rather than lowfat or nonfat, unless noted in the recipe or in a headnote or tip.
- Onions are yellow unless otherwise noted.
- Minced garlic is fresh.
- Vegetables are fresh unless otherwise noted.
- Fish, poultry, and meat are fresh. If you bought them frozen, you have thawed them before you begin cooking unless otherwise noted. Thaw frozen foods in the refrigerator, not on the counter.

✔ I take for granted that you have certain basic tools, such as saucepans, skillets, baking dishes, roasting pans, sharp, sturdy knives, a cutting board, wooden spoons, measuring cups, and measuring spoons. I also assume that you have a food processor. If you need a specific pan, I mention it in the special tools section of the recipe.

✔ All temperatures are in Fahrenheit. To convert to Celsius, use this formula: Celsius = (degrees Fahrenheit – 32) x ⅝. For metric conversions, see Appendix C.

✔ All herbs are fresh unless dried herbs are specified.

✔ Vegetable oil can be canola oil, grape seed oil, safflower oil, or any other oil except olive oil. It can also be from a bottle labeled simply "vegetable oil." Oil for brushing the pan is vegetable oil unless otherwise specified.

✔ When a recipe has a range of oil or another ingredient, the nutritional analysis assumes the smaller amount of oil.

✔ When a recipe has a range of servings, the nutritional analysis relates to the larger number of portions made from the recipe.

✔ When a recipe gives the yield in number of pieces as well as number of servings, the nutritional analysis is per piece.

How This Book Is Organized

Jewish Cooking For Dummies is like two books in one. The first is devoted to the Jewish holidays and includes helpful information on customs as well as festive recipes. The second part follows standard cookbook formats with recipes on all types of foods from appetizers to main courses to desserts. You can also take recipes from this section to supplement your holiday menus.

I have labeled each recipe according to whether it is Dairy, Meat, or Pareve, so you can use the book to easily create your own kosher menus.

Part 1: Jewish Food Origins: From Divinely Inspired to Downright Delicious

Part I tells you what Jewish cooking is and where it came from. Use it to identify Jewish dishes that you may have come across or heard about. In this part, you appreciate the richness and variety of the Jewish culinary experience. You also understand why Jewish cooking has so many substyles — after all, Jews have lived in so many regions of the globe. This section is full of information on Jewish ingredients and marketing. Here's where you turn to find out about the basics of keeping kosher and what it means for menu planning.

Part II: The Holidays

The major holidays of the Jewish calendar and their specialties are covered here. You find the time-honored dishes served during the week-long holiday of Passover and how to cook for this holiday. Here also are dishes perfect for a sweet beginning to the New Year and recipes to help fortify you before the fast of Yom Kippur. There are festive dishes for celebrating the holidays of Sukkot, Hanukkah, Purim, Shavuot, and the weekly holiday of Shabbat.

Part III: Beginning the Feast

This part covers appetizers and first courses of all sorts, as well as dishes that are perfect for snacks and parties. You find spreads, dips, and pastry appetizers great for celebrations. Here, too, are the hearty, warming soups for which Jewish cooking is so famous.

Part IV: The Heart of the Celebration

In this part, you find the main courses. First are the brunch type main courses, like blintzes and kugels, which often include dairy foods. In this part, you see the Jewish way with fish, chicken, and meats and how they're used in menus for special occasions as well as during the week. You discover many time-tested tips for making these entrees easy to prepare and to fit them into busy schedules.

Part V: Grains and Vegetables: Side Dishes and Pareve Entrees

This part covers all the side dishes but makes it clear that they're not secondary to the meal. In pareve menus, for example, many of them can play the role of entree, too. You discover how to prepare scrumptious kugels, a highlight of any meal. You also find recipes for delicious dishes from grains and pastas, as well as tasty, healthful legume dishes. A place of honor is reserved for vegetables on many Jewish tables, and you see how to make these nutrient-packed foods tempting for the whole family.

Part VI: Sweet Noshes

When you try some of these cakes, cookies, and sweet pastries, you'll see why Jewish baked goods are so famous. Those in this part are easy to make, and you'll find them a good introduction to the world of Jewish baking.

Part VII: The Part of Tens

Here you find ten tasty kosher menus, ten commandments of Jewish cooking, and ten useful Web sites for exploring Jewish food and culture further.

Icons Used in This Book

Throughout the book, I include five icons to highlight certain points that make food preparation easier or that deepen your understanding of Jewish cooking. Here's what they mean:

This icon gives you hints on easier, more efficient ways to cook or to prepare food ahead.

For keeping kosher, this icon suggests tasty ways you can include the dish in kosher menus or substitutions you can make in the recipe so that it can fit in certain kinds of kosher meals.

This icon explains why a certain custom grew up in the Jewish kitchen or clarifies a point that has its background in history.

When you need to be careful of possible dangers in the kitchen, as in deep frying, this icon warns you. It also alerts you to avoid taking a step that could cause a dish to be a flop.

In case you forget a guideline about cooking or keeping kosher, this icon serves as a reminder.

In addition, this little icon — ☺ — marks that the recipe is vegetarian. Vegetarian dishes are popular in the Jewish kitchen because plant-based foods are pareve. In addition, meatless dishes play an important role on traditional menus of several Jewish holidays.

Where to Go from Here

You can start reading this book anywhere. Want to find out what a knish is? Or where Sephardic Jews came from? Interested in keeping a kosher kitchen? Start with Part I. Is Passover coming up and you would like to prepare a Seder? Start with Chapter 8. Want a warming soup for supper? Read about soups in Chapter 12. Do you crave some tasty homemade rugelach as a treat with your coffee or tea? Begin leafing through Chapter 20. Just relax and enjoy!

Part I
Jewish Food Origins: From Divinely Inspired to Downright Delicious

The 5th Wave   By Rich Tennant

"Your latkes need work. The children are mistaking them for dreidels."

In this part . . .

*H*ere I survey the major Jewish festivals, most popular Jewish specialties, and special ingredients used in Jewish cooking. You find out what kosher food is all about. In this part, I also introduce the different styles of Jewish cooking and flavoring.

Chapter 1

Understanding Jewish Cooking

In This Chapter

▶ Discovering what lies behind Jewish cooking

▶ Enjoying the Jewish cycle of celebration

▶ Finding out how keeping kosher affects food choices and menu planning

● ●

In this brief overview, you discover what lies behind the guidelines of Jewish cooking. I give you a survey of the culinary culture of the Jewish home and the central role that holiday feasts play in family life. You see how food is selected, prepared, and enjoyed for everyday meals and for the many festive occasions on the Jewish calendar.

Tracing the Roots of the Jews

Jews have lived in many countries around the world. A quick glance at their ancient origins and history reveals what lies behind their holiday celebrations.

Where Judaism began

Judaism began in the eastern Mediterranean area. Some trace its origin to the Hebrew tribe living in Egypt. The Bible relates that the *Hebrews,* as the Jews were originally called, were slaves in ancient Egypt. Under the leadership of Moses, the scriptural account continues, they escaped from slavery and wandered in the Sinai Desert on their way to freedom in the Promised Land — Israel. These experiences are central themes of three major Jewish holidays — Passover, Shavuot, and Sukkot.

During their long sojourn in the desert, the Hebrews received the Ten Commandments and the *Torah,* also known as the Pentateuch, the first five books of the Old Testament. The Torah is the basis for Jewish religious law.

The age-old practice of keeping *kosher,* or observing the special dietary rules of Judaism, is outlined in the Torah.

Where modern Jewish cooking came from

In the course of history, invading armies vied for the Fertile Crescent. Eventually, the Romans conquered Israel and dispersed the Jews throughout their empire. This forced migration led to Jewish people living in many countries around the world.

In each country, the Jews found new foods instead of many of those they were used to. Some required different cooking methods. Jewish cooks adapted them to their dietary rules and developed new dishes to celebrate the holidays. After many years, the culinary styles of the Jews in many of these areas differed significantly from their relatives in other lands. A major distinction arose between the *Ashkenazic,* or eastern and central European, and the *Sephardic,* or Mediterranean styles (see Chapter 3).

Living by the Jewish Holidays

Holidays are the highlight of the Jewish calendar. Observing the holidays and preparing for them drive the daily schedule in the traditional home. Naturally, food plays a big part in these celebrations.

Principal festivals

The most important Jewish holidays, in their chronological order, are

- **Rosh Hashanah,** the Jewish New Year, which is celebrated for two days in September or October. Signature holiday ingredients include honey and other sweet foods.

- **Yom Kippur,** the Day of Atonement, a day of fasting and repentance. The holiday takes place in September or October. The fast is preceded and followed by traditional meals.

- **Sukkot,** the Feast of Tabernacles, a holiday expressing thanks for the harvest and honoring nature. The holiday is celebrated in a *Sukkah,* a special temporary hut with a leafy roof.

- **Hanukkah,** the Festival of Lights, an eight-day holiday celebrated with candles, gifts, and latkes, or pancakes usually made of potatoes. The festival usually occurs in December.

- **Purim,** the holiday of deliverance from danger, celebrated with costumes and sweet treats, notably three-cornered filled cookies called hamantaschen. Purim takes place in late February or March.

- **Passover,** the festival that honors freedom by commemorating the exodus of the Hebrew slaves from ancient Egypt. The signature food is *matzo,* an unleavened cracker-like bread that replaces leavened bread. Also known as the festival of spring, the eight-day holiday takes place in March or April.

- **Shavuot,** the holiday commemorating the receiving of the Torah. Dairy foods, notably cheesecakes and cheese blintzes, figure in the most popular holiday specialties. Shavuot occurs in May or June.

- **Shabbat,** the weekly festival, celebrated every Friday night and Saturday. Some popular foods include challah, chicken soup, and the overnight meat casserole called *cholent.*

If you're wondering why Passover sometimes comes out in March and sometimes in April, here is the reason: The Jewish calendar is based on the cycles of the moon, not the sun. That's why the Jewish holidays don't always appear in the same month of our usual calendar.

In the lunar calendar, each month begins with the new moon and lasts 29 or 30 days. Like the solar calendar, it has 12 months, but the total number of days is 354 instead of 365. To catch up from time to time and keep each Jewish holiday in its right season, a thirteenth month, or *leap month,* is added every two or three years.

To see when each holiday takes place, check out Table 1-1.

Table 1-1	Jewish Holidays and Their Months
Holiday	*Month*
Rosh Hashanah	September–October
Yom Kippur	September–October
Sukkot	September–October
Hanukkah	November–December
Purim	February–March
Passover	March–April
Shavuot	May–June

Family participation

Celebrating with the whole family is central to observing Jewish holidays. Naturally, enjoying the holiday meals together is important. For major holidays, the extended family gets together. Often, the table for Passover, Rosh Hashanah, or Sukkot is set for quite a large group.

Festivals determine the rhythm of activities of the entire households. When possible, parents buy new clothes for their children and use their best dishes for the holiday. Preparations in the kitchen do not involve solely the person in charge of cooking. Parents encourage children to participate. Often, they will help bake cookies or holiday bread or set the table. Grandparents contribute their cooking experience, too, by preparing their specialties. A popular custom today in busy families is to prepare *potluck dinners* where friends and relatives bring their own rendition of holiday specialities to share with the other guests.

The weekly menu cycle

Looking forward to the next holiday is a major consideration in menu planning. Naturally, the meals for holidays are more lavish than for everyday. Well in advance of the holiday, each family begins getting ready for the celebration. This includes the weekly holiday, Shabbat.

- ✔ **Planning weekend meals:** During most of the year, the focus of the week's menus among observant families is preparing for Shabbat. Shopping involves saving the most prized ingredients for the weekly holiday. Preparation may begin as early as Wednesday, proceeds in earnest on Thursday, and is completed early on Friday. Then everyone enjoys the festive meals on Friday night and Saturday.

- ✔ **Planning weekday meals:** Jewish cooking is for every day of the year, not just for holidays. After the family has feasted for Shabbat or other holidays, cooks make use of the leftovers for the meals for the next few days. Like efficient cooks everywhere, most follow the custom of planning to have extra food, to form the basis of later meals. Extra roast chicken from Shabbat dinner (see Chapter 10) may be made into a casserole or tossed with a pasta dish. New soups might be prepared based on meat or chicken broth from the holidays.

Inventive cooks are always coming up with new ideas for using up leftovers, depending on what they have at hand. Being creative is not a modern trend — it has been the custom in kitchens from time immemorial.

Keeping Kosher

Kashrut, or keeping kosher, is the guiding principle behind time-honored Jewish food traditions and remains so in observant homes today. Following these dietary laws is a basic precept of Judaism and is considered a divine commandment that was given to the Hebrews on Mount Sinai. Behind many of the rules is the desire to have compassion for animals and reverence for life.

Over the years, the basic framework, which is outlined in the Torah, has been interpreted and expanded by the rabbis. The rules of keeping kosher involve how you select food, how you cook it, and how you plan your menus.

Keeping kosher requires careful selection of meat, poultry, fish, and dairy products, as I outline in the following sections. It also involves keeping meat and dairy foods completely separate.

In addition to meat and dairy foods, a third category of foods, called *pareve,* exists. Pareve foods are neutral from a kosher standpoint, neither dairy nor meat. They include produce, grains, eggs, and fish. On kosher menus, you can serve pareve foods with either meat or dairy.

All the recipes in this book are kosher. To make menu planning easy, each one is labeled as meat, dairy, or pareve.

Keeping kosher also involves kitchen organization. In the homes of Jews who are Orthodox, or the most devout, there are separate dishes, pots, and cooking utensils for meat meals and for dairy ones. Cooks and members of the household are careful not to confuse them! The exception is dishes made of glass, which you can use for any meals, because, unlike other materials, glass is considered not to absorb foods.

Reading labels

Kosher cooks are avid label readers. They want to make sure that pastries, other baked goods, tortillas, and canned foods do not contain lard, which is made from pork.

Many also verify that the food is certified as kosher, which means it has been inspected by a rabbi or a kashrut inspector. Certification appears on the packaging label as a logo or stamp of a recognized certifying organization or a qualified rabbi.

The Union of Orthodox Jewish Congregations is the best known of these organizations. Its symbol is a U with a circle around it. Many nationally available foods carry its stamp of approval. Other organizations vary from one city to another. You can check with a local rabbi to find out the names of those in your area.

Choosing meat and poultry

The Torah defines kosher animals as those who chew their cud and have split hooves. Beef, veal, and lamb are kosher; pork is not. Poultry is also kosher.

How the meat is butchered also determines whether it is kosher. Butchers must be specially trained so they know how to prepare the meats and which cuts are kosher.

Shooting animals and poultry makes them not kosher. Thus, wild game is not kosher.

Before you can eat meat or poultry, it must be koshered, or salted. Salting removes as much blood from the meat as possible. Next, the meat is rinsed thoroughly to remove the excess salt.

If you are concerned about sodium, you can soak the meat or poultry in water for about 30 minutes before cooking it. You can also discuss the situation with a rabbi, who may suggest other solutions.

Coarse salt is used in the koshering process. It is known as kosher salt. Today many chefs use it for seasoning as well. They prefer kosher salt to table salt for its pure taste and coarser texture.

When I was growing up, my mother always koshered the meat at home. Today most kosher butchers and food packagers take care of the salting and soaking, making preparation much easier.

Livers are koshered by being salted and grilled until cooked through, instead of being soaked. Jewish cooks kosher livers at home, usually as the first step in a recipe. (See the recipe "Almost Old-Fashioned Chopped Liver" in Chapter 11.)

Kosher meat is available at kosher butcher shops and grocery stores. You can find packaged kosher poultry fresh or frozen at many supermarkets. It is labeled as kosher and certified.

Choosing dairy foods

Most dairy foods are kosher, unless they contain meat. You may find this fact surprising. However, a frequent step in the process of making hard cheeses, such as Parmesan, involves using a product called *rennet* to help coagulate the milk. Traditionally, rennet is an animal product and is considered meat, and therefore its presence makes cheese not kosher.

For kosher and vegetarian cheeses, other forms of rennet are available. Thus, you can find a variety of firm kosher cheeses at the market. You see them at kosher grocery stores, natural foods stores, and many supermarkets.

Another product that can make certain dairy products nonkosher is *gelatin,* which is made from the bones of animals. Gelatin is added to many yogurts and other dairy products. Yogurts made with other forms of gelatin list kosher gelatin in their ingredient list.

Choosing fish

Kosher fish must have scales and fins. Salmon, trout, tuna, sea bass, cod, haddock, halibut, flounder, sole, whitefish, and most other fish commonly available in markets are kosher.

Shellfish, mollusks, and squid are not kosher. *Surimi,* or imitation shellfish, can be kosher if it does not contain shellfish extract.

Monkfish, which does not have scales, is not kosher. Neither is eel.

Choosing other foods

Fruit, vegetables, legumes, and grains are kosher. Processed foods such as cake mixes and canned soups are kosher if they do not contain nonkosher components. For example, canned vegetable soups may contain chicken broth.

Many people feel that it's important that bread and wine be labeled as kosher because both are blessed at the beginning of holiday feasts.

Planning your menus

The principle of keeping meat and dairy foods separate determines how you cook and how you organize the dishes in a menu. Meat and dairy foods may not appear together in a single dish or even in the same menu. For example, you can't follow a chicken main course with a cheesecake for dessert.

Some people also wait a specified number of hours after eating meat before eating dairy. In many Orthodox families, the wait is six hours.

You can find kosher menus for holidays and every day in Chapter 22. In addition, I provide Menu Maven tips throughout the book to guide you in serving the recipes in kosher menus.

There are three types of kosher menus: those based on meat, those based on dairy foods, and those that are pareve.

- ✔ **Meat menus:** Serving meat in any form on a menu makes it into a meat meal. The meat may be the main course or may appear in an appetizer or a side dish. Meat products used in cooking also are included. If you make vegetable soup, for example, with chicken broth as an ingredient, the meal becomes a meat meal.

- ✔ **Dairy menus:** Any dairy product makes a meal into a dairy menu. Dairy products include such obvious candidates as milk and cheese as well as cakes made with butter.

- ✔ **Pareve menus:** You can serve pareve menus and dishes with meat, with dairy, or on their own. Pareve foods can be loosely described as vegetarian, but they do not include dairy foods and they do include fish and eggs. Fish is an important pareve food. For this reason fish appetizers are popular starters for festive menus, whether of meat or dairy. Other pareve foods are eggs, vegetables, grains, and fruit.

Chapter 2

Ingredients, Tools, and Techniques for Jewish Cooking

....

In This Chapter

▶ Shopping for Jewish ingredients

▶ Finding out which foods lend their special flavors to Jewish cooking, from herbs to condiments to grains

▶ Arming yourself with the basic tools and techniques to make it easy in the kitchen

....

*I*n this chapter, I highlight foods, tools, and cooking processes used often in the Jewish kitchen. You become acquainted with a few that may be new to you. I also offer tips on shopping for, preparing, and using foods, ranging from cumin to barley. Knowing about flavors will make your cooking a pleasure.

Most of the ingredients and cooking methods of Jewish cooking are probably familiar to you. Here, you find insights from Jewish cooks on how to use flavorings you already know in different ways, to enhance your cooking and to make your meal preparation easy. You also discover a few basic techniques for preparing foods that appear frequently on the Jewish table. I cover the preparation of any special ingredients in other chapters in the book.

Shopping to Stock Your Jewish Cooking Pantry

You can find most of the foods you need at the supermarket. Many supermarkets carry Jewish foods in several of their sections. In most markets, you can find such ingredients as Jewish-style egg noodles, soup bases, wine, and matzo in the aisle labeled kosher foods. You see refrigerated condiments, deli meats, and smoked fish in the market's deli section. Look for kosher chickens in the freezer section and cheeses and other dairy products in the dairy section. In well-stocked markets, you can find Jewish breads as well.

For a greater array of ingredients and a more interesting selection of each type of food, try these stores:

- ✔ **Gourmet and natural-foods stores:** Often, these shops carry a larger selection of kosher foods than the usual markets. Here, you can find many valuable ingredients for pareve cooking. (See Chapters 1 and 18.) You also can find a greater selection of kosher cheeses as well as kosher poultry, both fresh and frozen.

- ✔ **Jewish and kosher markets:** In communities with large Jewish populations, you will find that these types of stores carry the most extensive variety of foods for Jewish cooking. The better markets feature kosher butchers, which carry fresh meat and poultry and will often cut it to order. These markets also have many dairy products, baked goods, deli foods, pickles, prepared pastry doughs, and other kosher convenience foods.

- ✔ **Middle Eastern and Greek markets:** These stores carry many of the foods needed for Sephardic cooking, such as pita bread, spices, and grains.

- ✔ **Delicatessens:** In these shops, especially Jewish ones, you can find a variety of smoked fish, kosher deli meats, kosher cheeses, pickles, and other condiments.

- ✔ **Jewish bakeries:** Here, you can find the best selection of fresh baked challah, bagels, Jewish rye bread, pumpernickel, rolls, and other breads loved on the Jewish table.

Shopping at specialty markets is a fun learning experience because of the people you meet. Many are happy to give you hints and compare notes. Ask questions and exchange recipes!

Flavoring with Spices, Herbs, and Condiments

Jewish cooking, both Ashkenazic and Sephardic (see Chapter 3), depends on judicious seasoning for its flavor. Familiar flavorings like salt, pepper, paprika, cayenne pepper, onion, and garlic are important. Like all good cooks, you should always taste and adjust any seasonings before serving.

Here are some seasonings used in Jewish cooking. They are not necessarily standard ingredients in the typical American pantry, but if you have experimented with ethnic styles of cooking, you probably have used many of them.

✔ Kosher salt is a coarse salt originally used in the special process of making meat and poultry kosher (see Chapter 1). It is also good for seasoning and many prefer its taste to that of table salt because it is pure and contains no additives, which can give table salt a chemical flavor. Because it has larger grains than table salt, it is convenient for salting large amounts of water that you need to cook such foods as pasta and vegetables.

✔ Cilantro, or fresh coriander, is very popular in Israeli and Sephardic cooking. It lends its distinctive character to salads, soups, stews, and salsas. Be sure to use it fresh. When you chop cilantro, you can use the stems also. They are tender and have plenty of flavor. (Cilantro and other herbs are shown in Figure 2-1.)

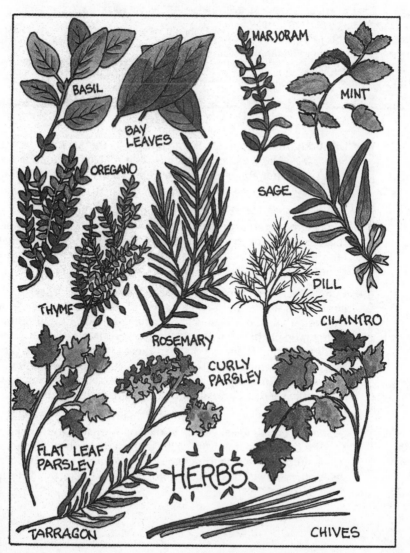

Figure 2-1:
A variety of herbs.

Horseradish

Horseradish is a long root vegetable with a hot, spicy taste. It is a popular condiment in the Ashkenazic kitchen, where its most common use is to accompany gefilte fish (see Chapter 14). Bottled red horseradish, made by blending the horseradish with beets, is the type most families prefer. You can find jars of ready-to-eat red horseradish at the deli section of many markets.

For Passover, fresh horseradish has a special place on the Seder plate (see Chapter 8). To prepare it, you buy a fresh horseradish root, peel it, and grate it coarsely on the large holes of a grater or with the grating disk of a food processor. In either case, open a window and avert your face; the fumes can be overpowering. Fresh horseradish is also good as a condiment. You can find it at Jewish and eastern European markets and at some supermarkets, especially in the spring.

Both fresh and bottled horseradish lose their pungency rapidly. Replace the lid on the jar of bottled horseradish as soon as you've removed the amount you like and refrigerate it promptly.

You can find Passover foods and recipes in Chapter 8, where you can also find descriptions of special ingredients for the holiday.

✔ Dill, both dried and fresh, is much loved in the Ashkenazic kitchen (see Figure 2-1). Many use it to perfume their matzo ball soup as well as a variety of other soups and stews. Sephardic Jews love fresh dill also and use it extensively, as do Israelis.

✔ Italian parsley, also known as flat-leaf parsley (see Figure 2-1), is a great favorite throughout the Jewish kitchen. Sephardic cooks, especially those from Morocco and the eastern Mediterranean, use Italian parsley lavishly, adding it by handfuls, not by tablespoons. When preparing it, remove the stems before chopping the leaves.

✔ Cumin is a favorite spice in the Sephardic and Israeli styles of Jewish cooking, as well as in the Mexican-Southwest U.S. kitchen. (Cumin, along with other spice options, is shown in Figure 2-2.) Cumin's pungent taste is dramatically better when it is fresh. For the best flavor, buy the cumin seeds and grind them as you need them in a spice grinder. If this suggestion isn't convenient, try to buy ground cumin in small amounts at a grocery story with a large turnover. You can find ground cumin everywhere, and whole seeds in Jewish, Middle Eastern, and Indian shops.

✔ Turmeric, also shown in Figure 2-2, is a bright orange spice favored in Sephardic cooking, especially in the southern Mediterranean and Middle Eastern branches. If you add a little turmeric to your chicken soup, it will acquire a lovely, warm golden hue and good taste. Turmeric is what gives curry powder its orange color. You can find ground turmeric at most markets.

✔ Chilies and hot sauce are popular in some versions of Sephardic cooking, especially the North African and Middle Eastern branches. Both fresh and dried chilies flavor soups and stews in these styles of Jewish cuisine.

In Israeli and some kosher markets, you can buy a very hot salsa called *zehug,* which is made of chilies and garlic. This bottled salsa is available in the refrigerated section of these markets. People often set some zehug on the table as a condiment for eating with soups or stews, for those who want extra kick, rather than adding it directly to the pot.

Figure 2-2:
A variety of spices.

Cooking with Beans, Grains, and Pasta

Legumes and grains figure prominently on the Jewish table. The Overnight Shabbat Stew known as *cholent* (see Chapter 10) is one of the most celebrated specialties and often contains both beans and grains. These foods also constitute the foundation for numerous pareve dishes.

Beans

Jewish cooks use all sorts of beans. White beans and chickpeas, also known as *garbanzo beans,* appear most frequently in traditional recipes. Lentils are also well liked, as are split peas. To save time, you can use canned beans in many dishes.

For more variety and better quality, cook dried legumes when you have a chance. (See the section "Using Techniques to Make Cooking Easy," later in this chapter.) Usually, you can find a greater selection of beans, both canned and dried, in Middle Eastern and Indian markets and in natural-foods stores than in the typical supermarket.

Dried beans are best when they are not old. Check whether packaged beans have a sell-by date. If you're buying them in bulk, choose a shop where people buy beans often.

Pastas and grains

In supermarkets and Jewish groceries, you can find a variety of egg noodles, which are useful for traditional Ashkenazic cooking. Cooks favor the finest ones for soups and medium or wide ones for kugels and other pasta dishes. *Couscous,* a tiny-grained pasta, is a great favorite in Moroccan and other styles of Sephardic cuisine.

Rice is the most popular grain staple in Jewish cooking, especially on the Sephardic table. Many prefer the wonderfully aromatic Indian basmati rice, which you can find in some supermarkets as well as in Israeli, Indian, and Middle Eastern groceries.

Kasha, or buckwheat groats, may be less familiar to you. It is cooked as a side dish in Polish, Russian, and other Ashkenazic cuisines. Kasha has an assertive flavor that goes well with meat and poultry and is often paired with pasta as well. Look for it in Jewish grocery stores and some supermarkets.

Bulgur wheat is a nutty tasting form of cracked wheat popular as an accompaniment in Middle Eastern Jewish cooking. You can find it in Israeli and Mediterranean grocery stores and some supermarkets.

Choosing Dairy Foods and Meats

Among the fresh cheeses, such as cream cheese and cottage cheese, many of the readily available brands at the supermarket are kosher. You can find farmers' cheese and other fresh cheeses at kosher markets.

Firm kosher cheeses such as Swiss and Parmesan are available at some delicatessens and at the dairy sections of supermarkets in communities with large Jewish populations. To find a good selection, go to a kosher market.

You can buy kosher poultry, especially chickens, turkeys, and Cornish hens, at many supermarkets and some natural-foods stores. Often, they are in the frozen foods department. To find them fresh, go to a kosher butcher shop, where you can also find ducks, geese, beef, lamb, and veal.

Getting to Know Special Vegetables

Here are a few vegetables that you may not have used. They are tasty and easy to prepare and worth adding to your menus.

Beets

Beets are used frequently in the kosher kitchen to make salads and soups. These root vegetables are easy to use and taste much better when you cook them fresh rather than using them from a can.

Good quality produce markets offer beets with their greens still attached. Opt for these over beets that have no greens. Choose beets with unblemished roots and with the freshest looking leaves.

You'll find it useful to consider beets and their greens as two separate vegetables. When a recipe calls for the root part, save the greens and cook them like spinach. Note that the greens keep only a few days and the root keeps longer.

Leeks

Leeks are popular throughout the Jewish kitchen for flavoring soups and stocks. They look like very large green onions. Some cooks use leeks instead of onions because leeks have a more delicate taste and aroma. Others prefer to use both. The flavor they contribute is most appealing in chicken as well as vegetable soups. In many Sephardic kitchens, braised leeks are popular, too, and are a traditional holiday dish.

When preparing leeks, be sure to clean them properly. See the section "Using Techniques to Make Cooking Easy," later in this chapter.

Parsley root

Parsley roots resemble parsnips in appearance and look like thin white carrots. Jewish cooks add them to chicken and meat soups, along with carrots, onions, and celery, to contribute a good taste. The flavor is a pungent combination of carrot, parsley, and celery.

Equipping Your Kitchen with Tools

For Jewish cooking, you need mostly the equipment used for basic cooking, such as good quality, sharp knives, slotted spoons, a colander, heavy saucepans like those shown in Figure 2-3, and baking pans in sizes that are convenient for you.

Figure 2-3:
Heavy
saucepans
work best.

Instead of following old-fashioned recipes that took grandmothers hours to prepare, you can take advantage of several tools that can help you prepare ingredients much more speedily. A food processor, blender, and electric mixer are the most useful.

A few other implements I find helpful:

- A hand-held, or *immersion blender,* to quickly puree soups and sauces with minimal cleanup
- A whisk for blending dressings in a bowl or sauces in a pot
- A peppermill for grinding black or white peppercorns to make freshly ground pepper (see Figure 2-4)

✔ A colander to efficiently drain cooked vegetables, pastas, and grains

✔ Slotted spoons for lifting a cooked ingredient out of its pan after boiling or frying it, when you want to leave the cooking liquid or oil in the pan

✔ A box grater that can stand on its own to grate ingredients directly into a bowl or onto a plate (see Figure 2-5)

Figure 2-4: A peppermill isn't a must, but it does improve flavor.

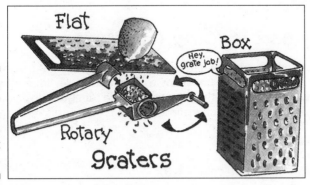

Figure 2-5: A box grater that stands on its own is the best choice.

In observant Jewish homes where the rules of keeping kosher are strictly observed, the same knives and saucepans are not used for meat and dairy foods. Therefore, many people have two of each of the major implements. They keep them in separate sections of their cupboard and try to purchase some that look slightly different — for example, with different handles. They label any tools that resemble each other to avoid confusion (see Chapter 1).

Using Techniques to Make Cooking Easy

Several cooking techniques used often in the book involve preparing vegetables and legumes. Knowing how to prepare tomatoes, peppers, greens, leeks, and legumes is helpful for making a great variety of dishes. You also can find useful tips on using box graters and seasoning kosher meats and poultry to create savory soups and entrees.

Peeling garlic

To peel garlic, crush each clove by holding a chef's knife flat above the clove and pounding on the knife with your fist to lightly crush the clove. This technique loosens the papery skin, and you can easily remove it, as shown in Figure 2-6.

Figure 2-6:
Peeling
garlic.

Use the side of a large chef's knife to press down on a garlic clove and loosen the papery skin...

(I'm free!)

Peeling and seeding tomatoes

Peel and seed tomatoes, shown in Figure 2-7, when you want a very smooth sauce or soup without skins and seeds to mar its texture. Squeezing out the seeds also removes much of the juice so that the tomatoes give you a thicker sauce. If you like, strain the juice and refrigerate it for drinking.

To peel tomatoes:

1. **Fill a large bowl with cold water.**

2. **Cut green core from each tomato with a sharp paring knife.**

3. **Turn each tomato over and slit skin on bottom of tomato in an X-shaped cut.**

4. **Put tomatoes in a saucepan containing enough boiling water to cover them generously and boil tomatoes 10 to 15 seconds or until their skin begins to pull away from their flesh.**

   Usually, the tomato's skin first pulls away in the spot where you slit it.

5. **With a slotted spoon, immediately remove tomatoes from the boiling water and put them in the bowl of cold water.**

   Leave for a few seconds so that they cool.

6. **Remove tomatoes from water and pull off their skins.**

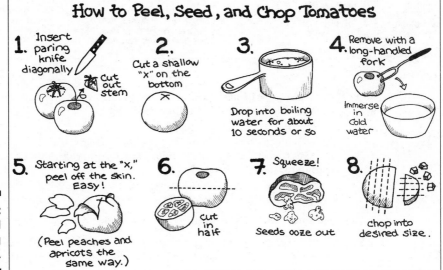

Figure 2-7: Peeling and seeding tomatoes.

To seed tomatoes:

1. **Cut tomatoes in half horizontally.**

2. **Hold each tomato half over a bowl, cut side down, and squeeze tomato to remove the seeds and juice.**

Grilling and peeling peppers

Grilling or broiling peppers gives them a wonderful taste by accenting their sweetness. This simple technique, shown in Figure 2-8, also makes them tender and loosens their skins so that you can peel them easily.

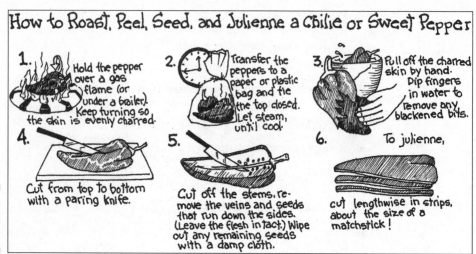

Figure 2-8:
Preparing a
pepper.

After the peppers are grilled, you put them in a bowl or bag and enclose them so that they steam. Then you take their peel right off!

Peel peppers when you want to serve them as an appetizer, to add them to salads or pasta dishes, or to puree them in order to make sauces. Here's an easy way to peel them.

1. **Leave peppers whole, with their stems still on.**

2. **Put peppers on grill or on broiler rack about 4 inches from heat.**

3. **Grill or broil peppers, turning every 4 or 5 minutes with tongs, until their skins are blistered and charred, about 15 to 20 minutes.**

4. **With tongs, transfer peppers to a bowl and cover them tightly.**

   Or you can put them in a bag and close the bag. A plastic bag works most easily, but you can use paper if you prefer.

   Some people rinse the grilled peppers to make it easier to remove the seeds and any bits of peel remaining. Avoid doing this because you'll make the peppers watery and lose some of their wonderful roasted flavor!

5. **Let peppers stand until cool enough to handle, about 10 minutes.**

6. **Peel peppers using a paring knife.**

   Be careful when peeling the peppers. They are still hot inside and may contain very hot liquid.

7. Discard pepper top, seeds, and ribs.

8. Drain well and pat dry.

Avoiding gritty greens

Fresh spinach and other greens, especially those for cooking, are often sandy or muddy. Here's the best way to rinse them to make sure that they're clean.

1. **Put greens in a large bowl of cold water.**

   Make sure that they are totally immersed.

2. **Swirl greens around to make sure that water reaches all the leaves.**

3. **Lift greens from water into a colander and then drain water.**

   If water is sandy, replace with new water and rinse leaves again.

4. **Repeat rinsing, if necessary, until you don't find sand on the bottom of the bowl.**

5. **Lift greens into colander and let excess water drain.**

   If using the greens for a salad, dry them by whirling them in a salad spinner or pat them dry.

Cleaning leeks

Leeks can be sandy and need to be cleaned thoroughly, as shown in Figure 2-9. Here's an efficient way to do it:

1. **With a sharp knife, split leeks lengthwise.**

2. **Start cutting in white part of leek about 1 inch from root end, moving the knife upward towards the green end.**

   Leave the root end attached so that the leek doesn't fall apart.

3. **Holding the uncut part of each leek, dip leek repeatedly in plenty of cold water; either a sinkful or a large bowl of water.**

4. **Check between the leek layers to be sure no sand is left; if any sand remains, soak the leeks in cold water for a few minutes and then rinse them thoroughly and drain.**

5. **Cut off leek roots.**

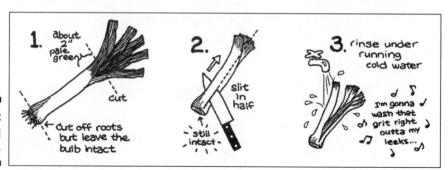

Figure 2-9:
Cleaning
leeks.

Mincing onions and shallots

To prepare onions and shallots for cooking, follow these steps, as shown in Figure 2-10:

1. **To peel the onion or shallot, cut off the stem and cut the onion in half from the stem through the root; gently lift off the dry outer layers of skin.**

2. **Put the onion or shallot halves on a cutting board, with their cut sides down. To chop or mince, make parallel lengthwise cuts with a chefs' knife, starting nearly at root end and cutting toward the stem end.**

   Leave the onion joined at its root end.

3. **Holding the knife horizontal to the board, cut the onion half in several horizontal slices, from top to bottom.**

   If cutting a shallot or small onion, one slice is enough.

   Again leave onion attached at root end.

4. **Slice the onion crosswise, forming small cubes to get chopped onion. To mince onion so that it's even finer, use a chopping knife to chop onion cubes in smaller pieces.**

Figure 2-10:
Mincing
onions and
shallots.

Preparing and cooking dried beans and chickpeas

Dried beans and chickpeas should be cooked slowly and gently so that they rehydrate and become tender. Use this recipe to cook dried white, red, pinto, or black beans or chickpeas.

Opinions are divided on whether to soak beans. Traditional cooks generally do so, while modern ones often skip this step. Soaking beans in water may cut their cooking time by 15 to 30 minutes and will improve their texture if they are old. You can soak the beans if you find it convenient.

Before you soak and cook the beans, you need to spread the beans out in a single layer on a plate and discard any pebbles or twigs. Then rinse the beans in a colander.

To soak the beans:

1. **Put the beans in a large bowl and cover them generously with water for 4 to 8 hours or overnight in a cool place or in the refrigerator.**

   They will expand and absorb much of the water.

2. **After soaking the beans, drain and rinse them.**

3. **Put the beans in a large saucepan and add water to cover generously.**

   For 1 pound dried beans or chickpeas, you will need about 2½ quarts of water. If you like, add 1 bay leaf, a few fresh thyme sprigs, 1 whole onion, and 1 whole carrot.

4. **Bring to a boil and then cover and cook over low heat until beans are tender, about 1 hour for most beans or 1½ to 2 hours for chickpeas. Add salt after beans have cooked about 30 to 40 minutes.**

   Begin tasting beans after about 45 minutes, and chickpeas after 1 hour. Before serving, remove the bay leaves, thyme sprigs, onion, and carrot.

If you're cooking the beans ahead, refrigerate them in their cooking liquid. Use the liquid in soups and stews.

Using a box grater

You need a grater mostly for three purposes — for grating vegetables, shredding cheese, and finely grating the zest of citrus fruits. For grating vegetables for salads, potato latkes, and vegetable kugels, use the large holes of a grater. You can also use the large holes for shredding cheese. Use the small holes to finely grate lemon or orange zest for desserts and for flavoring sauces and dressings.

The *zest* of a citrus fruit is the colored part of the rind, which has flavorful oils. Do not include the white pith underneath because it is bitter.

Seasoning kosher poultry and meat

Kosher poultry and meat has been salted in the koshering process (see Chapter 1). Some people feel this also gives them a finer flavor, especially for making soups.

Take the salt content into account when cooking these meats. If you're roasting them, it's best not to salt them. For soups, salt them lightly at first if you like and taste the soup once it is cooked. Whether to salt stews is up to you.

Chapter 3

Principal Branches of Jewish Cuisine

*I*n this chapter, I delve briefly into the origins of many deli delights and other Jewish foods still widely popular today, from potato latkes to challah to rugelach. You see who the Ashkenazic and Sephardic Jews are. In addition, you uncover the secrets to their most scrumptious savory and sweet treats.

Two major cultural groups make up the Jewish people — the Ashkenazic, or central European, and the Sephardic, or Mediterranean. Differing regional backgrounds are their most distinguishing characteristics. Neither category is homogeneous. Each is composed of numerous smaller communities, each of which has developed its own variations in their traditional dishes.

Unlike the regional cooking styles of such countries as France and Italy, the branches of Jewish cooking are very much a result of migration. Throughout their history, Jews have had to move from one place to another. Often, Jews of different backgrounds ended up in the same country and eventually adopted seasonings and recipes from each other.

Traditional Jewish recipes and menus, no matter what their country of origin, are kosher. To find out about kosher cooking, see Chapter 1.

Ashkenazic and American Style, from Kneidel to Kugel

The Ashkenazic Jews come from central and eastern Europe, notably Poland, the European parts of Russia, Germany, and the surrounding countries. They and their cooking style are the most familiar to Americans for a simple reason: It is mainly Jews from these countries who immigrated to North America. Ashkenazic Jews make up the majority of the Jewish population of the United States and Canada.

Ashkenazic Jews started the delis and bakeries so popular in the United States and helped to popularize such foods as matzo ball soup, challah, and cheesecake.

The word Ashkenazic comes from *Ashkenaz,* an old Hebrew word for Germany.

Seasonings

In their kitchens, Ashkenazic cooks prefer straightforward seasonings that emphasize the inherent tastes of foods rather than a large number of herbs and spices. This tendency may explain why so many of their specialties, from warming soups to roast chickens to potato pancakes to noodle casseroles, have become comfort foods.

Sautéed onions lend their savor to many appetizers and entrees. For many dishes, Jewish cooks like to brown the onions deeply to bring out their natural sweetness. Frequently, they sauté mushrooms with the onions, resulting in a tasty pair that's delicious as a first course on its own or enhances the taste of noodles, chicken, or meat.

Sweet-and-sour stews made of meat and vegetables are another hallmark of Ashkenazic cooking. Perhaps the most famous example is *tzimmes,* a stew of sweet vegetables such as carrots and sweet potatoes, dried fruit such as prunes or apricots, and often beef (see Chapter 4). To create the sweet-and-sour effect, cooks use sugar, honey, or raisins tempered with vinegar or lemon juice. They employ this flavoring technique for soups and meatless dishes as well.

Dill, bay leaves, parsley, and chives are the herbs of choice. Black pepper and paprika — both mild and hot — are the preferred spices. The food is tasty and not usually spicy but not bland. For more on flavorings in the Jewish kitchen, see Chapter 2.

Delights from the deli

When Ashkenazic Jews arrived in North America, some started small eateries so that their friends and neighbors could enjoy the foods they craved from the *Old Country,* or Europe. These eateries grew into the delicatessen-restaurants that are so loved today in the United States and Canada. The food was mainly simple home cooking, which I describe in the following sections.

Blintzes

Blintzes could be called crepes with a difference. They are composed of thin pancakes wrapped around savory or sweet fillings. One of the most requested deli desserts, blintzes are favored for brunches and for the Jewish holiday of Shavuot (see Chapter 9).

Kugels

Ashkenazic Jews are immensely fond of egg noodles and use them in inventive ways. Perhaps the most unique is the *kugel,* a delicious baked casserole combining the pasta with flavorful seasonings and eggs. You can make kugels savory with onions or other vegetables or sweet and fruity for dessert. For kugel recipes, see Chapter 17.

Matzo ball soups

Chicken soup with matzo balls may be the most celebrated Jewish specialty and vies for the title of best loved. The full-flavored chicken broth with the light *kneidel,* or matzo ball, floating in it, is irresistible on a cold day. A standard on deli menus, the soup with its tasty garnish is easy to make at home. (See the recipe in Chapter 8.)

Knishes

Knishes are pastry pillow turnovers traditionally filled with meat, potato, or other vegetable fillings. People enjoy these turnovers most when they are warm and serve them as substantial snacks or as first courses at dinners. For an easy version of knishes to bake in your kitchen, see Chapter 11.

Lox

Lox is salmon cured in brine so that it acquires a deliciously distinctive, slightly salty flavor. Many feel that a thin slice of lox on a bagel spread with cream cheese is practically a sandwich made in heaven! In Jewish homes, lox is the favorite brunch food and is enjoyed at many other occasions as well, from parties to light meals at home.

Lox is not smoked. Today, however, many substitute smoked salmon for lox in recipes such as spreads and egg dishes (see Chapter 13).

Gefilte fish

This famous fish dish is the standard starter at many festive meals. You can picture gefilte fish as meatballs made with fish instead of meat and served cold. Cooks season the fish mixture with onion, carrot, salt, pepper, and, in some families, a bit of sugar, and then poach it in a flavorful stock.

When I was growing up, gefilte fish was always on my family's table for Passover, Rosh Hashanah, and Shabbat. You can buy it at the deli or in jars at the kosher section of the supermarket, but homemade is always best. For an easy recipe, see Chapter 14.

Corned beef and pastrami

Sandwiches of corned beef and pastrami on rye bread rival lox and bagels as the most popular items at Jewish delis. Both are made of beef cured in brine and then cooked. Pastrami, made from brisket, is also smoked and tends to be richer and spicier than the leaner corned beef.

Both of these savory meats are best warm. People disagree on which meat they prefer, but some delis solve the problem by offering sandwiches that combine both. Sharp condiments like mustard, pickled cucumbers, and sauerkraut complement their richness.

Of course, you don't have to buy a deli sandwich to enjoy pastrami and corned beef. You can buy the meats already sliced at many supermarkets as well as delis to make your own sandwiches. You can also use them in egg dishes just like lox (see Chapter 13).

Kosher pickles

Dill pickles are sometimes labeled *kosher pickles* because this style of seasoning the cucumbers is a time-honored Jewish favorite. It is simply a name and does not refer to special rabbinical supervision. If a specific brand of pickles has been certified by a rabbinical organization as being processed with kosher equipment, there will be a certification symbol on the label.

Treats from the bakery

Jewish bakeries are renowned in America for their scrumptious cakes and pastries and tasty breads. Many of their specialties have become popular on the American table because they are now available at a wide variety of supermarkets, bakeries, and coffee shops.

Among the breads, challah, bagel, rye bread, and pumpernickel are the most popular. Cakes and desserts include cheesecake, honey cake, strudel, mandelbrot, and rugelach.

Many Jewish baked goods are made with oil rather than butter or other dairy products so that you can serve them at meals that include meat or poultry. Prudent kosher cooks always check the labels to be sure.

Most of the Jewish bakeries in America were started by Ashkenazic Jews. Today, Sephardic Jews enjoy these baked goods as well and serve them often.

Challah

A beautiful braided bread called *challah* graces the table of most Jewish holiday celebrations (see Figure 3-1). Challah, also called egg bread, is also enriched with oil. Usually the golden loaf is delicately sweetened with sugar and may contain raisins, too. For the Jewish New Year, round challahs (not braided ones) are baked. To bake your own challah, see Chapter 10.

Figure 3-1:
Challah is a delicious, slightly sweet, braided egg bread popular for Jewish holidays.

CHALLAH

Bagels

Bagels have become so much a part of the American scene that it's easy to forget that several decades ago it was mainly Ashkenazic Jews who appreciated these ring-shaped rolls. Many cities boast a large number of bagel bakeries, where it's easy to find warm, fresh-baked bagels. Until recently, the flavoring choices were limited, but today you can find an incredible variety, from onion to garlic to blueberry to cinnamon raisin walnut. The unique, slightly chewy texture of bagels is achieved by a special technique: The shaped rolls are briefly boiled before being baked.

For the traditional sandwich of bagels with lox and cream cheese, obviously the favorite bagel is a plain bagel or egg bagel rather than one with sweet seasonings. Purists prefer bagels fresh to enjoy their taste and texture and toast them only when they haven't just been baked.

Cheesecake

On Jewish tables, cheesecakes are one of the all-time favorite desserts. Jews from Poland, Russia, and Hungary did much to popularize their luscious cheesecakes, first in New York, and then across America. Cheesecakes even play a prominent part in a major holiday, Shavuot, described in Chapter 9.

I love baking (and eating!) cheesecake. Try my family's favorite, with its delectable sour cream topping. You'll find it easy to make. The recipe is in Chapter 9.

Strudel

Like cheesecake, *strudel* has become widespread in Jewish bakeries across the country because these pastries are so well loved on the dessert tables of

Jews from eastern and central Europe. Often prepared with fruit or nut fillings, strudel can easily be made pareve and is thus suitable at any time of day for Jews who keep kosher. You can find a strudel recipe in Chapter 5.

Mandelbrot and rugelach

These old-fashioned Ashkenazic Jewish cookies are beloved treats at any time of day. *Mandelbrot,* which means almond bread, are made of cookie dough that is baked as a loaf, then sliced, and baked again so that they come out very crunchy, much like Italian biscotti. Like biscotti, they're perfect for dunking in coffee. *Rugelach* are half-cookie, half-pastry, with a delectable, tender dough rolled around a sweet fruit, nut, or cinnamon filling. To make both these sweets in your kitchen, see the recipes in Chapter 20.

Sephardic Style, from Bourekas to Baklava

Sephardic Jews originated in the lands around the Mediterranean area and in the Middle East. Their cuisine is exuberant with the sunny flavors of this area.

Sephardic cooking is not only delicious, but is healthful, too. It could be considered a kosher branch of the style of eating known among nutritionists as the Mediterranean diet.

The word Sephardic comes from *Sepharad,* the Hebrew word for Spain. Many of the Sephardic Jews descended from the Spanish Jews who were exiled from Spain in 1492. They migrated mostly to other Mediterranean countries.

Seasonings

With plenty of herbs and sometimes generous use of spices, Sephardic cooking is aromatic. Lemon, garlic, tomatoes, and olive oil are its favorite flavors. Olives are popular, too, as appetizers and to lend their pungent flavor to stews. (See the Chicken with Green Beans, Mushrooms, and Olives recipe in Chapter 15.)

Cooks use herbs with a generous hand, especially Italian parsley and cilantro. Many love dill, thyme, and rosemary also.

Sephardic Jews from Morocco and other North African countries love cumin, ginger, and saffron, while some from the Middle East pair cumin with turmeric. Many like chilies, too, and their cooking can be quite hot. Jewish cooks from the eastern end of the Mediterranean are so fond of cinnamon that they use it as a savory accent for meat dishes, as well as to perfume their sweets.

Mediterranean favorites

Vegetables figure prominently on the Sephardic menu. Cooks prepare them in numerous ways, notably as an impressive array of salads to begin feasts. They use peppers, eggplant, zucchini, artichokes, and beans this way. Delectable vegetables braised in savory tomato sauce (see the Green Beans in Garlicky Tomato Sauce recipe in Chapter 19) and vegetables stuffed with fragrant meat and rice stuffings (see the recipe for Stuffed Eggplant with Nutty Lamb Filling in Chapter 5) are other highlights of their holiday tables.

Braised meats with rice or couscous are favorite main courses. For special occasions, the rice may be embellished with dried fruit and nuts, as in Rice Pilaf with Apricots, Almonds, and Cashews (see Chapter 18).

Pita, or pocket bread, is the best-known bread of Sephardic origin (see Figure 3-2). If you have tried only the mass-marketed types, try to taste fresh pita from an Israeli or Middle Eastern bakery. As with pizza, which is made from a similar dough, there is a world of difference between a fresh-baked pita straight from the oven and a packaged one designed to last a long time.

Figure 3-2:
Pita bread has a pocket and is perfect for falafel and sandwiches.

PITA

Sephardic cooks often bake their pastries, both savory and sweet, from filo dough. Bourekas are a popular appetizer pastry and often have feta cheese, spinach, or potato fillings. (For a recipe, see chapter 9). Baklava, a favorite sweet, features the dough layered with a nut and sugar filling and moistened with syrup.

Israeli Style, from Falafel to Foie Gras

Israel was the original homeland of the Jewish people before their wanderings divided them into the Ashkenazic and Sephardic groups. In modern days, members of both communities have come together in the Jewish State.

From a culinary standpoint, the result is an active melting pot. With people from so many different countries living in close proximity in a small space, maybe it should instead be called a melting pressure cooker!

Marriages among members of both groups have contributed to this trend, as in my family, which combines Ashkenazic influences from Poland and Russia with Sephardic ones from Morocco, Yemen, and India. With so many holidays, a lot of home cooking is going on. Neighbors and friends actively exchange recipes and try each other's favorite flavors.

Often, Israelis cook specialties of both culinary styles in their menus. A holiday dinner may begin with Ashkenazic Easy Gefilte Fish (Chapter 14) and then follow with a Sephardic style entree of Baked Chicken and Chickpeas in Garlic Tomato Sauce (Chapter 10). Often the sweet will be Ashkenazic, such as a strudel (Chapter 5).

By experimenting with each other's seasonings, some people gradually change their own recipes. My mother, who was born in Poland, now adds cumin, garlic, and cilantro to her chicken soup with matzo balls, after tasting how good it was at the home of my Sephardic sister-in-law.

Falafel is the most famous specialty of Israel. Originally an eastern Mediterranean appetizer, it became Israel's favorite light meal. In Israel, falafel is as common as hamburgers are in the United States. People eat falafel in pita sandwiches at casual falafel restaurants as a quick pick-me-up and also enjoy making it at home. (See recipe in Chapter 11.)

In just about every Israeli home, a salad of finely diced tomatoes, cucumbers, and onions dressed with olive oil and lemon juice is a staple. It's called simply *Israeli salad.* Most people eat it at least once a day, as a first course or to accompany an entree from roast chicken to a simple omelet. When I lived in Israel, I found this a healthy habit worthy of adopting.

This merging of culinary style is leading to plenty of creativity. Israelis enjoy a great variety of foods. Even *foie gras,* or rich goose liver, known worldwide as a specialty of France, has become a highlight of restaurant dining in Israel. Like many dishes, it's prepared with an Israeli twist — as kebabs on the grill served in pita bread, rather than as a European style pâté.

From chopped liver to hummus to sweet rugelach, Israelis have wholeheartedly embraced both traditional Jewish styles. As the center of Jewish culture, Israel also stimulates Jewish cooking in other parts of the world.

Part II
The Holidays

The 5th Wave — By Rich Tennant

"Today we celebrate Passover, which commemorates a long journey, and considering how far I had to travel for a good roast of veal, seems most appropriate."

In this part . . .

Turn to this part when you want to celebrate. I present festive specialties for enjoying each holiday to the fullest. Here you find foods and customs for every major joyous occasion on the Jewish calendar, from Rosh Hashanah to Hanukkah to Passover, as well as the weekly festival of Shabbat.

Chapter 4

A New Year as Sweet as Apples and Honey

In This Chapter

▶ Beginning the year sweetly for good luck

▶ Serving up symbolism

▶ Celebrating the bounty of the orchards and the fields

▶ Abstaining and then enjoying food on the most solemn day of the year

*J*ews celebrate Rosh Hashanah, the Jewish New Year, for two days in September or October. They are the first two days of the Jewish calendar, which is lunar. (For more about the Jewish calendar, see Chapter 1.)

Rosh Hashanah is both solemn and joyful. At the synagogue, people pray to be forgiven for misdeeds. The theme of repentance is echoed even more vigorously on Yom Kippur, which occurs ten days later. A variety of foods on the festive New Year dinners symbolize the hope for a good year.

Sweet Foods on Rosh Hashanah for Good Fortune All Year

The Jewish New Year menu is replete with sweet dishes. Fruit, sweet vegetables, and honey appear even in some main dishes and give the holiday meals their unique character. Sometimes it seems that the menus must have been designed with children in mind, especially in some Ashkenazic homes.

To ensure mellow meals and prevent a bitter future, some people avoid sour foods like vinegar and lemon juice. Others tone down peppery dishes, using fewer chilies than usual or omitting them.

Some say the Israelites adopted the idea of celebrating the new year with something sweet from the Persians. In ancient Persia, it was customary to eat sweet foods for the new year. Legend relates that one of the biblical prophets introduced this tradition to the Israelites. The sweet custom remains central to Rosh Hashanah festivities to this day.

Honey foretells happiness

Beginning the year on a sweet note seems to be taken literally by custom. Honey is used liberally, not only in desserts like honey cake, but even as a dip to begin the meal. Around the world, Jews start off their holiday meal by dipping apple wedges in honey. Some Jews dip slices of challah as well.

Honey was of great importance during the biblical era. There was no sugar then. The Torah frequently describes Israel as "the land of milk and honey" because honey represented the good life. For many people, it still does.

"I still spread my challah with honey every Friday night," a young Orthodox mother told me recently. She had learned from her mother that newlyweds should follow this custom to ensure a happy marriage. After a few years of marriage, she thought it was still a good idea. Why not?

Honey cake is one of the most convenient desserts to bake at home because it keeps so well, at least a week and sometimes longer. Unlike most cakes, it tastes even better two days after it is baked. The honey enables it to retain its good flavor and texture.

Orange Hazelnut Honey Cake

Ashkenazic Jews began the tradition of serving honey cake for Rosh Hashanah, but Jews of most origins have adopted it. Spices, especially cinnamon and cloves, are favorite accents. In Israel, coffee, cocoa, and citrus zest are popular, too. This cake doesn't have much oil or many eggs and is fairly low in saturated fat.

Special tools: *Mixer, 8 x 4-inch loaf pan*

Preparation time: *30 minutes*

Cooking time: *55 minutes*

Yield: *8 to 10 servings*

Keeping kosher: *Pareve*

1 teaspoon instant coffee granules	2 eggs
1/3 cup hot water	1/2 cup sugar
1 1/2 cups flour	1/2 cup honey
1 teaspoon baking powder	1/3 cup vegetable oil
1/2 teaspoon baking soda	1 1/2 teaspoons grated orange zest, orange part only
1/2 teaspoon ground cinnamon	
Small pinch of ground cloves	1/2 cup hazelnuts, coarsely chopped

1 Preheat oven to 325°. Lightly grease an 8 x 4-inch loaf pan, line it with parchment paper or waxed paper and grease paper.

2 In a cup, dissolve instant coffee in hot water. Let cool. Sift flour with baking powder, baking soda, cinnamon, and cloves.

3 Beat eggs lightly in large bowl of mixer. Add sugar and honey and beat until mixture is very smooth and lightened in color. Gradually add oil and beat until blended. Add orange zest.

4 Stir in flour mixture alternately with coffee, each in two batches. Stir in hazelnuts.

5 Pour batter into prepared pan. Bake for 55 minutes, or until a cake tester inserted in cake comes out clean. Cool in pan for about 15 minutes. Turn out onto rack and carefully peel off paper.

6 When cake is completely cool, wrap it tightly in foil and keep it at room temperature. Serve in thin slices.

Per Serving: *Calories 274.1; Protein 4.1 g; Carbohydrates 39.6 g; Dietary fiber 1.2 g; Total fat 11.9 g; Saturated fat 1.1 g; Cholesterol 42.5 mg; Sodium 115.1 mg.*

Carrots connote wealth

Carrots are popular items on the Rosh Hashanah menu because they stand for prosperity. Sliced carrots resemble gold coins. They might be used to garnish a fish, added to a meat entree, or served as a side dish.

Other vegetable favorites are sweet potatoes and winter squash because of their sweet taste. To accentuate this quality, Ashkenazic cooks like to glaze them with honey. Certain Sephardic Jews stew them with cinnamon and sugar.

Cinnamon Carrot Coins

The customary carrot rounds on the Jewish New Year table signify the wish for an upcoming year of prosperity. But there's another good reason to include them in the festive menu. Nobody can resist the alluring sweetness of glazed carrots, especially when honey is in the sauce. In fact, a bowlful of these sweet carrots is one of my most requested dishes for bringing to potluck dinners. I find that a touch of cinnamon complements the honey well. You can see a photo of this recipe in the color insert section of this book.

Preparation time: *20 minutes*

Cooking time: *25 minutes*

Yield: *4 servings*

Keeping kosher: *Pareve*

1 pound carrots, peeled and sliced about ¼ inch thick

1 cup water

Pinch of salt

1 tablespoon sugar

1 tablespoon honey

1 tablespoon vegetable oil

⅛ teaspoon ground cinnamon

1 Combine the carrots, water, and salt in a medium saucepan. Bring to a boil and simmer uncovered 10 minutes.

2 Add the sugar, honey, and oil. Cook over medium-low heat, stirring occasionally, about 15 minutes or until the carrots are very tender and only 2 tablespoons of liquid remain in the pan and coat the carrots. Do not cook until all the liquid evaporates. Add the cinnamon, stir gently, and remove from heat. Serve hot or at room temperature.

Per Serving: Calories 109.4; Protein 1.5 g; Carbohydrates 19.2 g; Dietary fiber 3.0 g; Total fat 3.4 g; Saturated fat 0.2 g; Cholesterol 0 mg; Sodium 93.3 mg.

Warning: *Watch the carrots carefully when only a little liquid is left in the pan, so that the sugar and honey do not scorch.*

Fruit foreshadows a sweet future

In addition to the traditional appetizer of apples dipped in honey, fruit might appear anywhere in the meal. Moroccan Jews enjoy an additional appetizer of syrupy quince, an apple-like fruit that is always served cooked. *Tzimmes,* a renowned stew of Jews of Central European origin, may include prunes, carrots, sweet potatoes, and beef.

Tzimmes can sometimes be quite elaborate. Therefore, the Yiddish word tzimmes also gave rise to the American-Jewish slang expression, "Don't make a tzimmes out of it," meaning "Don't make a big fuss or hullabaloo."

Tzimmes should be moist but not soupy. If you would like a thicker sauce, choose one of the following traditional techniques:

✔ **Baking:** Bake the finished tzimmes uncovered in a casserole dish in a 350 oven for 15 to 30 minutes.

✔ **Thickening with a flour slurry:** Heat the stew until the sauce begins to bubble. Remove it from the heat. Stir 1 tablespoon flour with 2 tablespoons apricot soaking liquid in a medium bowl. Gradually stir in about 1 cup of the sauce. Return the flour mixture to the pan and simmer it, stirring very gently, for 5 minutes.

Sweet Potato and Beef Tzimmes with Dried Apricots

Cooks prepare numerous versions of this sweet and savory stew, which originated among the Ashkenazic Jews of central and eastern Europe. Usually, tzimmes contains both fruit and vegetables. It often includes meat as well. Prunes are the time-honored fruit pick, but I find that people who are new to the dish prefer it when I use dried apricots instead. Carrots, sweet potatoes, and white potatoes are the most popular vegetable choices. If you would like to serve Cinnamon Carrot Coins as an accompaniment, omit the carrots in this recipe.

Honey or sugar lends a special flavor to the sauce, which may also be spiced with cinnamon. Tzimmes is not a sweet and sour dish, and therefore no vinegar or lemon juice is added. In my family, we add the sweetening agents with a light hand so that they season the stew discretely. You can see a photo of this recipe in the color insert section of this book.

Special tool: *Dutch oven or heavy stew pan*

Preparation time: *1 hour*

Cooking time: *2½ hours*

Yield: *4 to 6 servings*

Keeping kosher: *Meat*

2 pounds beef chuck	2 large white potatoes
2 tablespoons vegetable oil	1 pound orange-fleshed sweet potatoes (sometimes labeled yams)
2 onions, chopped	2 tablespoons honey
2 large carrots, peeled and cut in 1-inch chunks (optional)	¼ teaspoon ground cinnamon
Salt and freshly ground pepper to taste	1¼ cups dried apricots
3 cups water	1 tablespoon flour (optional)

1 Trim excess fat from beef. Cut meat into 1½-inch cubes.

2 In a Dutch oven or heavy stew pan, heat 1 tablespoon oil. Add half the beef and brown it well on all sides over medium heat, about 5 to 7 minutes. With a slotted spoon, transfer the beef to a bowl. Brown the remaining beef and remove it.

3 Add the remaining oil to the pan and heat it. Add the onions and sauté them over medium heat, stirring often, until they brown, about 5 minutes.

4 Return the beef to the pan and add any juices in the bowl. Add the carrots, a pinch of salt, and enough water to just cover the ingredients. Bring to a boil, skimming occasionally. Cover and simmer over low heat for 1 hour.

5 Peel both types of potatoes and cut them into large dice. After the meat and carrots have cooked for 1 hour, add both types of potato dice to the pan. Push them into the liquid. Bring to a boil. Partially cover the pan and simmer the stew for 30 minutes.

6 Meanwhile, in a small bowl soak the apricots in enough hot water to cover them for 15 minutes.

7 Gently stir the stew once. Remove the apricots, reserving their liquid in case you want to thicken the stew, and add them to the pan. Add the honey and cinnamon and stir gently. Uncover and simmer for 30 minutes, or until the beef is very tender.

8 Add salt and pepper to taste. Serve hot, from a deep serving dish.

Per Serving: Calories 659.1; Protein 32.5 g; Carbohydrates 61.8 g; Dietary fiber 6.7 g; Total fat 31.9 g; Saturated fat 11.0 g; Cholesterol 103.3 mg; Sodium 193.2 mg.

Jewish Mother's Tip: After adding the potatoes, avoid vigorous stirring so that they will not break up. Shake the pan occasionally to prevent sticking or stir very gently.

You can cook the stew up to two days ahead. Reheat it in a covered pan over medium-low heat or in a 300° oven. It is best to make it at least a few hours ahead to allow the flavors to intermingle and the sauce to thicken slightly.

Symbolic Foods with Mystical Meaning

Other foods at the traditional Jewish New Year table possess special significance unrelated to sweetness. Certain food customs have grown up only in some Jewish communities.

Some Sephardic families begin the dinner by sampling small tastes of these foods and reciting a blessing over each one. This ritual resembles a brief version of a Passover Seder. In some homes, families taste small portions of these foods in a ceremony, with a blessing said before each, rather like the Passover Seder.

Fish heads to prophesy getting ahead

Most people serve a starter containing fish, an age-old symbol of fertility and plenty. In modern days, fish is appreciated for its healthful qualities. Starting off the year with health in mind seems like a useful custom.

Some families follow a tradition of serving the fish with its head on. Two reasons are given for including the head of the fish.

✔ The literal meaning of the Hebrew words, "Rosh Hashanah" is "the head of the year." The fish head stands for this phrase.

✔ A Hebrew expression that you would rather be a head than a tail. The fish head represents this wish to get ahead.

For the following recipe, leave on the trout's head if you want to serve the fish according to custom.

Trout with Sweet Peppers

With its Moroccan-inspired seasonings, this fish dish is easy to prepare and tastes good hot or cold. Flavored inside and out with sweet peppers and garlic, the fish appeals to most palates. Choose small trout if you're serving them as a fish course followed by a meat entree.

Special tool: *Sturdy scissors, 13 x 9-inch baking dish*

Preparation time: *30 minutes*

Cooking time: *15 minutes*

Yield: *4 servings*

Keeping kosher: *Pareve*

4 trout, 9 to 12 ounces each, butterflied, heads removed if you like

3 tablespoons olive oil

2 teaspoons paprika

2 large garlic cloves, minced

¼ cup chopped cilantro

½ red bell pepper, diced small

Salt and freshly ground pepper to taste

⅓ cup water

Small cilantro sprigs, for garnish

1 Preheat oven to 425°. If the trout still have fins, snip them with sturdy scissors and trim their tails straight. Rinse them inside and out.

2 Mix the oil, paprika, garlic, and cilantro in a small bowl. Stir in the red pepper.

3 Lightly oil a 13 x 9-inch baking dish or another shallow baking dish in which the trout just fit in one layer. Put the trout inside with their skin side down. Sprinkle them with salt and pepper. Spoon about half the pepper garlic mixture evenly over them. Fold each one in half. Sprinkle them with salt and pepper and spoon the remaining pepper garlic mixture over them. Add the water to the dish.

4 Bake the trout uncovered about 20 minutes or until they are just tender and their flesh is opaque. Serve them hot or cold, garnished with cilantro sprigs.

Per Serving: Calories 286.6; Protein 26.6 g; Carbohydrates 2.3 g; Dietary fiber 0.7 g; Total fat 18.6 g; Saturated fat 2.8 g; Cholesterol 72.7 mg; Sodium 213.7 mg.

Jewish Mother's Tip: *For easiest eating, have the trout butterflied or boned at the market. If you want to remove any pinbones that may be left in the fish, do so before rinsing them. Run your finger along the trout flesh about ¾ inch from the backbone line, on both sides of this line. If there are pinbones, you will feel them and will see a row of small bones running parallel to the backbone. Use tweezers, small pliers, a pastry crimper, or a paring knife to gently pull them out.*

Taste of Tradition: *For Rosh Hashanah many highlight the holiday's sweetness by using bell peppers alone to flavor the trout. Some cooks add a dried small hot pepper or a minced jalapeno or serrano chile to the sauce for other occasions.*

Menu Maven Says: *If you'd like to make the fish a main course, serve with simple partners — seasonal vegetables and small steamed or boiled potatoes are perfect.*

Greens to augur grace

In some Sephardic homes, cooked greens such as spinach or chard appear on the table, either braised or made into omelets or small pancakes. They signify the hope for plenty of vegetables at the coming harvest.

Peas to promise plenty

Like in the American South, black-eyed peas are a New Year's favorite on the menus of Sephardic Jews. The peas symbolize abundance. You can prepare dried black-eyed peas following the recipe for Savory Beans with Tomatoes and Coriander in Chapter 18. Sometimes rice fulfills this function instead.

Beets and leeks to beat any enemies

The Hebrew words for beets and leeks evoke defense and, in Sephardic homes, are served to stand for heavenly protection from enemies. Ashkenazic Jews often eat beets also because they are sweet.

Be careful when handling, serving, and eating red beets. Their juice stains clothes, aprons, and tablecloths. This mishap doesn't seem to happen with specialty yellow beets.

Sweet Beet Salad with Orange

Instead of the usual vinegar, for Rosh Hashanah I dress these beets with orange juice and include a few orange segments, too. Steamed fresh small beets are much tastier than canned beets. You'll find it easiest to steam them in their skins and to peel them afterwards. You can see a photo of this recipe in the color insert section of this book.

Special tools: *Steamer, grater*

Preparation time: *10 minutes*

Cooking time: *50 minutes*

Yield: *4 servings*

Keeping kosher: *Pareve*

5 to 7 beets of 1½-inch diameter (about 1 pound, without greens)

1 green onion, minced

Pinch of salt

2 to 3 teaspoons sugar, or to taste

1 tablespoon orange juice, or to taste

1 navel orange, divided in sections

1 Rinse the beets, taking care not to pierce their skins. Trim off any long tails. If the greens are attached, cut off all but 1 inch of them.

2 Pour 1 inch of water into a steamer and bring to a boil. Place the beets on a steamer rack above the boiling water, without allowing the water to touch the beets. Cover tightly and steam them for 50 minutes or until tender, adding more boiling water occasionally as the water evaporates.

3 Cool the beets slightly. To remove their peels, hold them under cold running water while slipping off their skins.

4 Using the large holes of a grater, grate the beets. Add the green onion, salt, sugar, and orange juice to taste. Serve cold, garnished with the orange segments.

Per Serving: *Calories 72.9; Protein 2.2 g; Carbohydrates 17.2 g; Dietary fiber 3.0 g; Total fat 0.2 g; Saturated fat 0 g; Cholesterol 0 mg; Sodium 116.3 mg.*

Seasonal Produce Commemorates Biblical Harvest

One of my favorite Rosh Hashanah rituals is sampling a fruit for the first time in the year. It may be an exotic fruit or one that is seasonally available, such as a fig, date, or pomegranate. Before tasting the fruit, Jews recite a blessing expressing thanks for having lived to this day.

This custom is said to have originated in the agricultural cycle of ancient Israel. I can understand why the Hebrews of yore wanted to express appreciation for their fruit, ever since our backyard tree began producing figs!

Yom Kippur: A Fast Surrounded by Feasts

The holiest day of the Jewish year is Yom Kippur, which takes place ten days after Rosh Hashanah. A day of prayer, Yom Kippur's primary purpose is to atone for wrongdoing. To emphasize the earnest intention to ask for forgiveness, it is a full day of fasting.

Salt is enemy No. 1 because it provokes thirst. For this reason cooks use it with a light hand for the meal. Following similar logic, many people go easy on the spices too, preferring plainly prepared foods of uncomplicated flavors.

Some experts find an additional significance in observing a day of abstinence from food and drink. Personally, feeling famished promotes greater sympathy for the plight of people who are poor and hungry.

Yet Yom Kippur is a food holiday, too. Custom governs the menus preceding and following the fast.

Preparing a hearty prelude

The Yom Kippur fast lasts about 25 hours, from the evening before to nightfall on Yom Kippur day. During that time, adults do not eat or drink. Just prior to the fast, a substantial dinner is served.

Not surprisingly, chicken soup is the first course of choice. After all, Jewish lore has ascribed health-promoting powers to this broth for ages. Undoubtedly, Jewish mothers feel it helps to fortify their families for the fast. Besides, everyone loves it. In many homes, the pre-Yom Kippur chicken soup is the most richly flavored one of the year because cooks poach a whole chicken to make it. You can enhance the soup with rice, noodles, or kreplach, or Ashkenazic tortellini.

The entree is generally the chicken used to prepare the soup. Serving a simple poached chicken makes this menu different from other holidays, when roasting or braising is more common. Some present the chicken as a separate course with seasonal vegetables, while others may serve it in the soup.

As on Rosh Hashanah, the bread served is a round challah.

The rest of the menu is a matter of family preference. In my home a potato or noodle kugel has always been a popular partner for the chicken. Most people also enjoy a selection of salads. Dessert tends to be simple, perhaps stewed fruit, sponge cake, or pound cake.

Serve the following soup in two courses. First, serve a bowlful of soup embellished with egg noodles or matzo balls and then offer the chicken accompanied by the potatoes and the other vegetables. Provide shallow bowls for enjoying the main course so that you can moisten each portion with a little chicken broth.

Chicken in the Pot with Leeks and Potatoes

Savor the simple, pure taste of chicken soup made slowly by gently cooking a whole chicken. In our jumble of associating sharp tastes, we sometimes forget how good the basic, time-honored combinations can be. I find this is one of Yom Kippur's culinary lessons.

The French are not the only people who pair potatoes with leeks in their soups. Leek scented chicken soup is popular in Israel too. Poached potatoes are likely to be partnered with the Yom Kippur chicken and gain great taste from being simmered in the aromatic soup. To complete the dish, add carrots, green and yellow squash, and turnips. They will flavor the soup and complement the chicken.

Preparation time: *1 hour*

Cooking time: *2½ hours*

Yield: *6 servings*

Keeping kosher: *Meat*

1 whole chicken (about 4 pounds)

3 large leeks, split and rinsed

2 bay leaves

1 large onion, whole

Salt and freshly ground pepper to taste

About 6 cups water

4 medium-sized boiling potatoes (about 1 pound)

4 medium carrots, peeled and cut in 2-inch lengths (total ¾ pound)

2 garlic cloves, coarsely chopped

3 medium zucchini, halved and cut in 2-inch lengths (about ¾ pound)

8 ounces mushrooms, quartered (optional)

8 ounces fine egg noodles or My Mother's Fluffy Matzo Balls (see Chapter 8)

3 tablespoons chopped parsley or cilantro (fresh coriander)

1 Remove fat from chicken. Put chicken in a large pot. If chicken giblets are available, add neck and other giblets, except liver.

2 Rinse leeks thoroughly to remove any sand. Cut off dark green parts of leeks and add to pot. Cut white and light green parts of leeks in 2-inch lengths and reserve for later.

3 Add bay leaf, onion, salt, and enough water to barely cover ingredients. Bring to a boil. Skim foam from surface. Cover and cook over low heat 1 hour, skimming occasionally.

4 Peel and halve potatoes. Add potatoes, carrots, and garlic to pot. Cover and cook over low heat 30 minutes. Discard bay leaves, onion, and leek greens.

5 Add zucchini, mushrooms, and white and light green leek pieces to pot. Bring to a simmer. Cover and cook over low heat for 15 minutes or until chicken and vegetables are tender.

6 Meanwhile, cook noodles or prepare matzo balls. To cook noodles, add them to a medium saucepan of boiling salted water. Cook them uncovered over medium-high heat about 5 minutes or until tender. Drain well, rinse with cold water, and drain. Reserve the noodles in a covered container.

7 If you like, remove the chicken skin and cut the meat from the bones; return chicken to soup.

8 Skim off as much fat as possible from the soup. If you would like to skim the fat thoroughly, cool the soup at this point. Refrigerate it overnight. Refrigerate container of noodles or matzo balls.

9 If soup is cold, skim off the fat before heating it. Bring the soup to a simmer. Before serving, season to taste with salt and pepper.

10 Serve the soup as a first course with noodles or matzo balls. If desired, add parsley or cilantro to each bowl when serving.

11 In shallow bowls, serve the chicken and vegetables. Ladle a little soup over each portion to moisten.

Per Serving: Calories 615.2; Protein 42.8 g; Carbohydrates 53.9 g; Dietary fiber 6.0 g; Total fat 25.1 g; Saturated fat 6.7 g; Cholesterol 162.4 mg; Sodium 241.3 mg.

Jewish Mother's Tip: Clear chicken broth is customary in many traditional Jewish kitchens. To keep the potatoes from clouding the soup, cook them in a separate saucepan.

Finishing with a light finale

What to serve following the fast depends on family traditions. Often, the preference is for a meatless meal because many consider such a repast lighter on the digestion after an entire day without food.

When I was growing up, we broke our fast with typical "breakfast" foods. I am still partial to this type of menu. We enjoyed such easy-to-serve comfort foods as scrambled eggs with toast, or bagels with lox and cream cheese, followed by a scrumptious sour cream coffee cake.

Our menu is typical of many Ashkenazic tables. Some Sephardic Jews favor a meat-based rather than a dairy meal. The Moroccan Jewish tradition, for example, calls for a savory lentil and beef soup flavored with vegetables.

Chapter 5

Sukkot: When Camping Out Is a Commandment

*I*n this chapter, you discover the unique customs of the holiday of Sukkot. You find out what a Sukkah is and why the whole family enjoys it so much. Adding to the holiday cheer is the delicious food that goes with the Sukkah experience.

Sukkot could be considered Thanksgiving for a whole week. For many, Sukkot rivals Purim and Hanukkah as the Jewish festival that is the most fun. Its colorful customs involve activities for the whole family. In addition, it is an exuberant celebration of nature and a remembrance of the ancient Hebrews' exodus from Egypt.

Plants Express Appreciation of Nature

With its agricultural accent, Sukkot honors nature in three areas — in religious rituals, in making and decorating the traditional hut or *Sukkah,* and, of course, on the table.

In the Sukkah

Children adore Sukkot because it's a chance to camp out in the backyard for a whole week. Instead of a tent, people live in a Sukkah or temporary booth made especially for the occasion. This hut is crowned with leafy branches. To adorn the Sukkah, many like to string up fresh fruit and suspend it from this natural ceiling.

The sound of hammering is evident in many Jewish neighborhoods as people build family Sukkahs in their backyards and community Sukkahs on the synagogue grounds. To make the task easier, nowadays many buy a collapsible Sukkah frame. They finish the walls and top their Sukkah with fresh, green branches for the roof.

Children love to decorate the Sukkah. When I was a child, my brother and I helped my parents hang bunches of grapes, bananas, and pears from our Sukkah's ceiling. In my husband's Sukkah in Israel, the fruit selection was different — citrus fruit, guavas, and pomegranates were prominent. He and his brothers and sister also made a variety of paper ornaments for their Sukkah.

Among adults, only diehards sleep in the Sukkah all week instead of inside their home. Most observant Jews spend as much time in the Sukkah as possible — eating, meeting there with friends and relatives, and praying. The outdoor setting contributes to the special Sukkot ambiance.

An important purpose of making a Sukkah is to commemorate the flight of the Hebrew slaves from Egypt during the Pharaonic era. During this escape and their subsequent years of wandering in the Sinai Desert, they lived in transitory lodgings.

In the synagogue

Fruit and green plants figure prominently in the Sukkot ritual. The *citron*, known as an "etrog" in Hebrew and an "esrog" in Yiddish, is a wonderfully fragrant fruit that people hold during special Sukkot prayers, together with branches from three types of plants. In the United States, people buy an etrog especially for the holiday. Orthodox rabbis require that the citron be in perfect condition for the blessings. This old-fashioned citrus fruit is also used in the Middle East to make preserves. My husband fondly remembers the etrog jam his mother made when he was growing up in Israel, using fruit from their backyard tree. You can see a citron in the photographic insert section of this book.

Produce on the Menu Signifies Thanksgiving

I love Sukkot for an additional reason. This holiday celebrates the fresh fruit and vegetables of the season. Giving garden harvest parties may seem like a current craze, but, in fact, its roots go back to the Bible.

The agricultural theme runs throughout the Sukkot menu and makes perfect sense. Nature tells you that it's time for a party. In this season, gardens and farms are bursting with tomatoes, peppers, eggplants, squashes, plums, apples, and figs. Cooks make lavish use of vegetables and fruit to enliven their families' meals.

Vegetables with stuffing

Among many Jews, stuffed vegetables are Sukkot favorites. Popular choices in Israel for the vegetable containers are eggplant, zucchini, peppers, and cabbage leaves. Stuffings most often include beef or chicken mixed with rice and flavored with sautéed onions, garlic, herbs, and spices. For simmering and serving the filled vegetables, the two favorites are sweet and sour sauce or spicy tomato sauce.

Fruit in filo

To make use of the seasonal fruit, strudel is the Sukkot standard. Some Hungarian Jewish cooks still make their traditional strudel dough by hand, but making it properly requires practice and skill. Today, a more popular choice for enclosing fruit fillings is homemade pie dough, packaged filo, or puff pastry. Filo dough is often labeled strudel dough because it's ideal for making this tasty treat. This dough is also used by Jews of Greek extraction for wrapping sweet fillings of pumpkin, cinnamon, and nuts.

Strudel is a specialty of many Jewish bakeries. Classic strudel is a lot of work because it demands stretching the dough paper-thin over a tablecloth. Today, it's easy when you buy filo dough and use a simple fruit filling. When you're working with filo dough, follow these tips:

- Filo dough dries very fast. Always keep sheets covered with plastic wrap and a damp towel. Uncover to remove one sheet to work with and then cover remaining sheets.

- Work quickly when using filo so that it won't become brittle.

- If a filo sheet is torn or dried out, discard it and take another.

In addition, plenty of other sweet delights embellish the Sukkot table. The enticing aromas of carrot, apple, and plum cakes waft from many ovens. Chocolate lovers may enhance their cakes with applesauce to include the harvest theme. Fruit pies, honey cakes, and apple and quince compotes are other traditional desserts.

Stuffed Eggplant with Nutty Lamb Filling

A Sephardic favorite, this richly satisfying vegetable dish contains a meaty stuffing with rice and toasted almonds in a very tender eggplant shell. If you would like a leaner stuffing, you can substitute ground chicken for the lamb.

Preparation time: *1 hour*

Cooking time: *1½ hours*

Yield: *4 to 6 servings*

Keeping kosher: *Meat*

2 medium or 4 to 6 small eggplants (total 2½ pounds)	*4 garlic cloves, finely chopped, plus 6 whole garlic cloves*
Salt and freshly ground pepper to taste	*½ pound lean ground lamb*
⅓ cup slivered almonds	*¼ cup chopped Italian parsley*
3¼ cups water, plus more for baking eggplant	*½ teaspoon ground allspice*
½ cup long-grain rice, rinsed and drained	*½ teaspoon salt*
4 tablespoons olive oil	*½ teaspoon ground pepper*
1 medium onion, finely chopped	*2 tablespoons tomato paste*

1 Cut off the eggplant caps. Halve eggplants lengthwise. Use a spoon to scoop out centers, leaving boat-shaped shells about ½ inch thick and reserving eggplant you removed. Sprinkle eggplant shells with salt. Put them in a colander upside down and leave to drain for ½ hour.

2 Meanwhile, make stuffing: Preheat oven to 350°. Toast almonds on a baking sheet in oven for 5 to 7 minutes or until light golden. Transfer to a plate. Increase oven temperature to 425°.

3 In a small saucepan, bring 3 cups water to a boil and add a pinch of salt. Add rice and boil it uncovered for 10 minutes. It will be partly cooked. Drain in a colander, rinse with cold water, and drain well. Transfer to a large bowl.

4 In a medium skillet, heat 1 tablespoon olive oil. Add onion and sauté over medium-low heat about 7 minutes, or until soft but not brown. Stir in chopped garlic and remove from heat. Transfer mixture to a bowl and let cool.

5 Finely chop centers you removed from eggplant. Heat 2 tablespoons oil in the skillet, add the chopped eggplant, and sprinkle with salt and pepper. Sauté over medium-low heat, stirring often, about 10 minutes, or until nearly tender. Let cool.

6 To bowl of rice, add lamb, onion mixture, sautéed eggplant, parsley, allspice, ½ teaspoon salt, and ½ teaspoon pepper. Mix well. Mix in the toasted almonds.

7 Rinse eggplant shells lightly, pat them dry, and put them in a 13 x 9-inch or other shallow baking dish in which they fit in one layer. Fill them with stuffing. Mix tomato paste with ¼ cup water and spoon mixture over eggplant. Add enough water to baking dish to cover lower third of eggplant. Add whole garlic cloves to dish. Spoon remaining 1 tablespoon oil over eggplant.

8 Cover and bake 15 minutes. Reduce oven temperature to 350° and bake 15 more minutes. Uncover and bake, basting occasionally, 30 minutes or until eggplant is very tender. To serve, remove carefully from the baking dish with a slotted spoon. Serve hot or warm, with a little of the cooking liquid spooned over each piece.

Per Serving: Calories 315.6; Protein 11.2 g; Carbohydrates 30.2 g; Dietary fiber 6.1 g; Total fat 17.0 g; Saturated fat 3.7 g; Cholesterol 24.9 mg; Sodium 323.3 mg.

Jewish Mother's Tips: For stuffing, use fresh eggplanst with a smooth, shiny, unblemished peel.

Partly cooking the rice before adding it to the stuffing ensures that it will be tender in the final dish.

Pear Strudel with Chocolate Sauce

Many in Israel use the term *strudel* rather loosely to refer to a variety of rolled sweet pastries. For a simple strudel, my mother might use cookie dough or yeast dough that she happens to have from baking something else. She spreads it with jam, sprinkles it with diced fresh fruit or simply raisins and nuts, then rolls it up, and bakes it. We always enjoy the results.

Serving strudel with ice cream and chocolate sauce is my new twist on tradition, inspired by the French dessert pears Hélène that matches the fruit with vanilla ice cream and chocolate sauce. If you want to make the dark chocolate sauce pareve, make it with nondairy margarine rather than butter. The sauce also is terrific with vanilla or coffee ice cream or with plain cakes.

Preparation time: 50 minutes, plus time to thaw the filo dough if it's frozen

Cooking time: 30 minutes

Yield: 6 servings

Keeping kosher: Dairy if butter used to brush pastry and in sauce, Pareve if sauce made with pareve margarine

6 filo sheets

½ cup walnuts, chopped

⅓ cup raisins, finely chopped

1 pound ripe pears, peeled, halved, cored, thinly sliced, plus 2 whole ripe pears for garnish

⅓ cup sugar

2 teaspoons fresh strained lemon juice

1 teaspoon ground cinnamon

Pinch of ground cloves

2 tablespoons strawberry jam

⅓ cup butter or margarine, melted

6 tablespoons dry plain cookie or graham cracker crumbs

Powdered sugar (optional, for serving)

Vanilla ice cream (for serving)

1 If filo sheets are frozen, thaw them according to package instructions.

2 In a large bowl, mix nuts with raisins. Add pears, sugar, lemon juice, cinnamon, cloves, and jam and mix well.

3 Preheat oven to 375°. Lightly grease a baking sheet, using a little of the melted butter. Lay 1 filo sheet on a large sheet of waxed paper. Cover remaining filo sheets with plastic wrap and a very slightly dampened towel.

4 Brush the filo sheet on the waxed paper lightly with melted butter. Sprinkle with 1 tablespoon cookie crumbs. Top with a second sheet of filo, keeping the rest of the filo covered. Brush with butter and sprinkle with 1 more tablespoon crumbs. Top with a third sheet of filo and repeat the brushing and sprinkling.

5 Put half of filling near one end of top filo sheet, arranging it in a log shape and leaving a 1-inch border not covered with filling. Fold in both sides slightly to enclose filling. Starting with the filled end, gently roll dough toward the other end, using the paper to help support dough. Keeping the strudel with its seam side down, transfer it to the baking sheet. Brush top with butter. Make another strudel with remaining filling and remaining dough. Transfer it to the baking sheet.

6 Bake the strudels for 25 minutes or until golden.

7 Just before serving, slice the pears reserved for garnish. Serve the strudel warm, sprinkled with powdered sugar. To each plate add a few pear slices, a scoop of ice cream, and a little chocolate sauce. Serve remaining sauce separately.

Dark Chocolate Sauce

4 oz. semisweet chocolate, chopped

⅓ cup water

3 tablespoons sugar

3 tablespoons unsalted butter or margarine, cut in pieces

1 Combine chocolate and water in a small saucepan. Melt over very low heat, stirring occasionally.

2 Stir in sugar. Cook over low heat for 2 minutes. Remove from heat, add butter, and stir until it blends in.

3 Just before serving, reheat sauce in a bowl set in a pan of hot water over low heat. Stir until smooth. If sauce is too thick, gradually stir in a little water.

Strudel Per Serving: *Calories 410.91; Protein 4.3 g; Carbohydrates 60.1 g; Dietary fiber 5.3 g; Total fat 19.1 g; Saturated fat 7.4 g; Cholesterol 27.3 mg; Sodium 143.7 mg.*

Sauce Per Serving: *Calories 165.2; Protein 1.6 g; Carbohydrates 15.1 g; Dietary fiber 0.6 g; Total fat 13.3 g; Saturated fat 7.8 g; Cholesterol 15.5 mg; Sodium 1.4 mg.*

Jewish Mother's Tips: *If you want a pareve strudel, use margarine for brushing the dough and serve the strudel with nondairy ice cream made from soy or rice. You can find it at kosher or natural-foods stores.*

Slice strudel carefully with a serrated knife and a slow, sawing motion. It's easiest to cut after it has cooled. Don't worry if the slices aren't so neat — it will still be scrumptious.

Portable Food Spells Picnic-Like Fun

Bite-size appetizers are prepared in abundance for snacking on in the Sukkah and for serving friends who come by. They might be as simple as pickles, olives, and nuts. Most loved are the savory pastries, such as meat- or spinach-filled filo turnovers, a Sephardic standard for entertaining.

Sukkot dining is casual but festive. Because you need to bring the food from the kitchen to the Sukkah, most people opt for food that is easy to carry and serve. One-pot dishes like casseroles and stews are at the top of most cooks' lists. With all the food in a single dish, it helps avoid too many trips to the kitchen.

As on Rosh Hashanah, a stew called *tzimmes* (see Chapter 4), appears on Ashkenazic tables in numerous variations. This hearty one-dish meal fulfills both Sukkot needs — it is convenient for serving in the Sukkah and contains plenty of vegetables and fruits. Moroccan Jews make aromatic *tajines*, or stews of meat with vegetables or fruit.

Savory Drumsticks with Rice and Peppers

Israeli mothers love to cook chicken with rice because it is a favorite of children. Of course, adults also appreciate the wonderful flavor the chicken imparts to the rice as they cook. This savory one-pot dinner is perfect for carrying to the Sukkah table. (See the photo in the color insert section of this book.)

Including the season's luscious peppers and tomatoes makes the dish delicious and colorful as well as celebrating the holiday's harvest theme. In this dish, it's fun to experiment with the variety of peppers and tomatoes that become available at this time of year. Use any selection you like of sweet and hot ones. If you're serving young children, you'll probably want to go easy on the chilies or omit them.

Special tool: Large, deep, heavy skillet, 12 inches or more in diameter

Preparation time: 30 minutes

Cooking time: 1½ hours

Yield: 4 servings

Keeping kosher: Meat

2 to 2½ pounds chicken drumsticks

Salt and freshly ground pepper to taste

½ teaspoon turmeric

1½ teaspoons ground cumin

1 tablespoon olive oil

1 medium onion, thinly sliced

1 green bell pepper, cut in thin strips

1 red bell pepper, cut in thin strips

2 jalapeño peppers, chopped (optional)

2 large garlic cloves, chopped

1 cup long-grain white rice

½ teaspoon paprika

2 ripe medium tomatoes, peeled, seeded, and chopped

2 cups chicken stock or water

Cayenne pepper to taste

1 Sprinkle chicken with salt, pepper, turmeric, and 1 teaspoon cumin. Rub seasonings into chicken skin.

2 Heat oil in a very large heavy skillet. Add about half of chicken pieces and brown them on all sides over medium-low heat, about 10 minutes. Using tongs, remove them to a plate. Brown and remove remaining chicken.

3 Add onion to skillet and sauté about 7 minutes or until soft but not browned. Stir in bell peppers, jalapeño peppers, and garlic. Cook, stirring often, about 5 minutes. Add rice, paprika, and remaining cumin and cook over low heat, stirring, for 2 minutes.

4 Add tomatoes and stir into rice and vegetable mixture. Return chicken pieces to skillet.

5 In a small saucepan, bring chicken stock to a simmer and season it with salt, pepper, and cayenne. Pour 1¾ cups of the hot stock over mixture in skillet. Cover tightly and cook over very low heat, without stirring, for about 45 minutes or until chicken and rice are tender and liquid is absorbed. During the last 5 minutes, check on the amount of liquid. If all of it has been absorbed but the rice or chicken is not yet tender, add a few more tablespoons hot stock and simmer a few more minutes. Serve hot.

Per Serving: *Calories 507.4; Protein 34.5 g; Carbohydrates 49.1 g; Dietary fiber 3.0 g; Total fat 18.0 g; Saturated fat 4.0 g; Cholesterol 96.5 mg; Sodium 740.2 mg.*

Menu Maven Says: *Since this chicken entree already includes rice and vegetables, little else is needed to complete the meal. A green salad or diced vegetable salad adds a welcome fresh touch. For an additional cooked vegetable, boiled green beans or sautéed summer squash is fine, or serve the following recipe, Sautéed Zucchini in Tomato Dill Sauce. Fresh fruit is great at this season or serve a pareve cake or cookies.*

Sautéed Zucchini in Tomato Dill Sauce

This simple, tasty way of preparing zucchini is a favorite on Jewish tables. It's inspired by the Hungarian Jewish style of cooking and is much lighter than the familiar cream-laden Hungarian dishes. Bright and fresh flavored, this side dish complements just about any entree, from fish to meat to vegetarian. You can serve it hot or cold. For a colorful variation, use half zucchini and half yellow squash. (See the photo in the color insert section of this book.)

Preparation time: *30 minutes*

Cooking time: *25 minutes*

Yield: *4 servings*

Keeping kosher: *Pareve*

3 tablespoons vegetable oil

1¼ pounds ripe tomatoes, peeled, seeded and chopped

Salt and freshly ground pepper to taste

1½ teaspoons sweet paprika

1½ pounds zucchini

1 medium onion, chopped

Pinch of hot paprika or cayenne pepper (optional)

2 tablespoons chopped fresh dill, or 2 teaspoons dried

2 tablespoons chopped parsley

¼ teaspoon sugar (optional)

1 Heat 1 tablespoon oil in a deep skillet or casserole. Add tomatoes, salt, pepper, and 1 teaspoon sweet paprika. Cook, stirring often, over medium-high heat for 7 minutes or until thick.

2 Meanwhile, quarter zucchini lengthwise and cut each piece in 3 crosswise pieces.

3 Heat remaining oil in a medium sauté pan. Add onion and sauté over medium heat for 5 minutes or until golden brown. Add zucchini, remaining ½ teaspoon sweet paprika, hot paprika, salt, and pepper. Sauté 1 minute, stirring to coat. Cover and cook over medium-low heat, stirring occasionally, for 7 minutes or until barely tender. Check and add 1 or 2 tablespoons water during cooking if needed.

4 Add zucchini to tomato sauce and heat gently. Reserve 1 tablespoon fresh dill and 1 tablespoon parsley for sprinkling. Stir remaining dill and parsley into sauce; if using dried dill, stir in all of it. Adjust seasoning, adding sugar if needed. Serve hot or cold, sprinkled with the remaining dill and parsley.

Per Serving: Calories 141.7; Protein 3.1 g; Carbohydrates 10.9 g; Dietary fiber 3.6 g; Total fat 11.0 g; Saturated fat 0.8 g; Cholesterol 0 mg; Sodium 162.2 mg.

Jewish Mother's Tip: With the luscious ripe tomatoes and fresh zucchini at the peak of their seasons for Sukkot, you probably won't need sugar in the sauce, but it's always a good idea to taste tomato sauce to see whether you find it too tart. Tomatoes vary in their natural acidity and you might prefer a touch of sweetness in the sauce. A bit of sugar will also balance any bitterness in the zucchini, in case they're not in mint condition.

Old-Fashioned Potato Salad

Potato salad is perfect for the picnic-like atmosphere of Sukkot. Unlike deli potato salad, at home mayonnaise is the preferred dressing rather than sweet and sour boiled dressing. My Israeli-born sister-in-laws always add cooked peas and carrots to their salad. Pickles are a standard flavoring. These must be dill pickles, not sweet pickles.

Preparation time: *20 minutes*

Cooking time: *30 minutes*

Yield: *4 servings*

Keeping kosher: *Pareve*

2 pounds boiling potatoes, unpeeled	*⅓ cup finely chopped red or white onion*
Salt and freshly ground pepper to taste	*2 dill pickles, cut in small dice*
2 tablespoons mild white wine vinegar	*1 cup mayonnaise*
2 tablespoons water	*2 hard-boiled eggs, chopped*
2 cups frozen peas and carrots, or 1 cup of each	*3 tablespoons chopped parsley*

1 Scrub potatoes with a vegetable brush. Cut any large ones in half. Put them in a large saucepan, cover them with water by about ½ inch, add salt, and bring to a boil. Cover and simmer over low heat about 25 minutes or until tender enough so that knife pierces center of largest potato easily and potato falls from knife when lifted.

2 Meanwhile, mix vinegar, water, and a little salt and pepper in a small cup. Set aside for seasoning the warm potatoes.

3 Meanwhile, cook the peas and carrots in boiling water about 3 minutes or until just tender. Drain, rinse with cold water, and drain well.

4 Drain the potatoes in a colander. Peel them while they are hot and cut them in medium dice. Put potatoes in a large bowl and pour the vinegar mixture over them. Fold it in gently with a spatula. Let potatoes cool to room temperature.

5 Add onion, pickle, carrots, and peas to bowl of potatoes. Add mayonnaise and fold it in gently. Season to taste with salt and pepper. Add chopped eggs and parsley and fold them in gently. Refrigerate salad in a covered container until ready to serve.

Per Serving: *Calories 670.7; Protein 11.6 g; Carbohydrates 53.4 g; Dietary fiber 7.6 g; Total fat 47.0 g; Saturated fat 7.5 g; Cholesterol 138.6 mg; Sodium 997.1 mg.*

Jewish Mother's Tips: *When you're boiling potatoes for salad, the potatoes should be tender to taste good but do not overcook them, or they will fall apart when you cut them. To check them, pierce them with the point of a sharp knife. The knife should pierce the center of the largest potato easily. When you lift the knife, the potato should fall into the pot.*

If you prefer, make this salad with lowfat mayonnaise. For meatless meals, you can instead use half mayonnaise and half lowfat yogurt.

Chapter 6

Hanukkah: The Light-Hearted Festival of Lights and Latkes

- -

In This Chapter

▶ Making tasty treats and lighting festive candles to honor the holiday theme

▶ Turning vegetables into delectable latkes

▶ Dressing up your Hanukkah pancakes in sweet and savory ways

- -

Recipes in This Chapter

🍳 Pauline's Potato Pancakes

🍳 Spicy Vegetable Latkes

🍳 Fast, Lowfat Corn Latkes

🍳 Sweet Hanukkah Fritters

🍳 Homemade Cinnamon Applesauce

🍳 Leek and Mushroom Latke Topping

🥕 🥔 🍳 🧄 ✳ 🌿

anukkah is known as the Festival of Lights, but many food lovers think of it as the Festival of Latkes. These scrumptious holiday pancakes have become one of the best-known specialties of Jewish cooking. In this chapter, you discover how to present them in both customary and contemporary fashion. You will also find out what other treats are popular for Hanukkah.

Celebrating a Miracle Based on Oil

Hanukkah is an eight-day holiday that usually occurs in December and celebrates religious freedom. A miracle involving oil is Hanukkah's central theme and provides the background for its customs. In a historic event more than 2000 years ago, the Jews defeated a foreign army who had tried to deny them the right to practice their culture and their religion. Legend relates that when the Jews relit the light in the Jerusalem Temple, they had enough ritually pure oil for only one day. Miraculously, the oil turned out to be enough for eight days, and that's why Hanukkah is an eight-day holiday.

To symbolize the light in the temple, Hanukkah's main ritual is lighting candles. This is done in a specific way — one candle for the first night of the holiday, two for the second, and so on, culminating with eight. The candles appear in a Hanukkah candelabrum called a *hanukkiah* or *menorah,* with eight equal branches and a separate one to hold a candle that lights each of the others.

After the candle lighting, it's time for singing songs and feasting on latkes. So what's a latke? Look up *latke* in the dictionary, and it will tell you it's a pancake made from grated potatoes, and that the word is derived from Yiddish. Actually, latke in Yiddish means simply pancake. The potato pancake probably came from Russia, but there the Jews turned all sorts of ingredients, from buckwheat to noodles to cheese, into latkes.

In fact, it is the oil used for frying latkes that symbolizes Hanukkah because the miracle involved oil. Potatoes have nothing to do with the original Hanukkah theme. After all, the event that started Hanukkah occurred more than two millennia ago in Israel, where potatoes were unknown. They came from the New World and were brought to the Old World much later.

Most common are lacy-textured latkes made of grated raw potatoes mixed with onions and eggs and fried. Some people use mashed cooked potatoes instead for a pancake with a softer interior. At home, most people shallow-fry their latkes, but some cooks, especially at restaurants, deep-fry them and then they resemble fritters.

At Hanukkah parties, latkes star as a course on their own, served with sour cream and applesauce. For the kids (and some adults, too!), some also offer jelly, sugar, or cinnamon and sugar. Potato pancakes are also great partners for fish, chicken, or meat.

In kosher kitchens, sour cream is not served with latkes if they accompany meat or poultry dishes, but you may find applesauce on the table. Usually, you don't need additional toppings for latkes when they are companions for main dishes like stews or any that come with a sauce. You simply spoon some of the sauce over the latkes, too.

Keep these tips in mind when you're making potato latkes:

- **Most cooks recommend using baking potatoes.** They're a good choice because they tend to be less watery. When I don't have them, I find that large boiling potatoes give good results. too. My mother uses large potatoes and isn't much concerned about which type they are.

- **It might surprise you that potato latkes reheat beautifully, unlike most other fried foods. To make potato latkes ahead, fry them and put them on a cookie sheet and then refrigerate or freeze them.** Once they are frozen, you can transfer them to a freezer bag. Before serving, preheat the oven to 450 and, if your latkes are frozen, remove them from the freezer about 15 minutes before heating so that they partially thaw. Bake the refrigerated or frozen latkes on an ungreased cookie sheet for about 5 minutes or until they are hot. Frying potato latkes in advance is better than making the batter ahead, as the raw potatoes in the batter tend to discolor.

- **No matter what kind of latkes you are making, heat the oil well before adding the latkes.** That way, they don't stick.

- **Do not turn your latkes over too soon, or they will stick and break.** Once their bottoms have begun to brown, they don't stick. Check by lifting the edge of one carefully with a spatula when they appear to have begun browning at their lower edges.

↙ **When frying potato or vegetable pancakes, turn them carefully so that the oil doesn't splatter.** It's easiest to use two slotted spatulas or pancake turners to do this.

Pauline's Potato Pancakes

This is the way my mother, Pauline Kahn Luria, makes potato latkes, or pancakes, and I like to follow her tradition. They are lacy and crisp and always a hit at parties and dinners or as a savory snack. (You can see a photo of the recipe in the color insert section of this book.) My mother grates the potatoes by hand, but I use a food processor to save time. Serve them with their traditional partners — applesauce and sour cream. In our family, we often put out a bowl of plain yogurt, too. For an elegant dinner dish, crown them with Leek and Mushroom Latke Topping. (See recipe later in this chapter.)

Special tool: *Food processor with large grating disc or hand grater*

Preparation time: *20 minutes*

Cooking time: *30 minutes*

Yield: *4 servings (12 to 15 pancakes)*

Keeping kosher: *Pareve*

1¼ pounds large potatoes, peeled	*¼ to ½ teaspoon white pepper*
1 medium onion	*2 tablespoons flour*
1 egg, lightly beaten	*½ teaspoon baking powder*
1 teaspoon salt	*½ cup vegetable oil, more if needed*

1 Using coarse grating disc of a food processor or large holes of a hand grater, grate potatoes and onions, alternating them. Transfer the mixture to a colander. Squeeze mixture by handfuls to press out as much liquid as possible; discard liquid.

2 Put potato-onion mixture in a bowl. Add egg, salt, pepper, flour, and baking powder.

3 Heat ½ cup oil in a deep heavy 10- to 12-inch skillet. For each pancake, add about 2 tablespoons of potato mixture to pan. Add 3 or 4 more pancakes. Flatten with back of a spoon so that each measures 2 ½ inches. Fry over medium heat for 4 to 5 minutes. Using 2 pancake turners, turn them carefully. Fry second side about 4 minutes, or until pancakes are golden brown and crisp.

4 Drain on a plate lined with paper towels.

5 Stir potato mixture before frying each new batch. If all the oil is absorbed during frying, add 2 or 3 tablespoons more oil to pan. Serve hot.

Per Pancake: *Calories 97.5; Protein 1.2 g; Carbohydrates 6.4 g; Dietary fiber 0.6 g; Total fat 7.6 g; Saturated fat 0.6 g; Cholesterol 14.2 mg; Sodium 173.8 mg.*

Variations on the latke theme

Although potatoes are by far the most popular latke that everyone demands, you can make latkes from other vegetables, too. They become a welcome change in the course of the holiday; not everyone wants to eat potato pancakes every day.

The vegetables you choose depend on your own creativity. I've made them from corn, carrots, greens, zucchini, and mixtures of vegetables. You'll find it's fun to make up your own. Serve them the same way as potato latkes. With pancakes from some vegetables like cauliflower or spinach, you may prefer a spicy salsa or other topping instead of applesauce. (See the section "Topping alternatives" later in this chapter.)

Spicy Vegetable Latkes

You can make latkes from any vegetable you like. Some of those I've liked were sweet potatoes, leeks, spinach, squash, mushrooms, and cauliflower. If you'd like a variety of tastes and textures in each latke, you can combine a few vegetables for your latke mixture. Depending on the vegetable you choose, you either cook it and chop it, or you grate it raw. Then you mix the vegetable with seasonings, egg, and usually flour, bread crumbs, or matzo meal to hold it together. (You can see a photo of the recipe in the color insert section of this book.)

Preparation time: *20 minutes*

Cooking time: *30 minutes*

Yield: *4 appetizer or side-dish servings (12 to 14 small pancakes)*

Keeping kosher: *Pareve*

¾ cup coarsely grated zucchini

4 ounces small mushrooms

5 tablespoons olive oil, more if needed

1 medium onion, finely chopped

2 large garlic cloves, finely chopped

1 teaspoon ground cumin

¼ teaspoon turmeric

½ cup frozen peas, cooked

½ cup frozen corn, cooked

Salt and freshly ground pepper to taste

½ teaspoon dried oregano

Cayenne pepper to taste

2 large eggs, slightly beaten

3 tablespoons matzo meal

1 Put grated zucchini in a colander. Squeeze by handfuls to remove excess liquid; discard liquid. Leave zucchini in colander while preparing next ingredients.

2 Halve mushrooms, place them cut side down on board, and slice thin. Heat 1 tablespoon oil in a large skillet. Add onion and sauté over medium heat for 3 minutes. Add mushrooms and garlic and sauté for 2 to 3 minutes or until onions and mushrooms are tender. Add cumin and turmeric and stir over low heat for a few seconds.

3 Transfer mushroom mixture to a bowl. Add zucchini, peas, and corn and mix well. Add salt, pepper, oregano, and cayenne to taste. Stir in eggs and then matzo meal.

4 Heat 3 or 4 tablespoons oil in a deep heavy large skillet. For each latke, add 1 or 2 heaping tablespoons of vegetable mixture to pan. Flatten them slightly with back of a spoon. Sauté over medium heat for 2 to 3 minutes on each side, or until golden brown. Turn very carefully using two spatulas.

5 Drain on a plate lined with paper towels. Stir mixture before sautéing each new batch. If all the oil is absorbed during sautéing, add 1 tablespoon more oil to pan. Serve hot.

Per Latke: Calories 74.3; Protein 2.0 g; Carbohydrates 4.4 g; Dietary fiber 1.0 g; Total fat 5.7 g; Saturated fat 0.9 g; Cholesterol 30.4 mg; Sodium 59.1 mg.

Jewish Mother's Tip: *If your mushrooms are large, quarter them before slicing. Any large pieces of food in latkes can prevent them from holding together. Keep this point in mind when you create your own.*

Fast, Lowfat Corn Latkes

I created these pancakes at the request of a friend who wanted to celebrate Hanukkah with easy lowfat latkes. These fit the bill perfectly. I find that using corn in two ways — as a puree and as whole kernels — makes these latkes absolutely delicious. They're incredibly quick and easy, too. You can make them ahead and store them, layered with paper towels in a covered container, in the refrigerator for two or three days. Reheat them at 400° for about 5 minutes. (You can see a photo of the recipe in the color insert section of this book.)

The first time I made them, I was surprised at how little oil I could use, and they sautéed fine. You don't miss the fat at all. Their texture is tender with a delicate crust, somewhat like breakfast pancakes. It's hard to eat just a few of these small latkes. But remember, to keep the calories low, don't increase the portion size!

For a sweet treat, I love corn latkes topped with strawberry preserves or plum jam, which complement the corn's taste. They're also good with savory toppings like fruit-based salsas, roasted peppers, a light tomato sauce, or Leek and Mushroom Latke Topping (see recipe later in this chapter).

Special tool: *Nonstick skillet*

Preparation time: *10 minutes*

Cooking time: *25 minutes*

Yield: *4 appetizer or dessert servings (12 small pancakes)*

Keeping kosher: *Dairy*

2 cups frozen corn kernels	3 or 4 teaspoons canola oil
Pinch of salt	About $\frac{1}{3}$ cup nonfat yogurt or sour cream (for topping)
$\frac{1}{2}$ teaspoon sugar	
2 large egg whites	About $\frac{1}{3}$ cup strawberry preserves (for topping)
2 tablespoons flour	

1 Put corn in a saucepan of boiling salted water, return to a boil, and cook for 2 minutes or until tender; drain well and let cool. Puree $\frac{1}{2}$ cup cooked corn in a food processor; a few chunks may remain. Mix pureed corn with salt, sugar, and egg whites. Stir in flour and then corn kernels.

2 Heat 2 teaspoons oil in a large heavy nonstick skillet over medium heat; pan is hot enough when a drop of batter sizzles when added. For each latke, drop 1 rounded table-spoon of corn mixture into pan. Do not crowd them in pan. Flatten them slightly with back of a spoon. Cook over medium heat for 2½ to 3 minutes on each side or until light brown. To prevent sticking, turn latkes over only when their bottoms are cooked.

3 Transfer to a plate lined with paper towels. Stir corn mixture before cooking each new batch. Add more oil to skillet by teaspoons as needed. Serve latkes hot, with yogurt and preserves.

Per Latke: Calories 40.1; Protein 1.5 g; Carbohydrates 6.6 g; Dietary fiber 0.7 g; Total fat 1.3 g; Saturated fat 0.1 g; Cholesterol 0 mg; Sodium 22.2 mg.

Doughnuts for Hanukkah

To most Jews in North America, latkes mean Hanukkah. When I lived in Jerusalem, I was surprised to learn that to Israelis, *soofganiyot* say Hanukkah even more than *levivot,* the Hebrew word for latkes. Soofganiyot are light doughnuts without holes. They are made plain or filled with jelly. In Israel on Hanukkah, they are everywhere. You can buy fresh ones at bakeries, super-markets, and even tiny corner grocery stores throughout Israel. In recent years, soofganiyot have become popular in the United States and can be found at American Jewish bakeries during Hanukkah.

Because soofganiyot are fried in oil, they commemorate the Hanukkah mira-cle as well as latkes. Of course, plenty of people enjoy both!

Bakery doughnuts are made from yeast-leavened dough. At home, Israeli mothers make them, too. Some cooks prefer to make easier, faster versions using baking powder.

Soofganiyot probably came to Israel with the immigration of Jews from cen-tral Europe. This type of doughnut can be found from Alsace in France to Germany, Austria, Hungary, and other nearby countries.

Hot oil can be a fire hazard and can cause severe burns. To avoid any prob-lems, be sure to observe these points:

- ✔ **Fill the saucepan up to halfway with oil.** Do not add more, or it may boil over when you add the food.
- ✔ **Hold the food near the oil's surface and put it in gently.** Don't drop the food from high above the oil, or the hot oil may splash on you.
- ✔ **As you add the food, the oil will bubble vigorously.** Never crowd the pan so the oil will not come up too high.
- ✔ **Regulate the heat as needed to keep the oil at the right temperature.**
- ✔ **Give frying your full attention.** Never leave the pan unattended, even for a moment.
- ✔ **If possible, keep a fire extinguisher in the kitchen.**

Sweet Hanukkah Fritters

At home, many Israelis prepare other fried pastries instead of yeast-leavened soofganiyot, opting to buy the yeast type at the store. These fritters are made of batter or simple dough, and many have become family traditions.

You can make these easy puffs in a short time because they're made from a batter leavened with baking powder instead of yeast. Forming them is quick, too. Instead of rolling out dough with a rolling pin and cutting it in rounds, you shape the fritters with spoons, like making cookies.

Serve the fritters a short time after frying them. Accompany them with a small bowl of jam, jelly, or fruit preserves if you like.

Special tools: *Deep fryer or heavy deep saucepan, frying thermometer if possible*

Preparation time: *10 minutes*

Cooking time: *15 minutes*

Yield: *4 to 6 servings (16 to 18 small fritters)*

Keeping kosher: *Dairy*

1¼ cups flour	3 tablespoons cool melted butter or vegetable oil
1¼ teaspoons baking powder	½ teaspoon vanilla extract
2 large eggs	1½ teaspoons finely grated orange zest
3 tablespoons sugar	5 cups vegetable oil (for deep frying)
⅓ cup milk	Powdered sugar, sifted (for sprinkling)
¼ teaspoon salt	

1 Prepare a tray lined with paper towels. Sift flour with baking powder. Whisk eggs and sugar in a bowl. Whisk in milk, salt, butter, and vanilla until smooth. Stir in orange zest. Add flour mixture and stir slowly with the whisk to a smooth thick batter.

2 Heat oil for deep frying in a deep fryer or a deep heavy saucepan to 350 on a frying thermometer, or until a small piece of dough added to oil makes it bubble gently.

3 Take a rounded teaspoon of batter. Dip a second spoon in the oil and then use it to push the batter from the first spoon gently into the oil. To prevent hot oil splatters, do not drop dough from high above oil. Be careful not to crowd pan.

4 Fry 2 to 3 minutes on each side or until golden brown. Remove with a slotted metal spoon. Drain on paper towels. Pat tops gently with paper towels to absorb excess oil.

5 Check oil temperature and reduce heat if it has increased. Continue making more puffs with remaining batter. Serve fritters hot or warm, dusted with powdered sugar.

Per serving: Calories 94.8; Protein 1.8 g; Carbohydrates 9.0 g; Dietary fiber 0.3 g; Total fat 5.7 g; Saturated fat 1.7 g; Cholesterol 29.4 mg; Sodium 68.3 mg.

Lending Life to Latkes

Latkes are tasty on their own, but toppings or dips make them even more fun to eat. A selection of them lends a festive air to Hanukkah parties.

Conventional applesauce and contemporary innovations

Most people simply serve their latkes with applesauce from a jar. We used to have only sweetened or unsweetened applesauce to choose from, but now you're likely to find some new versions at many markets. You'll see cinnamon applesauce and others flavored with apricots, peaches, blackberries, and other fruit or made from specific varieties of apples. Choose whichever type appeals to you, remembering that children at the party tend to go for the simplest kind. For entertaining or to be true to tradition, you may enjoy serving your own homemade applesauce instead.

Topping alternatives

Today's diners often like savory sauces and spicy toppings with their latkes. There's no rule about choosing them. You can stay fairly close to custom by simply mixing a few herbs in your sour cream or substituting yogurt. Or go wild with toppings like pesto, Mexican salsa, or the French olive paste called tapenade.

Chefs of fancy eateries seem to have adopted potato latkes in a big way. They stuff latkes with fish, use them as a base for steaks, or top them with caviar.

Homemade Cinnamon Applesauce

Applesauce that you make in your own kitchen is much tastier than the kind in a can or jar. Besides, you can use the type of apples you prefer. I often use naturally sweet ones like Golden Delicious or Gala or semisweet ones like Jonathan so I don't need to add much sugar. Some cooks prefer tart apples, such as Granny Smith or Pippin. This way of making applesauce is convenient because you don't need a food mill. (You can see a photo of the recipe in the color insert section of this book.)

Special tool: *Food processor, nonstick skillet*

Preparation time: *12 minutes*

Cooking time: *30 minutes*

Yield: *6 to 8 servings*

Keeping kosher: *Dairy if made with butter; pareve if made with oil*

2 pounds sweet apples, such as Golden Delicious or Gala, or tart ones, such as Granny Smith or Pippin

2 tablespoons butter or vegetable oil

1 teaspoon lemon juice, or more to taste

1 teaspoon ground cinnamon, or more to taste

Pinch of ground cloves

¼ cup apple juice or water (optional)

2 tablespoons sugar, or more to taste

Pinch of freshly grated nutmeg (optional)

1 Peel and halve apples. Cut each in 6 to 8 wedges or in thick slices, discarding cores.

2 Melt butter in a large sauté pan. Add apples and sauté over medium-high heat, stirring occasionally, for 2 minutes or until they are coated with butter.

3 Add lemon juice, cinnamon, and cloves. Cover and cook over low heat for 5 minutes, or until liquid begins to come out of apples. If pan is dry, add apple juice and bring to a simmer.

4 Uncover and cook over low heat, gently stirring occasionally, for 20 minutes, or until apples are tender and beginning to fall apart.

5 Add 2 tablespoons sugar and cook over medium-high heat, stirring, for 2 minutes or until sugar dissolves. Remove from heat. Taste and add more sugar if needed and return to heat for another 2 minutes. Add nutmeg and more lemon juice or cinnamon if you like. Let cool.

6 Puree apple mixture in a food processor, leaving it chunky, if you prefer, or running machine until applesauce is smooth.

7 Serve warm, cold, or at room temperature, with potato pancakes.

Per serving: Calories 93.4; Protein 0.2 g; Carbohydrates 17.7 g; Dietary fiber 2.0 g; Total fat 3.2 g; Saturated fat 1.8 g; Cholesterol 7.8 mg; Sodium 0.5 mg.

Leek and Mushroom Latke Topping

This savory medley scented with cumin and thyme enlivens any vegetable or potato pancakes. If you're including dairy foods on the menu, top each latke with a spoonful of sour cream or yogurt and then with the topping.

Preparation time: *20 minutes*

Cooking time: *15 minutes*

Yield: *4 to 6 servings as topping*

Keeping kosher: *Pareve*

1 pound leeks, white and light green parts only	*Salt and freshly ground pepper*
2 tablespoons olive oil	*6 ounces mushrooms, halved and sliced*
4 to 6 tablespoons vegetable stock	*½ teaspoon paprika*
1 teaspoon dried leaf thyme, crumbled	*Cayenne pepper to taste*
1 teaspoon ground cumin	*1 tablespoon chopped Italian parsley*

1 Split and clean leeks. Cut them in thin slices.

2 Heat 1 tablespoon oil in a heavy sauté pan. Add leeks and sauté, stirring, for 1 minute. Add 4 tablespoons stock, thyme, ½ teaspoon cumin, salt, and pepper. Cover and cook over low heat, stirring often, about 10 minutes or until leeks are tender; add more stock if pan becomes dry. If mixture is soupy, uncover and simmer until excess liquid evaporates.

3 Heat remaining tablespoon oil in a large heavy skillet over medium heat. Add mushrooms, salt, and pepper. Sauté mushrooms, stirring often, about 2 minutes or until just tender. Add paprika and ½ teaspoon cumin and cook over low heat about ½ minute.

4 Add mushrooms to pan of leeks and mix gently. Heat over medium heat for 1 or 2 minutes to blend flavors. Season to taste with cayenne, salt, and pepper. Serve sprinkled with parsley.

Jewish Mother's Tip: For a lowfat variation to serve with Lowfat Corn Latkes (see recipe earlier in this chapter), use a total of 2 ½ teaspoons olive oil. Use 1 teaspoon with the leeks and 1½ teaspoons for the mushrooms. Sauté the mushrooms in a heavy, nonstick skillet.

Per serving: *Calories 70.0; Protein 1.5 g; Carbohydrates 6.2 g; Dietary fiber 1.3 g; Total fat 4.9 g; Saturated fat 0.7 g; Cholesterol 0.0 mg; Sodium 106.5 mg.*

Chapter 7

Purim: When the Mitzvah Is Merrymaking

Purim is a joyous festival celebrated in late February or March to commemorate the Jews' deliverance from danger in ancient Persia. It is a holiday of gaiety, games, and sweets, of costumes, cookies, and rum balls. In this chapter, you find out how to prepare delicious Purim treats that are good for any festive occasion.

How to Make Pleasure a Precept

All are urged, practically commanded to have fun on this holiday. Noisemaking, costume balls, treats, and wine add to the exuberantly joyous atmosphere.

Children are the stars of Purim. They especially love this holiday because they are not just allowed, but urged, to make noise. At the synagogue service, the reader chants the Book of Esther, who was the Jewish Queen of Persia. She helped to thwart the wicked scheme of the king's powerful adviser Haman, who wanted to murder the Jews.

Although this is a solemn story, there are moments of levity: Every time the leader pronounces Haman's name, the children in the congregation stamp and make lots of noise with special noisemakers called *groggers* designed for the occasion. There is a role to this racket — the children must listen carefully to the reading in order to play their part properly.

Purim is the merriest holiday on the Jewish calendar, and adults like it almost as much as children do. With the multicourse feast celebrating the occasion, adults are encouraged to drink wine.

Observing Purim with wine is not simply a suggestion. It is a recommendation of the rabbis because it is a hallmark of joyful celebrations.

Like Halloween, Purim involves dressing up. The children get to wear costumes and make-up to the synagogue and to school. Some dress as Queen Esther, Haman, or other characters of the Book of Esther, but others opt for their TV heroes or select funny subjects like cookies. Purim parades are popular in Israel, where costumed children also stroll around the neighborhoods and show off their outfits at the markets.

Some adults continue this jolly tradition at masquerade balls. Every Purim my mother dresses up, perhaps as a gypsy or a sari-clad Indian woman, and sometimes wins a prize for her disguise. One year my husband and I went to a Purim party as newlyweds and had fun wearing our wedding clothes again!

What a Jewish Girl Ate in a Persian Palace

The heroine of the Purim tale is Queen Esther, who was chosen by the King of Persia to be his wife. Food customs of the holiday commemorate her courage. Legend relates that she risked her life to beg the king to disregard the evil plan of his advisor Haman.

According to legend, the Jewish queen became a vegetarian when she moved into the king's palace because she could not obtain kosher meat. If the banquets at the king's palace were as good as the recent feast I enjoyed at the home of some Persian friends, these culinary delights were indeed difficult to resist!

Yet Esther had will power. She lived on legumes and seeds. Inspired by her example, some observant Jews also follow a meatless diet when traveling or when they cannot find kosher food.

Today many Jews still observe a custom of including chickpeas, beans, poppy seeds, and nuts in Purim menus and treats. Some people of North African origin begin the festive dinner with a plate of fava beans and hard-boiled eggs. An Ashkenazic Purim favorite is noodles with poppy seeds. In most homes, poppy seeds flavor the filling of choice for the holiday's traditional cookies, hamantaschen.

Chickpea and Green Soybean Salad

A plain plate of chickpeas, or garbanzo beans, appears on many Purim tables. Instead, I prefer to turn them into this healthful, savory salad. If I have time, I follow the holiday custom of cooking dried chickpeas for optimum texture. Otherwise, I find the canned ones are a good stand-in. When I brought this salad to a potluck Purim party, they were a hit. As a colorful variation, you can add four diced plum tomatoes. (You can see a photo of this recipe in the color insert section of this book.)

Green soybeans, also sold under their Japanese name, *edamame,* are available in Asian, gourmet, and natural-foods stores as well as many supermarkets. They cook quickly and are a great addition to the pareve pantry. You can buy them shelled or in the pod. Obviously, the shelled ones are the most convenient to use.

Preparation time: *20 minutes*

Cooking time: *5 minutes (plus 1 hour of marinating time)*

Yield: *6 to 8 servings*

Keeping kosher: *Pareve*

2 cups frozen shelled green soybeans	*2 cups cooked chickpeas, also called garbanzo beans, or a 15-ounce can, drained*
¼ large onion, chopped	
1½ tablespoons lemon juice	*½ cucumber, diced (1 cup)*
2 tablespoons extra virgin olive oil	*1 cup diced jicama, or 3 radishes, diced*
Salt and freshly ground pepper	*⅓ cup chopped Italian parsley*

1 Cook the soybeans in a saucepan of boiling water for 5 minutes or until tender. Drain, reserving liquid for vegetable soups if you like, and rinse to cool.

2 In a large bowl, mix the onion with the lemon juice, olive oil, salt, and pepper. Add the chickpeas, soybeans, cucumber, jicama, and parsley. Taste and adjust seasoning. Let stand about 1 hour to marinate before serving or refrigerate overnight. Serve cold or at room temperature.

Per serving: *Calories 202.7; Protein 12.3 g; Carbohydrates 21.0 g; Dietary fiber 6.9 g; Total fat 8.9 g; Saturated fat 1.1 g; Cholesterol 0 mg; Sodium 87.7 mg.*

Why You Share Sweets and Gifts

Everyone should share the joy of the holiday. For this reason, giving gifts to the poor is an important Purim precept. Another well-loved tradition is "Mishloah manot," a Hebrew phrase meaning "sending of portions." In practice, this custom has evolved into a Jewish "cookie exchange."

By far the most popular Purim sweet is a filled cookie called *hamantaschen,* Yiddish for Haman's pockets, also called "Oznei Haman," Hebrew for Haman's ears. These three-cornered cookies are filled with poppy seed, prune, or other dried fruit mixtures.

Fresh poppy seeds are not an everyday ingredient. Here are some hints for finding and using them.

- ✔ **Use fresh poppy seeds.** You can find them in Jewish, Polish, and Iranian markets and in some gourmet groceries.

- ✔ **Store the fresh poppy seeds in a cool place.** If they have been ground, refrigerate them and use them promptly.

- ✔ **If you prefer a smooth filling, grind the seeds in a spice grinder or coffee grinder.** Leave them whole for a more crunchy texture. I like both ways.

High on Hamantaschen, a poppy seed story

When I lived in the Tel Aviv area, I heard a Purim anecdote on the Israel army radio station about a little boy who ate over 20 poppy seed hamantaschen at one time and became high. His parent's took him to the hospital because they didn't know what to do.

Although poppy seeds do come from the opium poppy, I have my doubts about this story's reliability. Maybe the reporter was pulling a Purim prank on his listeners. According to *The Cook's Book* by Howard Hillman (Avon, 1981), "You can eat poppy-seed cakes and pastries forever without experiencing any narcotic effects, because the plant cannot form seeds until all the narcotic alkaloids have disappeared from the plants."

Poppy seeds have a pleasantly nutty flavor and aroma. Although I tend to associate poppy seeds with Ashkenazic sweets, poppies have been grown in the Near East since ancient times. In India, they are used to thicken sauces or combined with spices to flavor vegetables.

Crisp Cookie Dough

This delicately sweet dough is my favorite pastry for making hamantaschen. Paradoxically, the triangular treats begin with dough cut in circles. Basically, you take three arcs of each dough round and fold them over the filling. What you get is a three-cornered treat.

For ease in rolling, prepare the dough at least three hours ahead, wrap it in plastic wrap, and keep it in the refrigerator. You can keep it up to three days.

This dough also makes terrific flat cookies. Make them with the extra dough. They will need only about 8 minutes to bake.

Preparation time: *15 minutes, plus 3 hours to chill*

Cooking time: *None*

Yield: *Dough for 2½ dozen hamantaschen*

Keeping kosher: *Dairy*

3¾ cups flour	1 large egg
1⅓ cups powdered sugar	1 large egg yolk
1½ teaspoons baking powder	1¼ cups cold butter, cut in small bits
¼ teaspoon salt	1 to 2 tablespoons orange juice (optional)

1 Combine flour, powdered sugar, baking powder, and salt in a large food processor. Process briefly to blend.

2 Beat the egg with the yolk in a small bowl.

3 Scatter the butter pieces over the flour mixture in the processor. Mix using on/off pulsing motion until mixture resembles coarse meal.

4 Pour the egg mixture evenly over the mixture. Process with an on/off motion, stopping to scrape the mixture down occasionally, until the dough just begins to come together in a ball. If the crumbs are dry, sprinkle with 1 tablespoon orange juice and process briefly; repeat if the crumbs are still dry. The top of the dough may seem a little dry, but the bottom will be moist and will moisten the rest when you knead it.

5 Transfer dough to a work surface. Knead it lightly to blend the ingredients. With a rubber spatula, transfer the dough to a sheet of plastic wrap. Wrap it and push it together, shaping it a flat disk. Refrigerate the dough for three hours before using it.

Per serving: *Calories 146.4; Protein 2.0 g; Carbohydrates 16.4 g; Dietary fiber 0.4 g; Total fat 8.2 g; Saturated fat 4.9 g; Cholesterol 34.9 mg; Sodium 42.1 mg.*

Jewish Mother's Tip: *Unsalted butter gives the dough the finest flavor. This rich dough softens rapidly. Handle it lightly. If it becomes too soft while you are rolling it or shaping the cookies, refrigerate it to firm it before continuing.*

Menu Maven Says: *For a kosher finale to a meat meal, make the dough and the filling with pareve margarine instead of butter. For simmering the poppy seeds in the filling, substitute water for the milk, or use half water and half orange juice to complement the orange zest in the mixture.*

Hamantaschen with Poppy Seeds

To make a delicious, creamy filling for these three-cornered cookies, simmer the poppy seeds with milk and honey and accent the mixture with nuts and raisins. (You can see a photo of this recipe in the color insert section of this book.)

Special tools: *Rolling pin, 3-inch cookie cutter*

Preparation time: *1 hour, plus 2 hours to chill*

Cooking time: *30 minutes*

Yield: *About 2 to 2½ dozen*

Keeping kosher: *Dairy*

Crisp Cookie Dough, refrigerated (see preceding recipe)	*¼ cup sugar*
¾ cup poppy seeds (¼ pound)	*¼ cup raisins*
½ cup milk	*2 tablespoons butter*
¼ cup honey	*¼ cup pecans, finely chopped*
	1 teaspoon grated orange zest

1 For the poppy seed filling, grind the seeds in a spice grinder if you prefer a fine texture.

2 In small saucepan, combine poppy seeds, milk, honey, and sugar and bring to a simmer. Cook over low heat, stirring often, about 15 to 20 minutes or until it is thick. Add the raisins and butter and stir the filling over low heat until the butter melts. Remove from heat.

3 Stir in the pecans and orange zest. Refrigerate in a covered container for at least two hours before using.

4 Grease two baking sheets. To shape the cookies, use one quarter of the dough at a time. Roll it out on a lightly floured surface until it is about ⅛ inch thick.

5 Using a 3-inch cookie cutter, cut the dough in rounds. Brush their edges lightly with water. Put 1 teaspoon filling in the center of each one. Pull up the edges of each round in three arcs that meet above the filling, covering it, as shown in Figure 7-1. Pinch the dough above the filling to close the cookies firmly. Pinch the edges to seal them. Put them on a greased baking sheet and refrigerate them uncovered while shaping the remaining cookies. Pat the dough scraps together, wrap them in plastic wrap, and refrigerate them also. Save them for making flat cookies.

6 Roll the remaining dough and shape more hamantaschen. Refrigerate the cookies at least 30 minutes before baking to firm dough.

7 Preheat oven to 375°. Bake the hamantaschen for 14 minutes, or until they are light golden at the edges. Cool them on a rack.

Per serving: *Calories 200.5; Protein 2.9 g; Carbohydrates 22.6 g; Dietary fiber 1.0 g; Total fat 11.4 g; Saturated fat 5.7 g; Cholesterol 37.5 mg; Sodium 45.5 mg.*

Jewish Mother's Tip: *To get ahead with your holiday baking, you can keep the shaped cookies overnight in the refrigerator before baking them. Once baked, they keep for about four days in an airtight container at room temperature. You can also freeze them.*

Warning: *Resist the temptation to overfill the cookies, or they may burst. Also make sure that you bake the cookies only until they are pale golden at the edges. If the cookies are baked too long, the sugar in the dough may cause them to burn.*

FOLDING HAMANTASCHEN

Figure 7-1:
Folding traditional holiday cookies isn't as hard as you may think.

1. CUT DOUGH INTO 3-INCH CIRCLES AND BRUSH LIGHTLY WITH WATER.

2. PUT 1 TEASPOON OF FILLING INTO THE CENTER OF EACH CIRCLE.

3. PULL UP THE EDGES, IN 3 ARCS THAT MEET IN THE CENTER.

4. CLOSE FIRMLY AND PINCH EDGES TO SEAL.

Tidbits to bring your neighbors

Relatives, neighbors, and friends give each other decorative tins of treats. Often, children perform this pleasant task. In addition to hamantaschen, the pretty boxes may include favorite cookies, slices of cake, or candies. Preference is for home-baked delights but if time is short, bakery cookies do the job.

Chocolate Almond Rum Balls

In my family, chocolate stands for celebrations, and we always make these scrumptious sweets. They are great additions to the traditional Purim gift boxes of treats, if you manage to resist eating them while you're shaping them! (You can see a photo of this recipe in the color insert section of this book.)

I love the ease and versatility of this confection. The mixture takes moments to make, and you can prepare it from pantry staples — leftover cookies, cocoa, chocolate, and nuts. Depending on what you have on hand, you can vary the taste and texture according to your impulse. Graham crackers work well, as do basic sugar cookies and cake crumbs.

Preparation time: *1 hour*

Cooking time: *5 minutes*

Yield: *2½ dozen*

Keeping kosher: *Dairy when made with butter; pareve if made with pareve margarine*

4 ounces bittersweet or semisweet chocolate, chopped	5 tablespoons butter or margarine, room temperature, cut in pieces
2 tablespoons unsweetened cocoa	1¼ cupscookie crumbs (made from 4 to 6 ounces simple, unfilled cookies)
2 tablespoons sugar	
½ cup sweet wine	½ cup toasted almonds
2 tablespoons rum	1 cup coconut

1 Combine the chocolate, cocoa, sugar, wine, and rum in a heavy, medium saucepan. Heat the mixture over low heat, stirring often, until the chocolate melts. Remove from heat and add the butter. Stir the mixture until the butter melts and blends in.

2 In a food processor, grind the cookies to fairly coarse crumbs. Stir them into chocolate mixture. Add the almonds to the processor and process until finely chopped. Add them to the chocolate mixture and mix well. Transfer to a bowl. Refrigerate the mixture about 30 minutes, or until it is just firm enough to shape in balls.

3 Prepare a shallow bowl or tray and put the coconut in it. To shape the sweets, take about 2 teaspoons of the chocolate mixture and roll it quickly in your palms to a smooth ball. Set the ball in the coconut and roll it until it is completely coated. Set it on a plate. Refrigerate 1 hour or up to 1 week before serving. Serve the candies cold or at room temperature, in candy papers.

Per serving: Calories 92.3; Protein 1.2 g; Carbohydrates 8.1 g; Dietary fiber 0.9 g; Total fat 5.8 g; Saturated fat 3.0g; Cholesterol 5.4 mg; Sodium 29.4 mg.

Jewish Mother's Tips: *If you like, substitute orange juice for the wine and the rum. Also, use coconut that is finely grated. My favorite is the unsweetened type, sometimes sold as macaroon coconut in natural-foods stores.*

Children love to help roll homemade candies.

Chapter 8

Passover: What Happened When the Bread Didn't Rise

*T*he eight-day springtime festival of Passover, or *Pessah* in Hebrew, celebrates the ancient Hebrews' liberation from slavery in Egypt about 3,000 years ago. Passover food customs commemorate this milestone event.

On the Passover table, matzo is served instead of bread, as a reminder of the slaves' hurried escape. The Torah relates that the fleeing Hebrews did not have time to let their bread rise. To identify with their ancestors' flight and deliverance, the Jews eat *matzo,* a flat, unleavened cracker-like bread.

Creating the Passover Paradox

Passover meals are intentionally different from those of the rest of the year. Besides bread, several other foods are shunned. In spite of these constraints, most people look forward to Passover as a food holiday. Inventive cooks throughout the ages contributed to the holiday flavors and have produced a popular Passover repertoire. They developed tasty, out-of-the-ordinary dishes. The result is that Passover meals are not only the most festive of the year but the most interesting as well.

Meals without grains and beans

Grains are eliminated from most traditional Jewish tables during Passover. True, *matzo* (see Figure 8-1) is made of wheat, but it is a special exception. In some Sephardic communities, rice is allowed, too. Ashkenazic Jews and many Sephardic Jews avoid beans as well.

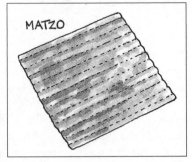

Figure 8-1: Matzo replaces bread on Passover.

Foods prohibited during Passover are called *hametz* in Hebrew, meaning leavened. In addition to bread, certain other foods are not allowed because they can *leaven,* or ferment naturally, upon contact with liquid. These foods include wheat flour, other grains, and legumes. This principle is the same one that's behind sourdough baking: When a mixture of flour and water is left to sit, it catches wild yeast from the air.

Matzo itself is made from wheat flour. To prevent its fermentation, it is inspected during its preparation to ensure that the dough is mixed quickly and baked immediately.

Menus highlighting matzo

Matzo does not simply play the role of bread replacer. Cooks turn it into an amazing variety of delicacies, from lasagna to chicken stuffing to cookies.

When I was a child, we had only white flour matzo and egg matzo. Matzo is now available in a variety of flavors, such as whole wheat, white grape, and chocolate.

Although most matzo is square, there are special *shmura matzos,* meaning watched-over matzos, which are usually round. Even more than other types of matzo, they are carefully scrutinized by rabbis or special inspectors at every stage of their preparation. Orthodox Jews prefer them for the Seder.

Certain flavored matzo varieties are not considered kosher for Passover. Check the labels on the packages.

A glance at the supermarket Passover displays reveals many foods made from matzo. Cooks find matzo meal, cake meal, and matzo farfel the most useful. (See Table 8-1 for descriptions and uses of basic Passover ingredients.) Passover pasta began recently appearing in the stores so that noodle lovers need no longer miss their favorite food during the holiday. You can also find numerous cake mixes and prepared cakes and cookies.

Table 8-1	Basic Passover Products	
Food	*Description*	*Main Uses*
Matzo meal	Flour made from ground matzos	Dumplings, breading, baked goods
Cake meal or matzo cake meal	Fine flour made from ground matzos	Cakes, other baked goods
Matzo farfel	Small matzo squares	Breakfast cereal, casseroles, stuffing
Potato starch	Flour made from potatoes	Cakes

My Mother's Fluffy Matzo Balls

Matzo balls are not just for chicken soup. Few people realize how versatile they are. My mother adds them to all sorts of soups, from creamy to chunky, and they enhance these soups beautifully.

Like my mother, I prefer my matzo balls light and airy. The secret is keeping the batter soft and shaping the balls with a gentle, light touch.

During most of the year, you can add ½ teaspoon baking powder to this recipe to make the matzo balls puff more. For Passover, people make their matzo balls without it because leavening agents are not allowed. (See the photo in the color insert section of this book.)

Preparation time: *20 minutes, plus 20 minutes chilling*

Cooking time: *30 minutes*

Yield: *6 servings*

Keeping kosher: *Meat or pareve*

2 eggs	*1½ teaspoons salt*
1 tablespoon vegetable oil	*3 tablespoons chicken or vegetable broth, or water*
½ cup matzo meal, plus 1 tablespoon more if needed	*About 2 quarts salted water (for simmering)*
Pinch of ground white or black pepper	

1 In a medium bowl, lightly beat eggs with oil. Add ½ cup matzo meal, pepper, and ½ teaspoon of the salt. Stir with a fork until batter is smooth. Slowly stir in 1 tablespoon chicken soup.

2 Cover the batter and refrigerate it for 20 minutes. It will thicken as the matzo meal softens and absorbs some of the liquid.

3 In a medium saucepan, bring 2 quarts of water to a boil and add 1 teaspoon salt. Reduce the heat so that the water barely simmers.

4 Check the batter for thickness. It should be very soft. With wet hands, take about 1 teaspoon of matzo ball batter and shape it lightly in a small, roughly round dumpling by transferring it from one hand to the other. The batter should be too soft to be formed into a neat, round ball. If it is firm, gradually stir another tablespoon of the chicken soup into the batter and make another dumpling.

5 If you're not sure whether the matzo balls will hold together, slip your test one into the simmering water and cook it over low heat for 10 minutes. Remove it with a slotted spoon and taste it for firmness. If it is too firm, stir a little more soup into the batter. If it falls apart, stir in another tablespoon of matzo meal. Taste it for seasoning and add more salt and pepper to the batter if you like.

6 Carefully slip the matzo ball into the water. Continue shaping matzo balls, wetting your hands before each one and using 1 teaspoon of batter for each.. Cover and simmer over low heat about 30 minutes or until firm. Cover and keep them warm until ready to serve.

Per serving: *Calories 71.6; Protein 3.0 g; Carbohydrates 5.8 g; Dietary fiber 0.3 g; Total fat 4.1 g; Saturated fat 0.7 g; Cholesterol 71.0 mg; Sodium 536.9 mg.*

Jewish Mother's Tip: *Do not worry if the batter does not form neat, regular rounds. Perfect spheres usually mean overly firm matzo balls.*

Prominence of potatoes

Because many of the usual carbohydrate foods are not permitted during the holiday, potatoes play a major part on Passover menus (see Figure 8-2). Potato starch replaces flour in some recipes.

A favorite way to prepare potatoes, especially for the Seder and for other festive meals, is to bake them around a main course of chicken, turkey, or meat, as in the recipe Garlic Roast Lamb with Potatoes, later in this chapter, or to roast them separately in a pan as in Rosemary Roasted Potatoes (see Chapter 10). Some prepare potato latkes, similar to those for Hanukkah (see Chapter 6), but with no baking powder and with matzo meal used instead of the flour. For an appealing accompaniment for fish or to serve at Passover dairy dinners, bake a Creamy Potato Kugel with Leeks (see Chapter 17).

Figure 8-2: Potatoes of all kinds are popular on Passover menus.

Preparing for Passover

In observant households, people start preparing for Passover at least several days ahead. Many do a thorough spring cleaning to be certain that no bread or cake crumbs are in the house.

Kitchen implements

To keep the food completely kosher for Passover, many people switch their eating and cooking utensils, including dishes, flatware, pots, and mixing spoons. This means two sets of Passover equipment, one for meat meals and one for dairy dining.

Using different dishes helps give this week's meals a special presentation and contributes to the festive feeling. So does the custom of buying new clothes for the whole family.

Special Seder foods

Passover begins with a ritual-rich dinner called a Seder. It involves ceremonial foods presented on a special Seder plate, which is divided into sections labeled in Hebrew indicating where to place each food. (See Table 8-2 and the Passover photo in the color insert section of this book.) Their purpose is to symbolize the Hebrews' bondage in Egypt, deliverance, and gaining their own land of Israel.

Table 8-2	Seder Plate Foods and Labels		
Food	*Hebrew Label*	*Ingredients Used*	*Symbolizes*
Bitter herbs	Maror	Grated fresh horseradish or leaves of bitter greens	Misery of servitude
Haroset	Haroset	Fruit and nuts made into spread (See Haroset recipe)	Mortar and bricks made by Hebrew slaves

Food	Hebrew Label	Ingredients Used	Symbolizes
Roasted bone	Zeroah	Roasted lamb shank or chicken neck	Sacred sacrifices at Holy Temple in Jerusalem
Egg	Beitzah	Hard-boiled egg	Temple offerings
Celery	Karpas	Stick of celery or sprig of parsley	Spring

A matzo plate is an essential Seder table element. On it are three matzos, often covered with or enclosed in a matzo cloth reserved for the occasion.

Wine is an important element of the Seder. During the ceremony, people drink four glasses of wine. Many families serve it in special small glasses, as shown in Figure 8-3.

Figure 8-3:
In the course of the Passover Seder ceremony, four glasses of wine are poured for each person.

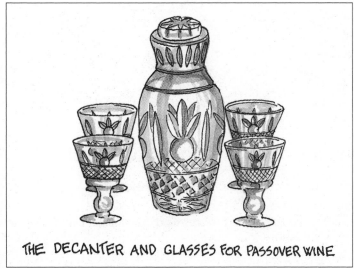

THE DECANTER AND GLASSES FOR PASSOVER WINE

The Levy Family's Favorite Haroset

One of the universal dishes of Jewish cooking, haroset is made in all families, no matter what their origins. (See the photo in the color insert section of this book.) Haroset is a spread or condiment made of fruits, nuts, spices, and wine. Its reddish-brown color is designed to recall the mortar and bricks that the Jewish slaves were coerced to make in Egypt. During the Seder ceremony, you taste the spread on a piece of matzo.

In spite of the sad memory it evokes, haroset is a highlight of the Seder because of its appealing sweet taste. You can use fresh or dried fruit. The top picks are apples, dates, or raisins. In our house, we often combine all three.

Any nuts and sweet spices can flavor haroset. Cinnamon is the spice of choice, but cloves, ginger, and even black pepper can be added. With all the possible permutations, it's no wonder that haroset comes in countless variations.

After the Seder tasting, most people leave the haroset on the table to be enjoyed throughout the dinner.

Special tools: *Grater*

Preparation time: *20 minutes*

Cooking time: *None*

Yield: *8 servings*

Keeping kosher: *Pareve*

½ cup walnuts	*¼ cup raisins, chopped*
½ cup pecans	*¾ teaspoon ground cinnamon*
1 medium or large apple, peeled, halved, and cored	*Pinch of ground cloves*
	2 to 4 tablespoons sweet red wine
¾ cup dates, finely chopped	*Matzos (for serving)*

1 In a food processor, grind walnuts and pecans by pulsing them until fairly fine, leaving a few small chunks. Transfer to a bowl.

2 Coarsely grate apple. Add to nut mixture. Stir in dates, raisins, cinnamon, cloves, and 2 tablespoons wine. Add more wine if needed so the haroset can spread easily.

3 Spoon into a serving bowl. Serve at room temperature or cold, accompanied by matzos.

Per serving: *Calories 165.4; Protein 2.1 g; Carbohydrates 21.1 g; Dietary fiber 2.8 g; Total fat 9.1 g; Saturated fat 0.9 g; Cholesterol 0.0 mg; Sodium 2.6 mg.*

Jewish Mother's Tip: *You may like to emulate this popular custom: Make enough haroset to last for several days. It makes a satisfying, healthful, sweet snack.*

Although the time-honored taste of Seder wine is sweet, any kosher-for-Passover wine is appropriate. American, Israeli, French, and Italian wine-makers prepare dry and semi-dry Passover wines as well as sweet ones.

Seder ceremony

For the Seder, there is a book of prayers and songs called the Haggadah. Either the leader reads from it or those at the table take turns. Most of the reading takes place before the actual dinner begins. The recitation is punctuated with pauses to taste or point out each of the special Seder foods.

Around the world, Jews prepare two Seders, one on the first and one on the second night of the holiday. Israeli custom calls for only one Seder, on the first night.

Planning Seder Menus

After spending an hour or more reciting the Haggadah, everyone is ravenous and eager for the Seder feast. Most cooks prepare the food ahead to making serving easy and to be sure that it is ready when it is needed.

In my family, like many others, the dinner begins with a selection of salads and is followed by matzo ball soup, the quintessential Passover dish. A braised or roasted poultry or meat course follows, often served with a savory matzo stuffing or a matzo and mushroom casserole. Baby carrots, new potatoes, asparagus, and other springtime vegetables are popular accompaniments.

Garlic Roast Lamb with Potatoes

On some tables, roast lamb is the Passover entree of choice. Other families opt for chicken. For this recipe, the lamb is flavored with garlic slivers that you slide into the meat. They become tender and lend good taste to the lamb. Garlic flavors the potatoes, too. (See the photo in the color insert section of this book. The photo shows the roast medium-cooked, but if you are strictly keeping kosher, continue to cook it until well done; see Step 5.)

To simplify the preparation, buy a boneless roast. If you don't find one that is already prepared, buy a 5 ½ to 6-pound lamb shoulder and ask the butcher to trim the lamb of skin and fat and to bone it. Then have him roll it and tie it to facilitate carving.

Special tool: *Roasting pan*

Preparation time: *30 minutes*

Cooking time: *2 hours, 10 minutes*

Yield: *8 servings*

Keeping kosher: *Meat*

6 large garlic cloves

3 ½-pound boneless rolled roast of lamb shoulder

Salt and freshly ground pepper to taste

6 large baking potatoes

2 large onions, sliced

2 tablespoons chopped fresh rosemary

About 1 cup water

¼ cup chopped Italian parsley

1 Preheat oven to 375°. Cut 10 very thin lengthwise slivers from garlic; chop remaining garlic.

2 Pierce lamb with point of a sharp knife to make a slit. With aid of knife, hold the slit open and insert a garlic sliver. Make more slits, spacing them fairly evenly, and insert remaining garlic slivers. Sprinkle lamb with salt and pepper. Set lamb in a roasting pan.

3 Peel and quarter potatoes and put them in pan around meat. Sprinkle potatoes with remaining chopped garlic, salt, and pepper. Add sliced onions, rosemary and ¾ cup water to pan.

4 Cover with foil. Bake 1 hour. Uncover and stir potatoes gently. Add ¼ cup water if pan is dry. Bake 30 minutes and stir again. Add a few tablespoons water if pan becomes dry.

5 Roast lamb another 10 to 30 minutes, basting lamb and potatoes occasionally, or until lamb is very tender. An instant-read or meat thermometer should register 150 for medium or 160 for well done. If potatoes are not tender and brown, remove lamb and bake potatoes uncovered for 30 more minutes.

6 Let meat rest on a board 15 minutes before carving. Meanwhile, spoon juices over potatoes and keep them warm in low oven. Remove strings from meat.

7 Carve lamb into ½-inch slices, using a very sharp large knife. With a small knife, remove excess fat from slices.

8 Sprinkle potatoes and lamb with parsley and serve hot. Season juices to taste with salt and pepper. Serve sauce separately.

Per serving: *Calories 396.4; Protein 44.0 g; Carbohydrates 22.4 g; Dietary fiber 2.4 g; Total fat 13.6 g; Saturated fat 5.1 g; Cholesterol 136.9 mg; Sodium 203.4 mg.*

Menu Maven Says: *Sephardic Spinach Casserole (see next recipe) is a good accompaniment. You may also like to serve seasonal vegetables such as asparagus or new carrots.*

Sephardic Spinach Casserole

Greens are a favorite food on the tables of Jews from Mediterranean and Middle Countries. Spinach flavors this matzo casserole along with garlic, mushrooms, nutmeg, a touch of cumin, and olive oil. Serve it as a savory casserole to accompany any meat or poultry dish. You can also use it as a stuffing by spooning it into chickens for roasting.

Special tool: *Two-quart casserole*

Preparation time: *45 minutes*

Cooking time: *1 hour*

Yield: *8 to 10 servings*

Keeping kosher: *Meat*

8 matzos	½ teaspoon ground cumin
1½ cups hot chicken stock	1 teaspoon paprika, plus a pinch for sprinkling
3 tablespoons plus 1 teaspoon olive oil	2 cups chopped clean spinach leaves
1 medium onion, chopped	2 medium zucchini, grated
4 ounces mushrooms, sliced	Freshly grated nutmeg to taste
4 large garlic cloves	2 large eggs, beaten
Salt and freshly ground pepper to taste	

1 Preheat oven to 350°. Crumble matzos into a large bowl and pour hot chicken stock over them. Lightly oil a 2-quart casserole.

2 Meanwhile, heat 2 tablespoons oil in a large skillet. Add onions and sauté over medium heat, stirring often, about 7 minutes or until they begin to turn golden. Add 1 tablespoon oil and heat briefly. Add mushrooms, garlic, salt, pepper, cumin, and paprika and sauté 3 minutes or until tender.

3 Add spinach and sauté, stirring, until it begins to wilt. Remove from heat. Stir in zucchini.

4 Add vegetable mixture to matzo mixture and let cool. Season to taste with nutmeg. Stir in eggs.

5 Spoon stuffing into casserole. Sprinkle with remaining oil and then with paprika. Bake for 45 minutes or until firm. Serve hot.

Per serving: *Calories 207.5; Protein 6.1 g; Carbohydrates 27.7 g; Dietary fiber 2.1 g; Total fat 8.3 g; Saturated fat 1.4 g; Cholesterol 54.1 mg; Sodium 285.2 mg.*

Warning: *If you want to bake the casserole as a stuffing inside a bird, be sure that the mixture is completely cool before spooning it into the bird's cavity. Stuff the bird just before roasting it.*

Asparagus and Carrots with Lemon Dressing

Naturally, asparagus is popular for Passover, the holiday of spring. It makes a tasty and pretty vegetable side dish when matched with carrots and a light Sephardic-style dressing of fresh lemon juice, fine olive oil, and herbs. If you find new baby carrots at your market, use them for this dish instead of cutting larger ones. Serve the vegetables hot as an accompaniment. You can also turn them into an appetizer by serving them cool or slightly warm on a bed of mixed lettuces. (See the photo in the color insert section of this book.)

Preparation time: *20 minutes*

Cooking time: *15 minutes*

Yield: *4 servings*

Keeping kosher: *Pareve*

¾ to 1 pound medium-width asparagus, trimmed

1 pound medium or wide carrots (about 5), peeled and cut in 2-inch pieces

3 tablespoons extra virgin olive oil

2 tablespoons strained fresh lemon juice (juice from 1 lemon)

½ teaspoon finely grated lemon zest

Salt and freshly ground pepper to taste

Cayenne pepper to taste

1 teaspoon chopped fresh thyme, or ½ teaspoon dried

2 teaspoons snipped fresh chives

1 Peel bottom ⅔ of each asparagus spear. Cut spears in 2-inch pieces. Quarter wide carrot pieces lengthwise; cut thinner pieces in two lengthwise. Put them in a medium saucepan with water to cover and a pinch of salt. Bring to a boil and simmer over medium heat for 10 minutes or until just tender. Remove with slotted spoon, leaving liquid in saucepan, and place the carrots in a strainer.

2 Meanwhile, in a small bowl, whisk oil with lemon juice and zest. Season to taste with salt, pepper, and cayenne. Bring carrot cooking liquid to a boil. Add asparagus and boil uncovered for 3 minutes or until just tender. Remove asparagus to a strainer with a slotted spoon; reserve cooking liquid if you like for soups, sauces, or stocks. If not serving hot, rinse asparagus with cold water; drain well.

3 Combine asparagus and carrots in a shallow serving bowl. Add dressing, thyme, and chives and toss lightly. Taste and adjust seasoning. Serve hot, warm, or cool.

Per serving: *Calories 153.2; Protein 2.6 g; Carbohydrates 14.2 g; Dietary fiber 3.7 g; Total fat 10.3 g; Saturated fat 1.4 g; Cholesterol 0.0 mg; Sodium 208.3 mg.*

Jewish Mother's Tip: *If you're preparing the vegetables ahead to serve as a cool salad, the color of the asparagus will be brightest if you add the lemon juice at the last minute.*

Apple and Matzo Kugel with Almonds

Like lasagna strips or noodles, matzos can be layered with other foods to create tasty casseroles like this one. They're even easier to use than most pasta because they require no cooking.

This scrumptious dessert tastes rather like apple pie with the crust mixed in. Choose tart apples such as Granny Smith or Pippin if you would like to serve this cinnamon-scented casserole as a sweet partner for roast chicken or turkey. Go for sweet ones like Golden Delicious or Gala if you prefer to present the kugel as a warm dessert.

Special tools: *Two shallow 2-quart baking dishes, preferably square*

Preparation time: *1 hour, 15 minutes*

Cooking time: *45 minutes*

Yield: *12 to 16 servings*

Keeping kosher: *Pareve if made with nondairy margarine*

10 matzos	*½ cup plus 5 tablespoons sugar*
6 eggs	*1½ teaspoons ground cinnamon*
½ cup margarine, melted	*8 medium apples*
Pinch of salt	*6 tablespoons chopped almonds*

1 Lightly grease two shallow, square, 2-quart baking dishes.

2 Break 5 matzos into quarters and put in a large bowl. Pour boiling water over them to cover and swirl to lightly moisten all the pieces. Drain in a colander. Cool slightly and then cut matzos in strips about ¾ inch wide. Put in another large bowl. Repeat with the other 5 matzos and add them to the first ones.

3 In a medium bowl, beat the eggs. Add to the bowl of matzos and mix well. Add 6 tablespoons melted margarine, salt, and ½ cup sugar and mix well.

4 Preheat oven to 350°. Mix 4 tablespoons sugar with 1 teaspoon cinnamon. Peel, halve, and core the apples and slice them very thin. Mix the apples with the cinnamon mixture. Add the apple mixture to the matzo mixture and mix well. Mix in the almonds.

5 Divide the matzo mixture between the baking dishes. Sprinkle each with 1 tablespoon of melted margarine.

6 Mix the remaining 1 tablespoon sugar with ½ teaspoon cinnamon. Sprinkle each kugel with half the mixture, or a bit more than 1½ teaspoons for each.

7 Bake uncovered for 30 minutes. Cover and bake for 15 more minutes or until the kugels are firm and the apples are tender.

8 While the kugels are still hot, carefully run a small sharp knife around each kugel's edges. Serve hot or warm. Cut carefully into portions, using a small sharp knife and an up-and-down motion.

Per serving: Calories 242.2; Protein 4.9 g; Carbohydrates 35.5 g; Dietary fiber 2.2 g; Total fat 9.5 g; Saturated fat 1.8 g; Cholesterol 79.7 mg; Sodium 98.9 mg.

Baking Flourless Treats

Over the ages, Jewish women have created an amazingly varied selection of Passover desserts. They prepare the batters for their cakes, cookies, brownies, and muffins by replacing the flour with matzos, matzo meal, cake meal, or potato starch. Cream puff dough for Passover is made from matzo meal instead of the usual flour. Crusts for fruit tarts and pies are made from matzos or matzo meal. These substitutions produce baked goods with a different taste and texture. Families look forward to these treasured, once-a-year treats.

For their baked goods, observant Jews opt for natural flavorings because extracts and other processed foods might contain ingredients that are not kosher for Passover. Instead, they use lemon and orange juice and zest, cinnamon, cocoa, nuts, coconut, and wine. Passover chocolate is popular, too, in all sorts of sweets, including modern flourless chocolate cakes, which are perfect for the occasion.

Cakes

Classic cakes for Passover are light in texture. With yeast and baking powder not permitted, cakes depend on whipped eggs to make them rise. A delicate citrus-flavored sponge cake is a welcome finale after the lavish Seder dinner. Nut tortes made with walnuts, pecans, almonds, or hazelnuts are also popular. (See Figure 8-4 for all the nut possibilities.) To emphasize the holiday's springtime theme, you may like to accompany each slice of cake with strawberry sauce or fresh berries.

For the Seder, Passover cakes are usually made without dairy products in observant households so that they can be served after a main course of meat or poultry.

Figure 8-4:
Cakes made with walnuts, pecans, almonds, and other nuts are favorite Passover desserts.

Passover Pecan Chocolate Cake

Most people vote for this moist, nutty gâteau over the standard holiday sponge cake. Instead of flour, it contains a small amount of potato starch. This makes it perfect for Passover but also contributes to its tender texture.

Special tool: *8-inch springform cake pan*

Preparation time: *25 minutes*

Cooking time: *1 hour*

Yield: *8 to 10 servings*

Keeping kosher: *Dairy or pareve, depending on choice of butter or margarine*

1 cup pecans

½ cup sugar

5 ounces semisweet chocolate, chopped

2 tablespoons orange juice

½ cup unsalted butter or margarine, cut in
8 pieces, room temperature, plus a little extra
for greasing the pan

4 large eggs, separated, room temperature

1 teaspoon finely grated orange zest

2 tablespoons potato starch

1 Preheat oven to 325°. Lightly grease an 8 x 2½-inch springform pan with margarine. Line pan's base with parchment paper or foil and grease the liner.

2 Grind pecans with 2 tablespoons sugar in a food processor until as fine as possible. Transfer to a bowl.

3 Melt chocolate in orange juice in a large bowl set above hot water over low heat. Stir until smooth. Add butter and stir until blended in. Remove from pan of water.

4 Whisk egg yolks to blend. Gradually add yolks to chocolate mixture, whisking vigorously. Stir in ¼ cup sugar, followed by orange zest, pecans, and potato starch. Mix well.

5 Whip egg whites in a large bowl until soft peaks form. Gradually beat in remaining 2 tablespoons sugar and whip at high speed until whites are stiff and shiny but not dry. Gently fold whites into chocolate mixture in three batches. Fold lightly but quickly, just until batter is blended.

6 Transfer batter to prepared pan and spread evenly. Bake for 45 minutes, or until a cake tester inserted in center of cake comes out clean.

7 Cool in pan on a rack for about 10 minutes. Run a thin-bladed flexible knife or metal spatula carefully around the edge of cake. Invert cake onto rack, gently release spring, and remove side and base of pan. Carefully remove paper and cool cake completely. Invert cake onto another rack and then onto a platter so that smoothest side of cake faces up. Serve it at room temperature.

Per serving: *Calories 304.6; Protein 4.8 g; Carbohydrates 20.0 g; Dietary fiber 1.1 g; Total fat 24.9 g; Saturated fat 10.4 g; Cholesterol 110.9 mg; Sodium 27.2 mg.*

Jewish Mother's Tip: You can make the cake up to two days ahead. Wrap it and keep it at room temperature or, during hot weather, in the refrigerator.

For dinners featuring a fish, dairy food, or vegetarian entree, frost this cake with whipped cream just before serving it. Make it with 1 cup of whipping cream and a little sugar and vanilla sugar (which is used on Passover instead of vanilla extract), as in Chapter 21. Then sprinkle the iced cake with a little grated semisweet chocolate. If you're frosting the cake, serve it cold.

Cookies

Macaroons are time-honored treats for Passover. For home baking, almond and coconut macaroons are the most frequent choices, but you can make these delicious cookies from any nut. I love to make them from macadamias as well as almonds.

Crunchy, airy meringues are another cherished holiday sweet. You can make them plain or fold in a small amount of chopped chocolate or nuts for accent.

Easy Almond Macaroons

Macaroons are the best-known Passover cookie. Although canned ones are widely available in the supermarket at Passover time, baking your own almond macaroons makes a lot of sense from the standpoint of taste as well as nutrition. Their homemade flavor makes them far superior to factory macaroons. Besides, most of the commonly available macaroons are made of coconut and are high in saturated fat. Almonds are much more healthful.

These lemon-scented macaroons keep well, need few ingredients, and are simple to make. They are fun to shape with the children and make for a pleasant pre-Passover activity. For the best flavor, purchase fresh almonds. You can use slivered or whole blanched almonds. If you store them in a cookie tin, they will keep fresh for a week.

Special tools: *Pastry brush, baking sheet, parchment paper or waxed paper*

Preparation time: *30 minutes*

Cooking time: *20 minutes*

Yield: *20 macaroons*

Keeping kosher: *Pareve*

1½ cups blanched almonds	*1 teaspoon lemon juice*
1 cup sugar	*1½ teaspoons grated lemon zest, yellow part only*
2 large egg whites	

1 Position rack in upper third of oven and preheat to 350°. Line a rimmed baking sheet with parchment paper or waxed paper; grease paper lightly with margarine.

2 Grind almonds with 4 tablespoons sugar in food processor by processing continuously until mixture forms fine, even crumbs. Add egg whites, lemon juice, and lemon zest and process until smooth, about 20 seconds. Add remaining sugar in two additions and process about 10 seconds after each or until smooth.

3 With moistened hands, roll about 1 tablespoon mixture between your palms into a smooth ball. Put on prepared baking sheet. Continue with remaining mixture, spacing cookies about 1 inch apart.

4 Gently press to flatten each macaroon slightly so that it is about ½ inch high. Brush entire surface of each with water. Bake 18 to 20 minutes or until very lightly but evenly browned; centers should still be soft.

5 Remove from oven. Do not let cool. Lift one end of paper and pour about 2 tablespoons water under it, onto baking sheet; water will boil on contact with hot baking sheet. Lift other end of paper and pour about 2 tablespoons water under it. When water stops boiling, remove macaroons carefully from paper. Transfer to a rack to cool.

Per serving: Calories 69.1; Protein 1.8 g; Carbohydrates 8.2 g; Dietary fiber 0.8 g; Total fat 3.7 g; Saturated fat 0.3 g; Cholesterol 0.0 mg; Sodium 5.8 mg.

Jewish Mother's Tip: *For an easy sweet pie crust, you can follow your graham cracker crust recipes, but substitute Passover macaroons for the crackers.*

Chapter 9

Shavuot — The Holiday Devoted to Dairy Delights

In This Chapter

▶ Celebrating with cheesecakes, blintzes, and kugels
▶ Glorifying grains and fruits

*I*f you're a dairy fan, you'll love *Shavuot*, a two-day festival held in early summer. During this holiday, cooks splurge on cheesecakes, blintzes, and cheese-filled pastries. In this chapter, you find out not only how to make these recipes but about lesser-known aspects of this holiday as well.

Celebrating Shavuot

Jews celebrate the two-day festival of Shavuot in late May or June to honor a major event in Jewish lore. On this day, Moses and the Hebrews received the Ten Commandments and the Torah, or Judaic scriptures, at Mount Sinai.

This occasion is truly a cheese lover's feast. On the menu, cheeses, butter, and cream take the center stage, appearing in appetizers, main courses, and desserts. Cooks use them in a variety of traditional treats, from blintzes to noodle kugels to cakes to savory turnovers.

What is Shavuot?

The word *Shavuot* means weeks in Hebrew, recalling that the holiday takes place seven weeks after Passover. Thus, Shavuot is sometimes called "The Feast of Weeks." Some call the holiday Pentecost, from a Greek word meaning the fiftieth day.

Naturally, the ancient Hebrews did not bake cheesecakes during their sojourn in the Sinai desert! Nor was there a divine decree saying "Thou Shalt Eat Cheesecake." The custom of eating dairy foods commemorates the Israelites' decision to abstain from meat on the day before receiving the Holy Scriptures for reasons of purity.

An agricultural explanation emphasizes the seasonal availability of dairy foods in previous ages. During this time of year cows, goats, and sheep give more milk.

Enjoying Dairy Products

Many families consider Shavuot the cheesecake holiday. Cheesecake fanciers rejoice when this delicious holiday arrives. For weeks before the date, neighbors share their favorite recipes for this delectable dessert. Families of Ashkenazic, or eastern European, origin also feast on delicately sweet, cheese-filled blintzes and sour cream noodle casseroles, called *kugels,* flavored with sugar and cinnamon. Sephardic or Mediterranean Jews opt for appetizer pastries called *bourekas* with feta cheese or spinach-and-cheese fillings.

Blintzes versus crepes

Blintzes are a hallmark of Jewish cooking and are made for other occasions besides Shavuot. They are most traditional for brunch, but you can serve them at any meal of the day when you want something particularly festive. Like crepes, *blintzes* are thin pancakes that usually are filled with cheese or fruit fillings, but may also contain meat or vegetable mixtures. Jews in France often celebrate the holiday with crepes, a renowned specialty of their country, and fill them with sweet or savory fillings.

Like crepe batter, blintz batter usually is composed of flour, milk, eggs, salt, and sometimes butter. Unlike classic crepes, blintz batter might contain water instead of milk, and oil instead of butter. To make blintzes, you use a slightly different technique from that of crepes. Sauté the wrappers on only one side before filling them, instead of browning them on both sides as for crepes. After filling the blintzes, you heat them again to be sure that the second side is cooked. This reheating is not necessary with crepes.

Usually blintzes look different from crepes, too. Crepes are often rolled up like cigars or folded in four. Blintz wrappers typically are first folded around the filling and then rolled in a cylindrical shape, so the filled blintzes are fatter than crepes.

Slightly sweetened cheese filling is the hands-down favorite for blintzes, especially for the Jewish holiday of Shavuot, but is rare in French crepes. For other main course and dessert fillings, see Chapters 13 and 21.

When you make blintzes, keep the following tips in mind:

- ✔ For small blintzes, use a 6-inch crepe pan or skillet. Use 2 tablespoons batter to make each blintz wrapper.

- ✔ To measure batter, use a quarter-cup measure: For an 8- or 9-inch pan, fill it three-quarters full to measure 3 tablespoons.

- ✔ If the first blintzes are thick, whisk a teaspoon of milk into the batter.

- ✔ If the blintzes are too thin and fragile to handle, sift 2 or 3 tablespoons flour into another bowl and gradually stir the batter into it.

- ✔ To make it easier to separate the wrappers before filling them, cover each with a sheet of waxed paper after you put it on the plate. The wax papers helps prevent them from sticking to each other as you pile them on the plate.

- ✔ When making blintzes for dinners containing meat, use water in the batter instead of milk, and vegetable oil or nondairy margarine instead of butter. Before baking the filled blintzes, dot them with margarine or brush them with oil.

Blintz Wrappers

Blintz wrappers resemble crepes or very thin pancakes. Use them to enclose sweet or savory fillings, from mushroom to cheese to blueberry. They are much thinner, more delicate, and more delicious than prepared, ready-to-fill crepes sold at the supermarket. Still, to make shortcut blintzes, you can roll packaged crepes around a homemade filling.

Special tool: *Blender (optional)*

Preparation time: *10 minutes, plus 1 hour to chill*

Cooking time: *25 to 30 minutes*

Yield: *6 servings (12 to 15 wrappers)*

Keeping kosher: *Dairy*

1¼ cups milk, plus a little more if needed to thin the batter

3 eggs

¾ cup flour, sifted

½ teaspoon salt

2 tablespoons butter

2 to 3 teaspoons vegetable oil for brushing pan

1 Combine 1¼ cups milk with the eggs, flour, and salt in a blender. Blend on high speed, scraping down sides of blender once or twice, about 1 minute or until batter is smooth.

2 Pour the batter into a bowl, cover, and refrigerate about 1 hour or up to 1 day.

3 After batter has chilled at least 1 hour, melt butter in a small saucepan over low heat. Cool slightly. Stir batter well. Gradually whisk melted butter into batter. (Batter should have consistency of whipping cream. If it is too thick, gradually whisk in more milk, about 1 teaspoon at a time.)

4 Heat an 8- or 9-inch pan over medium-high heat. Sprinkle the pan with a few drops of water. If the water immediately sizzles, the pan is hot enough. Brush the pan lightly with oil. Remove the pan from the heat and hold it near the bowl of batter. Quickly spoon 3 tablespoons of batter near the edge of the pan, tilting and swirling the pan until its base is covered with a thin layer of batter.

5 Return the pan to medium heat. Loosen the edges of the pancake with a spatula, discarding any pieces clinging to the pan's sides. Cook until the pancake's bottom browns very lightly. Slide it out onto a plate, with its uncooked side facing up.

6 Continue making wrappers, stirring batter occasionally with the whisk. Brush the pan with more oil if the wrappers begin to stick. If the batter thickens on standing, whisk in a little more milk, 1 teaspoon at a time. Pile the pancakes on the plate as they are done.

7 To use the wrappers right away, cover them with plastic wrap and a kitchen towel to keep them warm. To make them ahead, cover them tightly and refrigerate up to 2 days. Before filling them, bring them to room temperature to avoid tearing them.

Per serving: Calories 69.1; Protein 2.6 g; Carbohydrates 5.8 g; Dietary fiber 0.2 g; Total fat 3.9 g; Saturated fat 1.7 g; Cholesterol 49.4 mg; Sodium 100.4 mg.

Jewish Mother's Tip: *To make the batter in a bowl instead of a blender: Instead of Step 1, sift the flour into a medium bowl. Push the flour to the bowl's sides, leaving a large well in the center of the flour. Add the eggs, salt, and ¼ cup milk to the well and whisk the ingredients in the well briefly until blended. Using the whisk, stir the flour gently and gradually into the egg mixture until smooth. Gradually whisk in 1 cup milk. Strain the batter if it is lumpy. Continue with Step 2.*

Cheese Blintzes

Enjoy cheese blintzes as a main course or a brunch treat. You can also serve them for dessert. Top the blintzes with their time-honored partners: sour cream and fruit preserves. If you like, substitute a fresh strawberry sauce for the preserves. You can see a photo of this recipe in the color insert section of this book.

Preparation time: *30 minutes, plus time to make Blintz Wrappers*

Cooking time: *15 minutes*

Yield: *4 to 6 servings (12 blintzes)*

Keeping kosher: *Dairy*

Blintz Wrappers (see previous recipe)

2 cups farmers' cheese (about 1 lb.)

3 tablespoons cream cheese, softened

5 tablespoons cottage cheese

2 egg yolks

3 to 4 tablespoons sugar

¼ to ½ teaspoon ground cinnamon

3 to 4 tablespoons butter, cut into 24 pieces, plus a little more for brushing baking dish

Sour cream or yogurt, for serving

Fruit preserves, for serving

1 Prepare the wrappers, stack them, and keep them warm.

2 To make the filling, mash the farmers' cheese, cream cheese, and cottage cheese in a bowl. Add the egg yolks, sugar, and cinnamon and beat until smooth and blended.

3 Spoon 2½ to 3 tablespoons of filling onto the brown side (the cooked side) of each wrapper near one edge. Fold over the edges to the right and left of the filling so that each side covers about half the filling. Roll it in a cigar shape, beginning at the edge with the filling. If you're not baking them right away, cover them with plastic wrap and refrigerate them.

4 Preheat the oven to 425°. Butter a 13 x 9-inch baking dish.

5 Arrange the blintzes in one layer in the dish. Dot each blintz with 2 small pieces of butter. Bake for 15 minutes, or until heated through and lightly browned.

6 Serve the blintzes hot, with sour cream and preserves.

Per serving: Calories 287.6; Protein 12.8 g; Carbohydrates 11.4 g; Dietary fiber 0.2 g; Total fat 20.9 g; Saturated fat 13.3 g; Cholesterol 143.6 mg; Sodium 418.1 mg.

Jewish Mother's Tips: Farmers' cheese, a firm dry cheese, is a favorite ingredient in the filling to prevent it from being too soft. You can purchase it at Jewish grocery stores and well-stocked supermarkets.

To fry the filled blintzes instead of baking them, heat 3 or 4 tablespoons butter in a skillet. Add enough blintzes to make one layer, with their open ends facing down. Fry them over low heat for 3 minutes on each side or until brown and heated through. Do not let them burn.

Menu Maven Says: For serving cheese blintzes as dessert, use ⅓ cup sugar in the filling and add ¼ cup raisins if you like.

Cheesecakes

Whether plain or adorned with topping, there are cheesecakes for every taste. They may be sprinkled with a crumbly buttery streusel, coated with sour cream, or iced with meringue. Each family seems to have their favorites. Some are flavored with vanilla, orange, or lemon. Many are rich cream cheese creations; others are made lowfat with cottage cheese and yogurt. Any type can be a sweet welcome to the holiday of Shavuot.

Figure 9-1:
A springform pan.

A springform pan has a latch on the side and a detachable bottom.

Nutty Crumb Crust

This simple-to-prepare crust makes a tasty base for cheesecakes. You can also use it in pie pans for tarts filled with strawberries or other soft fruits. Instead of the graham crackers, you can make the crust from any crisp unfilled cookies by whirling them in a food processor until they turn into fine crumbs. If you already have cookie crumbs, you will need 1¼ cups for this recipe.

Special tools: *9-inch springform cake pan (see Figure 9-1)*

Preparation time: *15 minutes*

Cooking time: *10 minutes*

Yield: *Crust for a 9-inch cheesecake*

Keeping kosher: *Dairy*

5 ounces graham crackers, or enough to make 1¾ cups crumbs

¼ cup walnuts

3 tablespoons sugar

⅓ cup melted butter, plus a little for brushing pan

1 In a food processor, process the graham crackers to fine crumbs. Measure 1¾ cups crumbs and transfer them to a medium bowl. Combine the walnuts and sugar in the processor and finely chop them with a pulsing action of the processor. Add them to the cracker crumbs and mix well. Add the melted butter and mix well.

2 Preheat the oven to 350°. Lightly butter a 9-inch springform pan. Press the nut mixture in an even layer on the pan's bottom and about 1½ inches up its sides.

3 Bake the crust for 10 minutes. Let it cool to room temperature before adding filling.

Per serving: Calories 120.4; Protein 1.2 g; Carbohydrates 12.5 g; Dietary fiber 0.5 g; Total fat 7.6 g; Saturated fat 3.5 g; Cholesterol 13.7 mg; Sodium 72.2 mg.

My Mother's Creamy Cheesecake

Ever since my childhood, this cheesecake has been my family's favorite because of its luscious filling and vanilla scented sour cream topping. It's delicious and easy to make. My mother puts it together in no time. A colorful mixture of fresh berries makes a terrific accompaniment. You can see a photo of this recipe in the color insert section of this book.

Special tools: *Food processor, 9-inch springform cake pan*

Preparation time: *20 minutes, plus time to make Nutty Crumb Crust, plus 8 hours chilling time*

Cooking time: *55 minutes*

Yield: *10 to 12 servings*

Keeping kosher: *Dairy*

Nutty Crumb Crust (see preceding recipe), baked and cooled in its pan

1 pound cream cheese, cut in pieces and left to soften

2 cups sour cream

1 cup sugar

3 large eggs

Zest of 1 large lemon, finely grated, without any bitter white pith (about 1 tablespoon zest)

2½ teaspoons pure vanilla extract

1 Preheat the oven to 350°.

2 To make the filling, in a large bowl beat the cream cheese with ½ cup of the sour cream at low speed of the mixer until very smooth. Gradually beat in ¾ cup plus 1 tablespoon of the sugar. Beat in the eggs, one by one. Stir in the lemon zest and 1½ teaspoons of the vanilla.

3 Carefully pour the filling into the cooled crust. Bake for 45 minutes or until the cake's center is just firm to the touch; watch carefully and do not overbake, or the cake's surface may crack. Remove the cake from the oven and let it cool for 15 minutes. Raise the oven temperature to 425°.

4 Meanwhile, to make the topping, in a medium bowl mix together the remaining 1½ cups sour cream, 3 tablespoons sugar, and 1 teaspoon vanilla.

5 Carefully spread the topping mixture on the cake in an even layer. Do not let it drip over the crust.

6 Bake the cake for 7 minutes or until the topping just sets. Remove it from the oven and let it cool to room temperature. Cover the cake and refrigerate it overnight before serving. Remove the sides of the pan just before serving.

Per serving: *Calories 419.8; Protein 6.8 g; Carbohydrates 32.0 g; Dietary fiber 0.5 g; Total fat 30.1 g; Saturated fat 17.2 g; Cholesterol 125.3 mg; Sodium 220.3 mg.*

Bourekas

Bourekas, a specialty of Jews originating in Greece, Turkey, Lebanon, and Syria, are scrumptious filled pastries usually shaped like turnovers. As popular in Israel as pizza is in the United States, bourekas are increasingly being embraced by American Jews.

Home cooks stuff their bourekas with a variety of ingredients and serve them as appetizers or snacks. For Shavuot, many families favor a zesty cheese filling. A frequent choice for entertaining at other occasions as well, you can also stuff the turnovers with mixtures of mushrooms, meat, or greens.

You can shape bourekas one day ahead and refrigerate them on baking sheets or on plates. Cover them tightly with plastic wrap before refrigerating them.

Feta-Filled Bourekas

Most people purchase the dough to make these appetizer pastries. Flaky filo dough is preferred, but puff pastry and pie dough are used, too. You can form bourekas in rings or half-moons. Triangles are the most common shape because they are the easiest to make with filo dough.

For the filling, pair a pungent cheese such as feta or Parmesan with a mild one like cottage cheese. (You can see a photo of this recipe in the color insert section of this book.)

Special tools: *2 baking sheets, pastry brush*

Preparation time: *1 hour*

Cooking time: *20 minutes*

Yield: *15 small pastries*

Keeping kosher: *Dairy*

½ pound filo dough (about 10 sheets)	*Small pinch of salt*
¼ cup farmers' cheese or ricotta cheese	*Freshly ground pepper to taste*
½ cup finely crumbled feta cheese	*Pinch of cayenne pepper*
1 large egg, beaten lightly	*⅓ to ½ cup melted butter, for brushing dough*
⅓ cup grated cheddar or Swiss cheese	*1 teaspoon sesame seeds, for sprinkling*
½ teaspoon dried oregano	

1 If the filo dough is frozen, thaw it in the refrigerator for 8 hours or overnight. Remove it from the refrigerator 2 hours before using it, leaving it wrapped.

2 To make the filling, mash the farmers' cheese with the feta cheese in a medium bowl until blended. Add the egg, cheddar cheese, oregano, salt, pepper, and cayenne pepper and mix until combined.

3 Butter 2 baking sheets. Remove the filo sheets from their package and unroll them on a dry towel. With a sharp knife, cut the stack in half lengthwise, to make 2 stacks of 16 x 7-inch sheets. Cover them immediately with waxed paper and then with a slightly damp towel. Work with only 1 sheet at a time, keeping the remaining sheets covered with the waxed paper and towel so they don't dry out.

4 Remove 1 filo sheet and brush it lightly with melted butter. Fold it in half lengthwise, to make a 16 x 3½-inch strip. Dab it lightly with butter. Spoon 2 teaspoons cheese filling at one end of the strip. Fold the end of the strip diagonally over the filling to form a triangle and dab it lightly with butter. Continue folding it over, keeping it in neat triangle after each fold, until you reach the strip's end. Set the triangular pastry on a buttered baking sheet. Brush the pastry lightly with butter. Shape more pastries with the remaining filo sheets and filling.

5 Preheat the oven to 350°. Brush the pastries again lightly with melted butter and sprinkle them with sesame seeds. Bake them for 20 minutes or until golden brown. Serve them warm, not hot, or at room temperature.

Per serving: Calories 124.2; Protein 3.7 g; Carbohydrates 8.3 g; Dietary fiber 0.3 g; Total fat 8.3 g; Saturated fat 4.9 g; Cholesterol 35.5 mg; Sodium 176.6 mg.

Celebrating the First Fruits

Cheese is not the festival's only custom-favored food. Produce and grains gain prominence, too, because Shavuot is a harvest holiday. The Israelites of antiquity brought offerings to the Holy Temple to express gratitude for the grains and for the early fruits of the fields. When I taste the first peaches and nectarines from my trees during this season, I find it easy to understand how this tradition of thanksgiving came about.

Today, many people express this appreciation at the table. In my home, we enjoy such fresh-tasting medleys as sesame spinach salad with barley, peaches with mint, or strawberry sauce for our blintzes or our cheesecake.

Sesame Spinach Salad with Barley

A biblical grain, barley is fitting for the holiday feast because it is mentioned in the passages read at the synagogue on Shavuot. Barley has an added modern-day bonus. Nutritionists recommend it because of its healthful fiber. Sesame seeds, which have long been loved in the Holy Land, are a tasty match for this spinach melange. If you like, sprinkle the salad with crumbled feta cheese, another Eastern Mediterranean favorite. You can see a photo of this recipe in the color insert section of this book.

Preparation time: *10 minutes, plus 1 hour chilling time*

Cooking time: *30 minutes (begin tasting after 20 minutes)*

Yield: *6 servings*

Keeping kosher: *Pareve*

2 cups water

1 bay leaf

Salt and freshly ground pepper to taste

¾ cup pearl barley

2 tablespoons sesame seeds

½ mild white or red onion, chopped

3 to 4 tablespoons strained fresh lemon juice, or to taste

3 to 4 tablespoons extra virgin olive oil, or to taste

½ teaspoon dried thyme

4 ripe plum tomatoes, diced small

6 cups rinsed spinach leaves, lightly packed, chopped

1 In a 1½-quart heavy saucepan, bring 3 cups water to a boil with the bay leaf and a pinch of salt. Add the barley, cover, and simmer over low heat for 30 minutes or until it is tender; begin tasting after 20 minutes. Transfer to a large bowl and let it cool, about 1 hour. Discard the bay leaf.

2 Meanwhile, in a small, dry skillet, toast the sesame seeds over medium-low heat, shaking the pan occasionally, about 4 to 6 minutes, until golden. Pour them into a plate.

3 Add the onion, lemon juice, olive oil, thyme, salt, and pepper to the barley. Lightly stir in the tomatoes and spinach. Taste and adjust seasoning. Serve cool or at room temperature, sprinkled with toasted sesame seeds

Per serving: *Calories 190.3; Protein 3.9 g; Carbohydrates 24.3 g; Dietary fiber 5.5 g; Total fat 7.3 g; Saturated fat 1.0 g; Cholesterol 0 mg; Sodium 78.7 mg.*

Warning: *Do not leave the sesame seeds in the hot pan after toasting them, or they may burn.*

Chapter 10

Shabbat: A Weekly Excuse to Rejoice

. . . .

. . . .

*E*very Saturday, the Jews celebrate the Sabbath, or *Shabbat* in Hebrew, which means rest. It's the weekly chance to stop working and to enjoy relaxing and feasting with family and friends. All sorts of culinary customs for taking it easy in the kitchen have evolved around this holiday.

Cooking Meals Ahead

The most delicious dinners of the week are reserved for the weekly holiday. Traditionally, the woman of the house sets an attractive table, covering it with a pretty tablecloth, setting it with the family's best dishes and flatware, and gracing it with Shabbat candles in candlesticks, over which she says a blessing. Often, she decorates the table with fresh flowers too.

A beautiful braided *challah,* or egg bread, is one of the signature elements of the Shabbat table, no matter where Jews live. Next you may have an appetizer, followed by a fish starter, and a warming soup. Frequent main courses are roast chicken or a satisfying stew of meat and vegetables. To complete the meal, you have seasonal salads. A casserole called a *kugel,* usually of noodles or vegetables, is a beloved side dish. Last come fruit and homemade sweet treats.

When I was growing up, we enjoyed this menu every week. Obviously, today's busy cooks skip some of the courses or buy them prepared.

To prepare these meals, Shabbat food requires organization. During the holiday, which begins on Friday around sundown and ends on Saturday at nightfall, no cooking is permitted.

Observant families cook everything ahead. In these households, the rhythm of the whole week revolves around Shabbat.

Here's how a typical traditional schedule works. Obviously, those who work on Friday have to adjust their routine.

- **Wednesday:** Plan the multicourse menus for the two main Shabbat meals, Friday-night dinner and Saturday's midday meal.
- **Thursday:** Bake cakes or breads. Shop for the ingredients for the Shabbat menus.
- **Friday:** Cook all food for Friday night through Saturday.
- **Friday night:** Collapse!

Challah

Challah, or *hallah,* is a delicious bread that is a must for Shabbat meals and other Jewish feasts. It has a deep brown crust and soft white crumb and has become the best-loved egg bread in much of the United States.

Making challah dough in a food processor

A food processor with dough blade is best, but you can also make this dough using the usual metal blade.

1. Follow Step 1 in Challah — Egg Break recipe.

2. Combine 2¾ cups flour, remaining sugar, and salt in food processor fitted with dough blade. Process briefly to mix them.

3. Add yeast mixture, oil, and 2 eggs. With blades of processor turning, pour in remaining water. Process until ingredients come together to a soft dough. It will be too soft to form a ball.

4. To knead dough, process it for 30 seconds. Pinch dough quickly; if it sticks to your fingers, add more flour 1 tablespoon at a time, processing after each addition, until dough is no longer very sticky. Knead again by processing about 30 seconds or until smooth.

5. Remove dough and shape in rough ball in your hands.

6. Continue with Step 5 of the Challah — Egg Bread recipe.

Making challah dough in a mixer

If you decide to make challah dough using a mixer, keep in mind that you need one with a dough blade. A heavy-duty mixer is best.

1. Follow Step 1 in Challah — Egg Break recipe.

2. Sift 2¾ cups of flour into bowl of mixer fitted with dough hook. Make large deep well in center of flour. Add yeast mixture, remaining sugar, oil, 2 eggs, remaining water, and salt to well.

3. Mix at medium-low speed, pushing flour in often at first and scraping dough down occasionally from bowl and hook. Continue mixing about 7 minutes, or until ingredients come together to a dough that just begins to cling to hook. Dough should be soft and sticky.

4. To knead, increase speed to medium. Let machine run about 5 minutes, or until dough is smooth, partially clings to dough hook, and almost cleans sides of bowl. During kneading, stop mixer and scrape dough down 2 or 3 times.

5. Pinch dough quickly; if it sticks to your fingers, beat in more flour, 1 tablespoon at a time, until dough is no longer very sticky. If you have added flour, knead dough again by mixing at medium speed about 2 minutes. Dough should be soft, smooth, and springy.

6. Continue with Step 5 of the Challah — Egg Bread recipe.

Making challah does demand time. Like most yeast breads, it requires kneading. When you do have a chance, you'll find kneading fun to do by hand. Otherwise, you can take shortcuts to make kneading quick and effortless.

You can make the dough by any of three techniques: by hand, in a mixer, or in a food processor. Each has its advantages.

- Using a food processor is the fastest.

- A mixer is efficient for a large or two loaves because you can mix more dough at one time in a mixer than in a processor. You do need a mixer that has a dough hook.

- Making the dough by hand demands only the most basic of kitchen equipment — a bowl and a spoon. The dough in the following recipe doesn't need much kneading, and you'll find it easy to make in a bowl, too.

Homemade challah is best on day it is made; after all, it has no preservatives. You can wrap and keep it overnight at room temperature if you like. It also freezes well.

Challah — Egg Bread

Baking challah at home is a joy because of its tantalizing aroma and wonderful fresh taste. Fortunately, the dough is not difficult to make, and you can mix it in minutes if you use a food processor. Generally, the dough is enriched with oil rather than butter so that the bread will be pareve.

If you've ever braided hair, forming a braided challah will be a snap. If braiding isn't your thing and you want a faster way to shape the loaf, simply put it in a loaf pan and bake it following the variation, Basic Loaf-Pan Challah.

Special tool: *Small brush*

Preparation time: *30 minutes, plus rising time*

Cooking time: *40 minutes*

Yield: *1 medium loaf (about 16 servings)*

Keeping kosher: *Pareve*

½ cup plus 2 tablespoons warm water (105° to 115°)	*6 tablespoons vegetable oil, plus a little for bowl and baking sheet*
1 envelope dry yeast	*3 eggs*
1 tablespoon plus 2 teaspoons sugar	*1½ teaspoons salt*
About 2¾ cups unbleached all-purpose flour, more if needed	*2 teaspoons sesame seeds or poppy seeds (optional)*

1 Pour ¼ cup of warm water into small bowl. Sprinkle yeast over water. Sprinkle 1 teaspoon of sugar over yeast. Let stand until foamy, about 10 minutes. Stir if not smooth. Oil a large bowl.

2 Sift 2¾ cups flour into a large bowl. Make large deep well in center of flour. Add yeast mixture, remaining sugar, oil, 2 eggs, remaining water, and salt to well.

3 With a wooden spoon, mix ingredients in well until blended. Begin mixing in flour with spoon. Continue mixing it with your hand, as soon as it feels like this will be easier. Mix until ingredients come together to a dough. Dough should be soft and sticky.

4 To knead dough, push the dough away from you against the work surface with the palm of your hand. Turn dough and fold the top third down toward you. Continue kneading dough vigorously, adding flour by tablespoons if necessary to prevent excessive sticking, until dough is smooth and feels elastic, or springy. This will take about 7 minutes.

5 Put dough in oiled bowl and turn dough over to oil all surfaces. Cover with warm, slightly damp towel or plastic wrap. Let rise in warm draft-free area until doubled in volume, about 1¼ hours.

6 Remove dough with rubber spatula to work surface. Knead dough again, this time lightly. Clean bowl to remove any bits of dough. Return dough to bowl, cover, and let rise again until doubled, about 1 hour.

7 Lightly oil baking sheet. To braid dough, knead it lightly on work surface, flouring lightly only if dough sticks.

8 Shape dough in rough log. Cut dough in 3 equal parts. Knead 1 part briefly and shape in log. Roll back and forth firmly on working surface, pressing with your hands and elongating log from center to edges as you roll, to form a smooth rope about 20 inches long and ¾ inch wide. Taper rope slightly at ends. Repeat with other two parts of dough.

9 Put ropes of dough side by side, with one end of each closer to you. Join ends far from you, covering end of rope on your right side with end of center rope and then with end of left rope. Press to join. Bring left rope over center one. Continue bringing outer ropes alternately over center one, braiding tightly. Pinch each end and tuck them underneath. Set braided bread carefully on oiled baking sheet.

10 Cover shaped loaf with a warm, slightly damp towel. Let rise until nearly doubled in size, about 1 hour.

11 Preheat oven to 375°. Beat remaining egg in a small bowl with a pinch of salt. Brush loaf gently with beaten egg and sprinkle with seeds.

12 Bake challah about 40 minutes, or until top and bottom of bread are firm and bread sounds hollow when tapped on bottom. Carefully transfer bread to rack and cool.

Per serving: Calories 136.7; Protein 3.4 g; Carbohydrates 16.0 g; Dietary fiber 0.6 g; Total fat 6.4 g; Saturated fat 0.7 g; Cholesterol 39.8 mg; Sodium 230.1 mg.

Variation: For a basic loaf-pan challah, follow Steps 1 to 6. Oil an 8 x 4-inch or 9 x 5-inch loaf pan. On work surface, pat dough into a rough rectangle of about 8 x 4 inches (for smaller pan) or 10 x 5 inches (for larger pan), flouring lightly only if dough sticks. Beginning at longer side, roll up dough firmly, jelly roll fashion, to a log. Pinch ends and seam tightly. Then roll log again on work surface to press seam further. Place dough in pan seam side down. Bake bread about 40 minutes for a 9 x 5-inch pan or 50 minutes for an 8 x 4-inch pan. Turn bread out of pan. If it sticks, run a thin knife around bread and then unmold it.

Jewish Mother's Tips: To give challah a light texture, the dough needs to rise several times, both before and after you shape the bread. If you are in a rush, you can skip the second rising (Step 6).

Try to keep the dough soft, to give the challah a tender, cakelike texture rather than a dense chewy feel that hearty breads have. Adding the right amount of flour to make the perfect challah takes a little practice because flour varies from place to place, and the ratio of flour to eggs needed depends on the humidity. During kneading and shaping, go easy on the flour to keep the dough soft, and your bread will be terrific.

Don't worry if you don't get it perfect. Yeast dough is forgiving. With a little attention, you will get a good-tasting challah!

Shopping for Shabbat

Visit markets in Israel on Thursday, and the whole city is there. Everyone is purchasing fresh produce, meat, and fish for Shabbat. Those who are less organized have to shop on Friday, which makes it another busy day at Jewish markets around the world.

Time is short for Friday shopping because Jewish markets close early. Observing Shabbat also means closing the store on time to get home and prepare for the holiday. All kosher businesses are closed during Shabbat. Observant Jews do no work on Friday night or Saturday.

Families follow differing customs as to how to enjoy hot food on the holiday. According to the Orthodox regulations, turning on the stove is prohibited. People either keep the food hot or reheat it, depending on their degree of strictness. To keep it hot, you can use a low oven, a hot plate, or a slow cooker. To reheat food, you either set it on a hot plate or in the oven, which you turn on before Shabbat begins.

A recipe for relaxation

With everything done ahead, what's left to do on Shabbat is to eat, read, and catch up on your sleep. Shabbat is definitely a holiday of eating. In addition to the Friday night and Saturday midday meals, many families look forward to a homemade coffeecake or special pastry for Saturday's breakfast. After all this food, many enjoy a long Saturday afternoon nap. The occasion also provides a perfect chance to walk over to see your neighbors and nearby friends and relatives. Observant Jews also attend services at the synagogue.

An education in entertaining

Cooks have created many festive dishes for the holiday. You can imagine how many recipes have developed over thousands of years. In many families, the Shabbat specialties have become heirloom recipes, cherished and passed down from one generation to the next.

Shabbat food reflects the special holiday rules. Because you can't cook during the holiday, you can't make soufflés or last-minute sautés. Rather, the food runs to slow-cooked types of dishes, such as savory soups, fragrant stews, and hearty casseroles. In the course of preparing these dishes, cooks discover valuable lessons in cooking food ahead and reheating it properly.

Another popular category of foods is those designed for serving cold. Every family has its favorite first courses. Fish appetizers appear on many tables. Naturally, salads figure prominently on the menu, too.

If you're serving a cold dish made with olive oil, remove it from the refrigerator ten or 15 minutes before serving so that the sauce will become more fluid again. Chilled olive oil often congeals.

Rosemary Roasted Potatoes

On many tables, roasted potatoes are a frequent accompaniment for Shabbat roasted or baked chicken. You can simply season them and roast them, but to shorten their cooking time, I like to first cook them slightly in water. Whether or not to peel the potatoes is up to you. Other fresh herbs like thyme or sage also make good flavorings for the potatoes. You can see a photo of this recipe in the color insert section of this book.

Special tool: *Heavy roasting pan*

Preparation time: *10 minutes*

Cooking time: *1 hour, 10 minutes*

Yield: *6 servings*

Keeping kosher: *Pareve*

2 pounds baking potatoes, halved or quartered	*Freshly ground pepper to taste*
6 tablespoons vegetable oil	*½ teaspoon paprika*
¾ teaspoon salt	*1 or 2 large rosemary sprigs*

1 Preheat oven to 350°. Choose a heavy roasting pan that can hold potatoes in one layer. Put potatoes in a saucepan and add water to cover. Bring to a boil. Cover and cook over medium-low heat for 10 minutes. Drain gently.

2 Heat 3 tablespoons oil in roasting pan in oven for 5 minutes. Add potatoes and sprinkle them with salt, pepper, paprika and remaining oil. Put rosemary sprigs in base of pan.

3 Roast potatoes uncovered, carefully turning them over two or three times, for about 50 minutes or until tender. Serve hot.

Per serving: *Calories 253.9; Protein 2.9 g; Carbohydrates 31.1 g; Dietary fiber 3.0 g; Total fat 13.7 g; Saturated fat 1.9 g; Cholesterol 0 mg; Sodium 300.6 mg.*

Baked Chicken and Chickpeas in Garlic Tomato Sauce

Baked chicken is one of the most popular Shabbat entrees. By using chicken pieces, you avoid having to carve a whole chicken, and your main course is ready to serve. Another plus for Shabbat cooking is that the sauce keeps the chicken moist so that it reheats well. Chicken dark meat — thighs and drumsticks — give the most succulent results.

First, I like to roast the chicken without sauce, which is a much easier way to brown it than sautéing on the stovetop, and it can use the same baking dish. Next, I spoon in the savory sauce, which gains extra flavor as the chicken bakes in it.

This easy dish features Mediterranean flavors, which were originally particular to the Sephardic style. Now they are universally loved by Jews everywhere, from Tel Aviv to Los Angeles.

Preparation time: *20 minutes*

Cooking time: *1 hour, 10 minutes*

Yield: *4 servings*

Keeping kosher: *Meat*

2½ to 3 pounds chicken pieces

1 teaspoon paprika

2 tablespoons plus 1 or 2 teaspoons olive oil

1 large onion, chopped

1 carrot, diced

1 celery stalk, diced

4 large garlic cloves, chopped

One 28-ounce can whole tomatoes, drained and chopped

1 bay leaf

¼ teaspoon hot red pepper flakes, or cayenne to taste

Salt and freshly ground pepper to taste

4 tablespoons chopped cilantro or Italian parsley

15-ounce can chickpeas (garbanzo beans), drained and rinsed

1 Preheat oven to 425°. Sprinkle chicken with paprika on both sides. Put it in a 13 x 9-inch or other shallow baking dish in one layer. Drizzle chicken lightly with olive oil, using 1 or 2 teaspoons. Bake uncovered for 10 minutes. Turn pieces over and bake 7 more minutes to brown lightly. Reduce oven temperature to 375°.

2 Meanwhile, heat remaining 2 tablespoons oil in a large skillet. Add onion, carrot, and celery and cook over medium-low heat about 7 minutes, or until onion softens. Stir in garlic, then tomatoes, bay leaf, pepper flakes, salt, and pepper. Cook over medium heat, stirring often, about 10 minutes or until thick. Discard bay leaf. Add 2 tablespoons cilantro.

3 Gently mix sauce with chickpeas. Taste for seasoning. Pour mixture over chicken and mix gently.

4 Cover tightly and bake 20 minutes. Check and add ¼ cup water if sauce looks dry. Cover and bake about 25 more minutes, or until chicken is tender. Stir in 1 tablespoon cilantro. Serve sprinkled with remaining cilantro.

Per serving: Calories 510.1; Protein 42.4 g; Carbohydrates 24.6 g; Dietary fiber 5.9 g; Total fat 26.9 g; Saturated fat 6.1 g; Cholesterol 148.6 mg; Sodium 568.8 mg.

Menu Maven Says: *In choosing accompaniments for the baked chicken, I like to stay with the Mediterranean theme. All you need for this satisfying entree is a simply cooked vegetable, such as sautéed zucchini, roasted peppers, baked eggplant, or green beans in olive oil vinaigrette. Rosemary Roasted Potatoes (see next recipe) and rice pilaf are other tasty partners that complement the chicken's savory sauce. For a kosher meal, prepare these dishes without dairy products.*

Golden Baked Fish with Sautéed Peppers

Like many Shabbat fish dishes, this one makes a good cold appetizer for starting the meal. Still, it tastes better at room temperature than thoroughly chilled. If you make it ahead and refrigerate it, remove it from the refrigerator at least 15 minutes before serving. For other occasions, you can serve it hot as a main course.

Use any fish fillets you like for this dish. Lean fish like cod and halibut are good because the olive oil and vegetables keep it moist. Choose whatever fish is freshest at your market. The sautéed peppers and the touch of spice lend a reddish-gold hue to the tasty sauce. I make this tasty, colorful dish often for entertaining.

Preparation time: *20 minutes*

Cooking time: *30 minutes*

Yield: *8 appetizers, or 4 to 6 main-course servings*

Keeping kosher: *Pareve*

3 or 4 tablespoons extra virgin olive oil, plus a little more for oiling the baking dish

½ small onion, chopped

1 red bell pepper, diced (½-inch dice)

1 yellow bell pepper, diced (½-inch dice)

5 large garlic cloves, chopped

½ teaspoon paprika

½ teaspoon turmeric (optional)

2 pounds fish fillets, 3/4 to 1 inch thick, cut in 4 to 8 pieces

½ teaspoon dried oregano

Salt and freshly ground pepper to taste

Cayenne pepper to taste

2 tablespoons chopped cilantro or Italian parsley

1 Preheat oven to 400°. Heat 3 tablespoons oil in a large skillet. Add onion and sauté over medium-low heat for 5 minutes, or until softened but not brown. Add red and yellow peppers and sauté 5 minutes. Remove from heat and stir in garlic, paprika, and turmeric.

2 Lightly oil a 13 x 9-inch baking dish or another baking dish large enough to hold fish in a single layer. Set fish in dish. If you like, sprinkle it with 1 tablespoon oil and then with oregano, salt, pepper, and cayenne pepper. Spoon pepper mixture around and over fish. Cover and bake 18 to 20 minutes, or until fish is opaque inside; check with a small knife. Stir half of cilantro into cooking liquid. Taste liquid and adjust seasoning.

3 Serve fish lukewarm or at room temperature. Serve it topped with the peppers and cooking liquid and sprinkled with remaining cilantro.

Per serving: Calories 122.5; Protein 12.9 g; Carbohydrates 3.7 g; Dietary fiber 0.7 g; Total fat 6.2 g; Saturated fat 0.9 g; Cholesterol 29.7 mg; Sodium 116.5 mg.

For the next recipe, it's helpful to know how to dice an eggplant:

1. **Cut off cap and then cut eggplant in half lengthwise, as shown in Figure 10-1.**

2. **Slice each eggplant half parallel to the cutting board.**

3. **Cut each slice into lengthwise strips.**

4. **Cut each strip into cubes.**

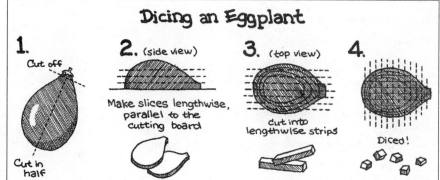

Figure 10-1:
Cutting an
eggplant
into cubes.

Spicy Eggplant

This flavorful dish is good hot or cold so is ideal for Shabbat. Serve it as an appetizer or an accompaniment for roast chicken. If the flavors appear Indian to you, you're right. It is inspired by a dish I learned from my sister-in-law, Mati Kahn, who was born in India. She finishes the sauce with fresh dill, a favorite herb in Israel. It you prefer eggplant that is not peppery, omit the jalapeño peppers, the pepper flakes, or both.

The stew is very convenient for making ahead of time. You can keep it in a covered dish for three days in the refrigerator, or you can freeze it.

Preparation time: *20 minutes*

Cooking time: *50 minutes*

Yield: *4 servings*

Keeping kosher: *Pareve*

1 medium eggplant, unpeeled (1 to 1¼ pounds)

3 tablespoons vegetable oil

1 medium onion, chopped

4 large garlic cloves, minced

1 or 2 jalapeño peppers, minced

2 teaspoons ground coriander

2 teaspoons ground cumin

½ teaspoon turmeric

¼ to ½ teaspoon hot red pepper flakes, or to taste

Salt to taste

28-ounce can tomatoes, drained and chopped

1 tablespoon tomato paste

½ cup water

2 tablespoons chopped fresh dill

1 Cut eggplant into ¾-inch dice (refer back to Figure 10-1). In a heavy wide casserole, heat oil, add onion, and cook over low heat 7 minutes, or until soft but not brown. Add garlic, jalapeño peppers, coriander, cumin, turmeric, and pepper flakes. Cook, stirring, 1 minute.

2 Add eggplant and salt and stir over low heat until eggplant is coated with spices. Add tomatoes and bring to boil over high heat. Mix tomato paste with water and stir into mixture. Cover and simmer over low heat, stirring often, for 30 to 40 minutes, or until eggplant is very tender and mixture is thick. Stir in dill. Taste and adjust seasoning, adding cayenne pepper if desired. Serve hot, cold or room temperature.

Per serving: Calories 173.7; Protein 3.2 g; Carbohydrates 18.0 g; Dietary fiber 5.5 g; Total fat 11.2 g; Saturated fat 0.8 g; Cholesterol 0 mg; Sodium 349.3 mg.

Developing the Ancestor of Baked Beans

One of the best-loved Shabbat dishes is *cholent*, known in Hebrew as hamin. This tasty, rich, rib-sticking stew is composed of meat and beans that cook very slowly all night long to be ready for Saturday at midday. It is a staple on observant Jewish tables because it follows the most stringent Shabbat regulations for heating food.

Over the years, Ashkenazic and Sephardic Jews alike have developed an incredible number of variations of this dish. Some are thick, others soupy. They may use white beans, red beans, chickpeas, or mixtures of beans. At the Jerusalem outdoor market, you can see sacs of beans of different colors and shapes, with such labels as "for Persian hamin" or "for Sephardic hamin." Occasionally, I see mixtures of several beans sold as "beans for cholent" in kosher grocery stores.

Although beans are central to most versions, some cholent recipes call for potatoes, whole-wheat kernels, or buckwheat instead of or in addition to them. Beef is the meat of choice; it's either cut into large cubes or ground and made into meat loaf or sausage type mixtures. Some prefer boneless beef, while others opt for cuts with bones to add flavor to the sauce, which forms during the cooking.

Seasonings vary from one kitchen to another, from the spicy Yemenite type with plenty of garlic, cumin, and turmeric to the milder tastes of some Ashkenazic recipes that rely on the meat to flavor the dish, enhanced only with salt, pepper, and onion. People basically created an overnight stew from the food at hand. If they couldn't afford much meat, they put in just a bit. These days, many are opting for chicken or making the dish meatless for health reasons.

Because of cholent's long history, some food historians believe it was the precursor of other slow-cooked bean casseroles, such as American baked beans or the French bean and meat casserole known as *cassoulet.*

Be sure to serve cholent hot, not lukewarm, for safety as well as for good flavor. If you have leftovers, refrigerate them promptly. A crock pot or slow cooker (see Figure 10-2) is useful for cooking overnight Sabbath stew.

Figure 10-2:
A slow cooker can save you time and energy.

Cholent — Overnight Shabbat Stew

The quintessential Shabbat stew, this beef and bean dish is the ultimate slow-cooked dinner-in-a-pot. During the super-gentle simmering, the flavors and aromas of the ingredients meld to give the cholent a rich taste. Jews around the world prepare versions of this stew according to the local ingredients and the community's spicing preferences.

Known by many names, the most common ones are cholent among Jews from Russia and central Europe, defina among Jews from Morocco, and hamin in Israel.

To make the stew the traditional way, you put it in the oven, on a hot plate, or in a crock pot or slow cooker (see Figure 10-2) on Friday just before sundown and serve it on Saturday for an early lunch. The cooking time varies according to the time the sun sets.

This is a well-spiced version of cholent that our family enjoys. Putting eggs in their shells on top of the stew mixture is a popular custom among many Jews of Middle Eastern origin. They turn light brown inside as the stew cooks and are a tasty addition. If I happen to have whole-wheat berries, which you can buy at kosher or Middle Eastern grocery shops or natural-foods stores, I add 1 cup with the other ingredients.

Preparation time: *30 minutes*

Cooking time: *About 16 to 18 hours (mostly unattended)*

Yield: *6 to 8 servings*

Keeping kosher: *Meat*

2 pounds beef chuck, trimmed and cut into 2-inch pieces

1 cup Great Northern, navy, or other white beans, picked over and rinsed

1 cup dried chickpeas, picked over and rinsed

6 medium boiling potatoes, halved

1 large onion, cut in thick slices

6 garlic cloves, coarsely chopped

2 small dried chilies such as chilies japones, left whole (optional)

2 teaspoons salt

½ teaspoon ground black pepper

4 teaspoons ground cumin

2 teaspoons turmeric

1 teaspoon paprika

1 or 2 beef bones (optional)

6 eggs in shells, rinsed

1 Preheat oven to 200°. In a large heavy stew pan or Dutch oven, combine meat, beans, chickpeas, potatoes, onion, garlic, and chilies. Sprinkle with salt, pepper, cumin, turmeric, and paprika. Mix thoroughly. Add beef bones to pan. Add 7 cups water or enough to barely cover the ingredients.

2 Bring to a boil. Cover and cook over very low heat, without stirring, for 20 minutes. Remove from heat. Set eggs gently on top of stew and push them slightly into liquid.

3 Cover tightly and bake stew, without stirring, overnight. Serve stew from its casserole or carefully spoon it into a large serving dish.

Per serving: Calories 596.1; Protein 37.7 g; Carbohydrates 52.2 g; Dietary fiber 10.9 g; Total fat 26.2 g; Saturated fat 9.5 g; Cholesterol 236.5 mg; Sodium 687.7 mg.

Preparing the Sweet of the Week

Baking cakes, cookies, and breads for Shabbat is a popular pastime. When I lived in Jerusalem, I always wrote down the recipe from the weekly radio show called "A Cake for Shabbat." Unlike the plethora of information you can easily get at your fingertips today, recipes then were somewhat scarce. I had only three cookbooks (in Hebrew) suited to the Israeli ingredients. These were my college years, and the show came on during my hours at my part-time job. The boss allowed me to take a break for this, on condition that I type up copies for her and the others at the office! After Shabbat, we compared notes on how the cakes turned out.

Most people bake cakes and cookies that are pareve, made without dairy products, so that they can be served after a meat main course. The exception is the Shabbat breakfast pastries and cakes, which may contain butter, milk, or sour cream. Often, the cakes are made in generous amounts so that some is left for later in the week.

Moist Cocoa Cake with Macadamia Nuts

Using macadamia nuts is my new twist on a long-time family favorite for Shabbat dessert. The cake is scrumptious, simple to prepare, and keeps for three days or longer in the refrigerator. Adding plenty of applesauce is the secret to its moistness.

The thin layer of chocolate frosting that tops the cake serves basically to stick whole macadamia nuts on it. I prefer unsalted macadamia nuts, but the choice is yours. If you have plenty of macadamia nuts, you can chop a few more and sprinkle them over the center of the cake for garnish. You can see a photo of this recipe in the color insert section of this book.

Special tools: *Mixer; 9-inch square cake pan*

Preparation time: *30 minutes*

Cooking time: *35 minutes*

Yield: *8 to 10 servings*

Keeping kosher: *Dairy if frosting is made with butter; pareve if made with nondairy margarine*

1½ cups flour, plus a little more for flouring the pan

⅓ cup unsweetened cocoa

1½ teaspoons ground cinnamon

1 teaspoon baking soda

½ cup vegetable oil, plus a little margarine or more oil for greasing the pan

1 cup sugar

1 large egg

1 teaspoon grated orange zest

1 cup unsweetened applesauce

½ cup macadamia nuts, chopped, plus 10 or more whole macadamia nuts for garnish

3 ounces semisweet chocolate, chopped

2 tablespoons butter or margarine, cut in 4 pieces, softened

1 Preheat oven to 350°. Grease and flour a 9-inch square baking pan. Sift flour with cocoa, cinnamon, and baking soda.

2 In a large bowl, beat oil, sugar, and egg with an electric mixer until mixture becomes somewhat pale and fluffy. Stir in orange zest.

3 Alternately stir cocoa mixture and applesauce into egg mixture, each in three batches, mixing after each addition just until batter is smooth. Stir in chopped macadamia nuts.

4 Pour batter into greased pan. Bake for 22 to 30 minutes, or until a cake tester inserted in cake comes out clean. Turn cake out onto a rack or, if you prefer, leave it in the pan; cool completely.

5 For the frosting, melt chocolate in a medium bowl set above hot water over low heat. Remove from heat and stir in butter. Cool frosting for 2 minutes, or until it is thick enough to spread. Spread it evenly over the top of the cake in a thin coating. Garnish with a circle of whole macadamia nuts.

6 Refrigerate cake for about 1 hour before serving, or until the frosting sets. Serve at room temperature.

Per serving: Calories 378.5; Protein 3.7 g; Carbohydrates 45.9 g; Dietary fiber 2.8 g; Total fat 21.2 g; Saturated fat 5.2 g; Cholesterol 27.5 mg; Sodium 140.6 mg.

Jewish Mother's Tips: Because I often prepare this cake to bring to a potluck dinner, I follow my family's custom and cool the cake in its pan instead of inverting it onto a rack. Because it's not a deep cake, it doesn't come out soggy. I frost only the top so that the cake is easy to carry right in its pan.

If you want to frost both the top and sides of the cake, make the frosting from 5 ounces of chocolate and 3 tablespoons butter or margarine.

Part III
Beginning the Feast

The 5th Wave   By Rich Tennant

"Walt took up baking just after retiring from the Navy. That's why all his blintzes look like submarines."

In this part . . .

Here I cover the many ways to begin a meal, from a savory soup to an array of colorful salads as the first course of a feast. This part gives you old-fashioned European-Jewish favorites like mushroom barley soup, tasty Israeli treats like falafel and hummus, and spicy Mediterranean-Jewish dips.

Chapter 11

Spreads and Savory Noshes

In This Chapter

▶ Converting humble elements into delectable pâtés

▶ Making the time-honored sauces for dunking

▶ Discovering Jewish secrets to savory pastries

▶ Transforming beans and vegetables into tempting treats

A s in many cuisines, meals for celebrating or entertaining in the Jewish kitchen start with a selection of appetizers. They include spreads, dips, marinated vegetables, and tasty pastries, but the variety is limited only by the cook's creativity with the available ingredients. Of course, these appetizers are great for snacking on at afternoon or late-night get-togethers with friends. The family finds them an enticing nosh at any time. In this chapter, I tell you what you need to know to make delicious appetizers.

A Plenitude of Pâtés

Spreads and pâtés may be the most favorite starters for making at home. After all, they're so delicious and so versatile. Whether they're meaty pâtés of liver or cooked chicken or bean spreads like hummus, most are simply stirred together or whirred in a food processor. So many foods can form the basis of spreads, from meats to cheeses to beans to vegetables to avocados. Good quality fresh or toasted bread or crackers are an essential accompaniment.

Chopped liver and wannabees

In the Jewish repertoire, the best known spread is chopped liver. The basic formula is just chicken liver blended with sautéed onions, hard-boiled eggs, salt, and pepper. Each cook has his or her own personal preferences for turning the liver into the perfect pâté. In my opinion, the secret to success lies in sautéing the onions until they brown well and in seasoning the mixture with plenty of salt and pepper. Chicken liver is the most common choice for home cooking, but at some delis, where this scrumptious spread is a well-loved item, they make it with beef liver.

In kosher cooking, chopped liver differs from typical French liver pâté in two important ways:

- ✔ To make chopped liver, you don't sauté the liver as in French pâté recipes. Instead, you broil it. Unlike other meats, liver can be koshered only by broiling or grilling over an open flame.

- ✔ Chopped liver never contains butter, because combining dairy and meat foods automatically makes the food nonkosher.

So popular is this pâté that it has spawned numerous imitators over the years. Their primary purpose is to provide a pareve pâté when you want to serve meatless meals. Eggplant, peas, green beans, walnuts, and lentils are some of the ingredients used to make the various versions. Many are wonderful and have become family treasures in their own right.

Hard-boiled eggs appear in many pâtés (like the following recipe) and salads. Here's a convenient way to make them.

1. **Put the eggs into a saucepan and cover them with water.**

2. **Bring to a boil, uncovered.**

3. **Remove from heat, cover, and let stand for 18 minutes.**

4. **Carefully pour off hot water. Rinse eggs with cold running water to cool them and stop the cooking.**

5. **If making them ahead, refrigerate them in their shells in a covered container up to five days.**

Almost Old-Fashioned Chopped Liver

You can buy this pâté at a deli, but your homemade chopped liver will be fresher and tastier. Besides, it's so simple to make. You can make it two days in advance and keep it in a covered container in the refrigerator.

This version has the old-fashioned taste without the toil. Instead of making it in an old-time meat grinder or chopping the ingredients with a knife, I use a food processor. Depending on your preference, you can puree it until smooth or pulse it to keep it chunky.

Old-fashioned recipes call for chicken fat for sautéing the onion, but I follow my family's tradition and use vegetable oil and the result is delicious. Another possibility is following an Alsatian Jewish formula and using goose fat or duck fat. Whichever fat you use, it is essential to sauté the onions slowly until they are deeply browned to develop their sweetness.

To serve the liver, put a scoop or large spoonful on a bed of lettuce. Garnish it with a selection of vegetables and pickles, such as onion rings, cucumber slices, tomato wedges, radishes, dill pickles, pickled peppers, and olives. Use any bread you like. The most frequent choices are challah, rye bread, and, for Passover, matzo.

Preparation time: 10 minutes

Cooking time: 30 minutes

Yield: 4 to 6 servings

Keeping kosher: Meat

¾ pound chicken livers	2 medium onions, chopped
Kosher salt	2 hard-boiled eggs, coarsely grated or chopped
3 tablespoons vegetable oil or chicken fat	Salt and freshly ground pepper to taste

1 Preheat broiler with rack about 3 inches from heat. Rinse livers and pat dry on paper towels; cut off any green spots. Put livers on foil in broiler and sprinkle with kosher salt on both sides. Broil 3 minutes per side or until completely cooked. Cut with a small knife to check that their color is no longer pink. Discard any juices. Cool livers slightly.

2 Heat oil in large heavy skillet. Add onions and sauté over medium-low heat, stirring occasionally, for 10 minutes. Continue cooking over medium-low heat for 7 to 10 more minutes or until tender and deep brown.

3 Put the liver and the onion mixture in a food processor. Chop with on/off pulses until finely blended or chunky, according to your preference. Transfer to a bowl and lightly mix in grated eggs. Season to taste with salt and pepper. Serve cold.

Per serving: Calories 137.8; Protein 8.2 g; Carbohydrates 3.9 g; Dietary fiber 0.7 g; Total fat 9.9 g; Saturated fat 1.5 g; Cholesterol 217.2 mg; Sodium 177.3 mg.

Jewish Mother's Tip: Using chicken fat: Rendered chicken fat sometimes separates in two layers. If yours has done so, stir it until blended before using it.

Pretend Chopped Liver

Call this mock liver, as my mother and her friends do, or use a more gentle term like vegetarian pâté if the word liver makes your friends squirm. Whatever you name it, this spread is easy and delicious. It's not the newfangled idea of a health-crazed Californian, but a legitimate Jewish dish in its own right. People have been making it for years when they're eating pareve or dairy dinners and want a festive appetizer. Serve it the same way as chopped liver.

Preparation time: *30 minutes*

Cooking time: *20 minutes*

Yield: *10 to 12 servings*

Keeping kosher: *Pareve*

¾ pound green beans, broken in 2, ends removed

¼ cup vegetable stock, more if needed (optional)

3 tablespoons vegetable oil

2 large onions, chopped

¼ pound mushrooms, diced

3 cups cooked chickpeas (garbanzo beans), or two 15-ounce cans, drained and rinsed

½ cup pecans

2 hard-boiled eggs, coarsely grated

Salt and freshly ground pepper to taste

1 Cook green beans in a medium saucepan of enough boiling salted water to cover them for about 10 minutes or until very tender. If you don't have vegetable stock, reserve ½ cup of the beans' cooking liquid. Drain beans, rinse with cold water, and drain well. Cool the reserved cooking liquid to room temperature or refrigerate it to cool it quickly.

2 In a large skillet, heat the oil, add onions, and sauté over medium heat for 7 minutes or until beginning to brown. Raise heat to medium-high, add mushrooms, and sauté, stirring often, for about 10 minutes, or until mushrooms and onions are well browned. Let cool.

3 In a food processor, chop green beans. Add chickpeas, onion and mushroom mixture, pecans, and stock or ¼ cup bean liquid. Process until smooth. If spread is too thick, add more stock or bean liquid, 1 tablespoon at a time, processing after each addition.

4 Transfer to a bowl. Lightly stir in hard-boiled eggs. Season to taste with salt and pepper. Serve cold.

Per serving: *Calories 161.6; Protein 6.0 g; Carbohydrates 16.5 g; Dietary fiber 4.9 g; Total fat 8.7 g; Saturated fat 0.9 g; Cholesterol 35.3 mg; Sodium 63.4 mg.*

Jewish Mother's Tip: *If you like, garnish the mock liver pâté with whole pecans. For extra flavor and aroma, toast the pecans — both those for the spread and any you want for garnish. Put them on a baking sheet and toast them in a 350° oven or toaster oven for 5 minutes.*

Great garbanzos

From its humble beginnings as cheap street food, the golden Middle Eastern chickpea spread called *hummus* has become famous in the U.S. and Europe. This fame is largely thanks to Israelis who spread the word about this delectable dip. Garlic and fresh lemon juice give the mixture its spirited flavor, and usually olive oil and *tahini* (sesame paste) is included as well. Generally, hummus is a smooth puree, but in Jerusalem I've found chunky versions, too.

Whatever you do, use fresh garlic. Many appetizers, such as garlic spreads, pâtés, dips, and uncooked sauces, gain a zesty flavor from raw garlic. Be sure your garlic is very fresh and minced finely or pressed with a garlic press. If it's old or the pieces are too big, the garlic will dominate the spread too much and give it an unpleasant taste.

These days you can easily find ready-to-eat hummus, even in different flavors and colors, but you can make homemade hummus in no time. If you use canned chickpeas, it requires no cooking. You don't have to do any chopping either. You just blend everything quickly in a food processor. In your own kitchen, you'll have natural, fresh-tasting hummus, made with lemon juice that you squeeze from a lemon and chopped fresh garlic.

Serve hummus the traditional way on plates for scooping up with pita bread. Or spread it in sandwiches, or as an appetizer, on small bread slices or on crackers. For a festive presentation for entertaining, Israelis spread hummus on a plate rather than serving it on a bowl. They use a large spoon to spread it and make the edges a bit higher than the center. Next they drizzle fine olive oil over the hummus. Often, they also spoon a dollop of tahini sauce (see the upcoming Tahini Sauce recipe) next to the hummus on the plate. Last, they sprinkle the hummus with paprika or cayenne pepper, and finally with chopped Italian parsley and sometimes toasted pine nuts.

If you're health conscious, you'll find homemade hummus valuable for lowfat meals because you can keep it on hand as a spread for bread instead of butter. For Hanukkah, you might like to serve it as an appetizer surrounded by raw vegetables like cucumber and carrot sticks and cauliflower florets. Because it helps satisfy hunger pangs, hummus can deter you from eating too many latkes!

You can make hummus ahead and keep it about four days in a covered container in the refrigerator. It thickens on standing. Stir in a little water before serving to lighten it.

Because hummus is pareve, it is suitable for kosher meals featuring either meat or dairy.

Hummus — Chickpea or Garbanzo Bean Dip

Israelis serve this inexpensive party dish at just about any occasion where friends and family members get together. They also like it for quick sandwiches and snacks. If you would like to cook dried chickpeas instead of using canned ones, see Chapter 18. Be sure to the spread with enough salt to balance the taste of the garlic. You can see a photo of this recipe in the color insert section of this book.

Preparation time: *10 minutes*

Cooking time: *None, if using canned chickpeas*

Yield: *2½ cups, or 6 to 8 servings*

Keeping kosher: *Pareve*

3 to 3½ cups cooked chickpeas (garbanzo beans) with about 1 cup of their cooking liquid, or two 15-ounce cans

2 or 3 large garlic cloves, peeled

¼ cup strained fresh lemon juice, or 1 or 2 tablespoons more to taste

¼ cup tahini paste

About ½ cup chickpea cooking liquid or water

Salt to taste

Cayenne pepper to taste

1 If using cooked chickpeas, drain them but reserve their cooking liquid. If using canned chickpeas, drain and rinse them.

2 In a food processor, mince garlic. Add chickpeas and process to chop them. Add lemon juice, tahini paste, and ¼ cup chickpea cooking liquid (or water if using canned chickpeas). Puree until finely blended. Taste and add 1 or 2 tablespoons more lemon juice if you like. If necessary, add more chickpea cooking liquid or water so that mixture has the consistency of a smooth spread. Season to taste with salt and cayenne pepper.

Per serving: Calories 148.3; Protein 6.8 g; Carbohydrates 19.4 g; Dietary fiber 5.1 g; Total fat 5.6 g; Saturated fat 0.7 g; Cholesterol 0 mg; Sodium 224.9 mg.

Jewish Mother's Tip: *If you're opening a jar of tahini paste, before measuring it, always stir it to be sure that the oil is blended with the solid sesame part. If you refrigerate it afterwards, the texture will remain uniform.*

Delectable Dips

Dips in Jewish homes tend to be meatless, and many serve double-duty as sauces. The most popular ones are made of sesame paste, cooked tomatoes, and hot and sweet peppers. You can serve one dip as an appetizer or snack or a selection of them at a party with various breads, chips, and vegetables for dunking. Make them ahead and keep them in the refrigerator, ready when you need them.

Sensational sesame

A frequent appetizer on the tables of Israelis is tehina or *tahini,* a sesame dip. Originally from the eastern Mediterranean, it is composed of ground sesame paste blended with lemon juice and garlic. For dunkers, you can use the customary pita bread, or you might like to opt for raw vegetables.

Tahini sauce is pareve, and Israelis and Sephardic Jews enjoy it in countless ways:

- ✔ As an appetizer dip
- ✔ As a sauce for spooning over falafel and other patties and fritters
- ✔ As a salad dressing, especially for Israeli Salad of tomatoes, cucumbers, and onions (see recipe in Chapter 19)
- ✔ To accompany grilled fish or meats
- ✔ To coat boiled vegetables, such as cauliflower, greens, and potatoes

Tahini labels can be confusing. Some may be called sesame butter, sesame paste, tahina, and various other spellings, or sesame sauce. Be sure to use the pure paste for the following recipe, and not one that has been mixed with other ingredients. Only one ingredient should be in the jar: sesame seeds.

You can keep tahini sauce for two days in a covered jar in the refrigerator. It thickens on standing, so stir in a little water before you serve it.

Tahini Sauce — Sesame Sauce

Tahini sauce is creamy-white, rich, and has a delectable flavor with a slight touch of bitterness. Made of sesame paste thinned with water and flavored simply with fresh lemon, garlic, and salt, it's easy to make and requires no cooking. Most often, it's used as an accompanying sauce or a dip for pita bread. Some people use it as a salad dressing. I have Israeli friends who prefer it to mayonnaise and use it in the same ways.

When tahini sauce is used as a dip for pita bread, it is made fairly thick and spread on a plate, like hummus, rather than being poured into a bowl for dipping. Israelis describe the action as wiping the plate with their piece of pita to scoop up the tahini. For serving as an appetizer, people sprinkle the tahini with olive oil, paprika or cayenne, and Italian parsley, following the same presentation as for hummus. (See recipe earlier in this chapter.)

Preparation time: *5 minutes*

Cooking time: *None*

Yield: *1½ cups, or 6 to 8 servings*

Keeping kosher: *Pareve*

¾ cup tahini (sesame paste)

¾ cup water, more if needed

¼ to ½ teaspoon salt, or more to taste

¼ cup strained fresh lemon juice, or more to taste

4 large garlic cloves, minced

Cayenne pepper to taste (optional)

¼ teaspoon ground cumin (optional)

1 If you are opening a jar of tahini, stir it to blend the two layers before measuring it. Stir it slowly to avoid splashing. Refrigerate the remaining tahini, and it will stay blended.

2 Spoon tahini paste into a medium bowl. Slowly whisk in ¾ cup water. Add salt, lemon juice, garlic, cayenne, and cumin. Taste and add more salt, lemon juice, and cayenne if you like. If sauce is too thick, stir in more water, 1 tablespoon at a time. Serve cool or at room temperature.

Per serving: *Calories 137.3; Protein 4.0 g; Carbohydrates 6.0 g; Dietary fiber 1.1 g; Total fat 11.9 g; Saturated fat 1.7 g; Cholesterol 0 mg; Sodium 80.9 mg.*

Jewish Mother's Tip: *If you prefer, you can combine the ingredients in a blender and blend it until smooth. A blender mixes it more quickly, but when you're making this relatively small amount, stirring the ingredients together in a bowl takes only a few minutes. I find washing a bowl and spoon easier than washing a blender. The choice is yours.*

Yemenite starters

On the tables of Jews originating in Yemen, you can find three standard dips — blazing hot *zehug,* a raw garlic-pepper paste; fresh and fiery smooth tomato salsa; and a bitter fenugreek seed dip called *hilbeh.* Yemenites much prefer homemade zehug, but you can buy it at Israeli grocery stores in the refrigerator case.

The tomato salsa is always prepared a short time before serving because it doesn't keep. It has only two ingredients — raw grated tomatoes and plenty of zehug.

Old-time cooks make their own hilbeh, but many purchase it from specially skilled hilbeh makers, who know the intricacies of soaking, grinding, and whipping the seeds to a smooth mixture.

Tangy tomato

Uncooked tomato makes a tasty dunk for breads. (See the sidebar "Yemenite starters.") More often, dips are made from cooked tomatoes because you can store them for much longer. Cooks combine the tomatoes with salt, oil, and a member of the allium family — either onion, garlic, or both — and simmer the mixture until it thickens. Depending on the their taste, the cook may be gentle with the seasonings or add an exuberant pepper flavor from black pepper, cayenne, or fresh or dried chilies. The result resembles a flavorful, concentrated, thick, chunky tomato sauce. You serve it cold as a dip or spoon it into sandwiches of fish and meats in pita bread.

Bourekas versus Knishes

Pastry appetizers are special treats for holidays and other festive occasions. Each Jewish community has developed their own favorites with a wide range of fillings made from vegetables, meat, or cheese. Jews from Russia make yeast-risen pastries called *piroshki,* which may be fried or baked. In the Moroccan Jewish tradition, the favorite is a rolled fried pastry called *cigars.* By far the best known of Jewish pastry appetizers are *knishes* and *bourekas.*

Filo savories from the Sephardic kitchen

A specialty of Jews originating in the eastern Mediterranean, bourekas baking in the oven are one of the most anticipated appetizers. These triangular or half-moon shaped pastries may be made of flaky filo dough, pie dough, or puff pastry and usually are sprinkled with sesame seeds before they go into the oven. Spinach, cheese, and potato are the most popular fillings, but some bourekas use meat or mushroom fillings as well. To make your own bourekas, see Chapter 9.

Pastry turnovers from the Ashkenazic kitchen

From Eastern Europe come *knishes,* a beloved savory pastry filled with meat, potato, or kasha (buckwheat groats). Today some Jewish knish bakeries have come up with a great variety and feature stuffings from broccoli to blueberry to chocolate with cheese. Obviously, the sweet ones are intended for dessert. The dough resembles pie dough, and the typical form is pillow-shaped, although a standard turnover shape is also common.

Knishes can be quite substantial. Good ones have a thin layer of dough enclosing plenty of filling.

Usually knish pastry is less flaky than bourekas pastry, but the two are starting to have a lot in common. One thing they share is that today's busy cooks often opt for dough you can buy. In fact, recently I saw prepared pastry sold at a kosher market that was labeled "for knishes or bourekas."

Cheaters' Spinach Knishes

I have to admit, I often take the easy way out and buy the dough for my knishes. At least I'm not alone. You can purchase pie dough, which resembles the traditional pastry more closely, but with a spinach filling, I prefer the flavor of puff pastry.

Cheese complements this filling well. If you want to add some to your knishes for meatless meals, add ½ cup grated cheese of your choice — Swiss cheese and cheddar complement the filling well in my opinion.

Special tool: *Pastry brush*

Preparation time: *2 hours*

Cooking time: *1 hour*

Yield: *About 40 small pastries, or about 10 servings*

Keeping kosher: *Pareve, if pastry is pareve; dairy, if pastry contains butter*

½ pound boiling potatoes, halved

Salt and freshly ground pepper to taste

1 cup cooked spinach, or a 10-ounce box frozen chopped spinach, thawed, drained

2 tablespoons vegetable oil

1 onion, chopped

Freshly grated nutmeg to taste

2 large eggs

2 pounds puff pastry, well chilled if fresh, thawed if frozen, or frozen puff pastry sheets

1 Put potatoes in a saucepan with water to cover and a pinch of salt and bring to a boil. Cover and simmer over low heat for 25 minutes or until very tender. Drain and leave until cool enough to handle.

2 Meanwhile, squeeze spinach by handfuls to remove excess liquid. Chop spinach fine.

3 In a medium skillet heat oil, add onion, and sauté over medium-low heat, stirring often, for 7 minutes or until well browned. Add spinach, salt, and pepper and sauté over low heat, stirring, for 1 minute.

4 Peel potatoes. Put in a bowl, cut each in a few pieces, and mash with a potato masher. Lightly stir in spinach mixture. Season filling generously with salt, pepper, and nutmeg so it will not be bland inside the pastry. Let cool.

5 Beat 1 egg in a small bowl. Stir egg into filling. Refrigerate in a covered container until ready to use.

6 Sprinkle 2 baking sheets with water. In a small bowl, beat remaining egg with a pinch of salt to use as glaze.

7 On a cool, lightly floured surface, roll half of dough about ⅛ inch thick. With a 3-inch round cutter or a sharp glass, cut rounds of dough. Separate rounds from rest of dough, reserving scraps. Roll each round to elongate it slightly to an oval. Put 1 teaspoon filling in center of each oval. Brush half of oval, around a narrow end, with beaten egg. Fold in half to enclose filling, joining plain pastry side to egg-glazed side. Press to seal well.

8 Set knishes on a baking sheet. Refrigerate at least 30 minutes. Shape more knishes from remaining pastry and filling. Refrigerate scraps at least 30 minutes and use them also. Cover remaining egg glaze and refrigerate until ready to bake knishes.

9 Preheat oven to 425°. Brush knishes with egg glaze. Bake for 10 minutes. Reduce oven temperature to 375 and bake for 12 minutes, or until pastries are puffed and brown. Serve warm or at room temperature.

Per serving: *Calories 143.1; Protein 2.3 g; Carbohydrates 11.9 g; Dietary fiber 0.6x g; Total fat 9.7 g; Saturated fat 1.4 g; Cholesterol 10.6 mg; Sodium 78.5 mg.*

Jewish Mother's Tip: *You can use frozen leaf spinach for the filling or frozen puff pastry for the dough. Or you can freeze these knishes before or after baking them. If they are unbaked, put the frozen knishes on a baking sheet and bake them as in the recipe, adding about 5 more minutes to their baking time. If they are baked, reheat them in a 325° oven until they are hot.*

Falafel and Friends — Treats to Tuck in Your Pita

Simple plant foods like chickpeas, vegetables, and olives are the basis for some of the most loved appetizers of all. They also make terrific pick-me-ups at any time of day, especially when you have some great pita bread on hand to enjoy them to their fullest.

Ever-popular falafel

Falafel, the Israeli fried chickpea nuggets, are most often served as a sandwich in pita bread together with Israeli diced vegetable salad, pickles, tahini sauce, and hot sauce. They also make a beloved appetizer for parties and other get-togethers. You can pass them around as hot hors d'oeuvre with tahini sauce for dipping, or put them on a platter with a selection of colorful thick dips and marinated vegetables, with pita wedges on the side.

Falafel

Israel's national snack, falafel, has become popular in North America and Europe as well in the last 20 years or so. When I was growing up in Washington, D.C., I was not familiar with these delectable, spicy chickpea balls. I first tasted them when I visited Israel.

Falafel is made of soaked dried chickpeas, not cooked or canned ones. When the falafel balls are deep fried, the chickpeas become cooked. Before frying them, review the rules for safe frying (see Chapter 6).

Serve falafel balls inside the pocket of a cut pita bread. Inside the pita, spoon a little of the eastern Mediterranean sesame dip, Tahini Sauce (see recipe in this chapter), and Israeli Salad (see Chapter 19). Serve hot sauce on the side, and hot pickled vegetables if you like. You can also include falafel on an appetizer platter with Hummus and Eggplant Spread (see recipes in this chapter), in addition to the sesame sauce and the Israeli salad. If possible, buy fresh pita bread from an Israeli or Middle Eastern bakery. You can see a photo of this recipe in the color insert section of this book.

Special tool: *Deep frying thermometer*

Preparation time: *25 minutes, plus 12 hours soaking time*

Cooking time: *10 minutes*

Yield: *8 servings as appetizer*

Keeping kosher: *Pareve*

2 cups dried chickpeas (also called garbanzo beans) (12 ounces)

16 large garlic cloves, peeled

¼ cup small cilantro sprigs

1 slice stale unsweetened white bread, crusts removed

2 tablespoons ground coriander

1½ tablespoons ground cumin

2½ teaspoons salt

2 teaspoons ground black pepper

¼ teaspoon cayenne pepper

2 tablespoons flour

About 6 cups vegetable oil (for frying)

1 Spread chickpeas on a plate and discard any stones. Put chickpeas in a bowl of cool water to generously cover. Soak them in the water overnight or for 12 hours; drain in colander and rinse.

2 Mince garlic in a food processor. Add cilantro to processor and chop it with garlic. Sprinkle bread with about 2 tablespoons water; squeeze dry. Add bread and chickpeas to processor and grind mixture until fine. Add ground coriander, cumin, salt, pepper, cayenne, and flour. Process to mix. Transfer to a bowl. Knead thoroughly with your hands to be sure mixture is well blended and evenly moistened. If mixture feels too dry to shape in balls, add more water, 1 tablespoon at a time, until it is lightly moistened.

3 To shape falafel, take 1 tablespoon of mixture and squeeze to compact it. Then press it to a ball. Roll ball lightly between your palms to give it a smooth round shape.

4 Heat deep fat to about 350° on a deep frying thermometer. Carefully slip in ¼ to ⅓ of the falafel balls. Do not drop them into oil from high up so that oil won't splash. Fry for 3 minutes, or until falafel balls are deep golden brown and coating is crisp. Drain briefly on paper towels. If oil temperature has decreased, reheat it before adding more falafel balls. Serve hot.

Per serving: Calories 270.9; Protein 10.6 g; Carbohydrates 35.6 g; Dietary fiber 9.5 g; Total fat 10.3 g; Saturated fat 0.8 g; Cholesterol 0.2 mg; Sodium 759.0 mg.

Versatile veggies

Over the ages, Jewish cooks have created countless meal starters out of vegetables. They are perfect for kosher cooking as they are naturally pareve and can be served at any time. Two vegetables — peppers and eggplant — seem to come up most often on the appetizer table.

✔ **Peppers with pizzazz:** Cooks love to grill and marinate peppers with garlic and olive oil, to sauté them and serve them warm or cold, or to stuff them and simmer them in a savory sauce. Some prefer sweet peppers, while others opt for the hot ones.

✔ **Extraordinary eggplant:** So versatile is this vegetable that some Israeli eateries feature an eggplant platter of five or six items, each amazingly different from the others. For appetizers, eggplant may be pickled, fried, and topped with tomato sauce; breaded and sautéed; marinated; or grilled and made into a spread. They may be seasoned with anything from hot peppers and tahini sauce to onion and mayonnaise and may be paired with other vegetables, meat, or cheese.

No-work noshes

On just about every holiday table, you find olives and pickles. People care about their quality. The supermarket across the street from my mother's home in Jerusalem offers an array of olives in bins, with little slotted spoons and cups for tasting — pitted and unpitted green and black olives of all sizes, cracked olives with herbs and garlic, spicy ones with dried hot peppers, large stuffed green olives, wrinkled oil-cured black olives. Good olives are important in the Jewish kitchen.

Pickles and marinated vegetables are equally important. Besides the ever-popular dill pickles made of cucumbers, there are pickles made from just about every vegetable, even tiny eggplants.

Many people also served roasted nuts. Jews of Middle Eastern origin also buy roasted chickpeas.

Good quality marinated fish is another much appreciated appetizer. The selection begins with herring in a sweet and sour sauce, tuna in olive oil, and sardines in a spicy sauce but a glance at a Jewish deli case reveals much more.

Avoid exploding eggplants!

Don't forget to prick the eggplants before cooking them. Otherwise, the steam that builds up inside can cause it to explode. That happened to me once, before I knew what I was doing in the kitchen, and I will never forget to prick it again! There was a loud boom from my oven, where my eggplant was baking. When I opened the oven, there was nothing left of it. It had blown apart!

Two-Way Eggplant Spread

Wildly popular in Israel, eggplant salad, as it is known there, is prepared in numerous renditions, and each person has his or her favorite. Many appreciate a smoky tasting eggplant and grill it over coals. Others broil or bake it. The cooking is easy because you grill the eggplants whole. Keep this spread on hand in the refrigerator for a tasty snack.

Once the eggplant is tender, you scoop out the pulp, mash it, and add garlic, lemon juice, and plenty of salt and pepper. Then you enrich it. The two best-loved flavorings are tahini and mayonnaise, although olive oil is a close third. Leave it plain or stir in strips of roasted peppers or a mixture of diced tomato, cucumber, and chopped onion. Fresh pita bread is the usual accompaniment. You can see a photo of this recipe in the color insert section of this book.

Preparation time: *25 minutes, plus time to prepare Tahini Sauce if using*

Cooking time: *40 minutes to 1 hour*

Yield: *6 to 8 servings*

Keeping kosher: *Pareve*

2½ pounds eggplants (2 medium or large)	*Salt and freshly ground pepper to taste*
2 large garlic cloves, finely minced	*Hot sauce to taste*
⅓ cup mayonnaise, or ½ cup Tahini Sauce — Sesame Sauce (see recipe), or more of either one to taste	*Chopped Italian parsley or parsley sprigs (optional garnish)*
2 to 3 tablespoons strained fresh lemon juice	

1 Prick eggplant a few times with fork. Put eggplant on an outdoor grill or in a shallow baking dish in the broiler. Turning eggplant often, broil it for 40 minutes or grill it for 1 hour, or until it is tender when pierced. Eggplant will look collapsed when it's done.

2 Cut off eggplant caps. Leave eggplant until cool enough to handle. Cut eggplant in half lengthwise. If eggplant is very soft, simply scoop flesh out of peel with a spoon. Otherwise, cut away peel with a paring knife. Chop eggplant fine with a knife, almost to a puree; or put it in a food processor and chop it with on/off pulses to a chunky puree or a smooth one, as you prefer.

3 Put eggplant puree in a bowl. Add garlic and mix well. Stir in mayonnaise, sesame sauce, and 2 tablespoons lemon juice. Season generously with salt, pepper, and hot sauce. Taste and add more mayonnaise, tahini sauce, or lemon juice if you like. Serve cold or at room temperature, garnished with parsley.

Per serving: *Calories 104.8; Protein 1.3 g; Carbohydrates 9.7 g; Dietary fiber 3.4 g; Total fat 7.5 g; Saturated fat 1.1 g; Cholesterol 5.4 mg; Sodium 128.8 mg.*

Jewish Mother's Tip: *If you're going to use the broiler, be sure to choose eggplants that are slim enough to fit.*

Chapter 12

Soups, the Jewish Mother's Secret Cure-All

*J*ewish cooking has long been known for its savory soups. Chicken soup with noodles or matzo balls is the best known, but many others are out there. In this chapter, you find out Jewish secrets for preparing soups not only from chicken but from beef, mushrooms, vegetables, and legumes.

Over the ages, frugal Jewish cooks have created tasty soups, both smooth and chunky, from a great variety of ingredients. By turning meats, poultry, and vegetables into soups, they made satisfying dishes from them in an economical way. Today, many of these soups have remained favorites for another reason. As ingredients gently simmer together, they exchange flavors, and the resulting soups are delicious. In this chapter, you see how to cook such tasty soups.

Chicken Soups — Jewish Mothers' Aspirin, Penicillin, and Antidepressant

Just about everyone knows that chicken soup is the supreme Jewish comfort food. Jewish mothers have long held the opinion that a bowl of steaming hot chicken soup always makes you feel better, whether or not you're in a great mood or in good health.

In spite of the mystique surrounding it, chicken soup is simple to prepare. All you need is chicken, water, a few aromatic vegetables, and time to simmer them.

My mother flavors her soup with onions, carrots, celery, bay leaves, parsley, and sometimes dill. Generally, she serves it as a clear soup with a few carrot slices and either matzo balls or noodles. If you've tasted chicken soup at a Jewish deli, you are most likely familiar with this style of seasoning, which stems from the Ashkenazic tradition. Chicken soups of completely different tastes come from Sephardic kitchens, where leeks, cumin, tomato, and cilantro are popular flavorings.

A stock pot is the most efficient pot for preparing chicken and meat soups (see Figure 12-1). The deep pot is ideal for long, slow simmering and for cooking any ingredient that needs a substantial amount of liquid.

Figure 12-1:
Use a stock pot to make soups and stocks, especially those made from chicken and meat.

stock pot

Miraculous matzo balls

Dumplings made of matzo meal and eggs, also called *kneidelach* in Yiddish, are chicken soup's most famous associates. There are numerous versions, from substantial, firm dumplings to airy, fluffy ones. In most families, the definition of the ideal matzo ball is simply a matter of tradition.

Skim the fat from your soup

Chicken and meat give off plenty of fat to the soup as they cook. Some people feel the fat contributes to the flavor. With today's nutritional knowledge, most people agree that removing at least some of the fat is a good idea.

To remove the fat from chicken or meat soup (see figure), first chill the soup in the refrigerator or freezer so that the fat will rises to the top and congeal. Chilling takes several hours. The soup chills fastest if you transfer it from the pot to a shallow bowl. Spoon off the congealed layer of fat. If there is enough fat, it forms a whitish layer on top of the soup.

You'll probably find it convenient to make the soup a day ahead and refrigerate it overnight, so that you can remove the fat the next day.

SKIM THE FAT FROM CHICKEN SOUP!
☆ FOR A QUICK ALTERNATIVE, PUT THE PAN IN THE FREEZER...
THE FAT
SPOON OFF THE CONGEALED LAYER OF FAT (THE WHITISH LAYER THAT COVERS THE SOUP)

Some people feel that matzo ball making is a mystery and that success in getting them to rise is practically a miracle. My mother taught me to handle the batter lightly to prevent them from being heavy and to poach the dumplings gently to keep them from falling apart. See recipe in Chapter 8.

Soothing noodles

After matzo balls, egg noodles are the most popular addition to chicken soup. To please everyone in the family, some cooks may serve their soup with both. Most people opt for very thin egg noodles, although when I was growing up, alphabet noodles appeared just as often in our soup. Serving noodles is a common way to entice children to enjoy the soup.

Some cooks of eastern European origin embellish their soup with homemade *kreplach,* or Jewish tortellini, made with egg noodle dough enclosing a meat filling. Preparing them is time consuming and generally reserved for holidays. You can buy them in some well-stocked kosher grocery stores.

Grandma's Chicken Soup with Noodles

Every Thursday my mother follows the time-honored Jewish practice of preparing chicken soup for the Friday night dinner. This is her recipe. Once she stuck to the pure Ashkenazic tradition of flavoring her soup with onions, carrots, celery, and bay leaves. Since she has been living in Jerusalem, she has adopted the Sephardic habit of adding small amounts of cilantro and cumin. Because of the long simmering, they do not dominate the taste of the soup.

The secret to sensational chicken soup is to use plenty of chicken for the amount of water in the pot. I find that chicken legs, thighs, wings, and backs produce more richly flavored soup than white meat pieces. You can see a photo of this recipe in the color insert section of this book.

Preparation time: *30 minutes*

Cooking time: *1¾ hours*

Yield: *6 servings*

Keeping kosher: *Meat*

2 pounds chicken legs or wings

1 large onion, quartered

2 celery stalks, cut in 3-inch lengths

2 large carrots, cut in 3-inch lengths

2 bay leaves

Salt and freshly ground pepper to taste

8 cups water

½ teaspoon ground cumin

2 tablespoons chopped cilantro

1½ cups fine egg noodles

2 tablespoons chopped parsley

1 Put chicken pieces in a large pot and add the onion, celery, carrots, bay leaves, salt, and pepper. Add enough water to cover the ingredients. Bring to a boil over high heat, skimming the foam from the surface as it accumulates. Cover and cook over low heat for 1 hour.

2 Add the cumin and cilantro and simmer 30 minutes more, or until the chicken is very tender and the soup is well flavored.

3 Remove the chicken and reserve it for other purposes. If you like, remove some of chicken meat from bones and return it to the soup. Remove the carrot pieces. Slice 3 or 4 of them and return the slices to the soup. Remove onion, celery, and bay leaves. Refrigerate the soup. Thoroughly skim fat from the top.

4 Cook the noodles in a large pan of boiling salted water about 5 minutes or until just tender. If you are preparing them ahead, drain them and rinse them with cold water. Refrigerate them.

5 Before serving, remove the noodles from the refrigerator so that they come to room temperature. Bring the soup just to a simmer and add the parsley. Season the soup to taste with salt and pepper.

6 At serving time, add noodles to each bowl of hot soup.

Per serving: Calories 68.0; Protein 1.8 g; Carbohydrates 9.8 g; Dietary fiber 1.4 g; Total fat 2.6 g; Saturated fat 0.7 g; Cholesterol 9.5 mg; Sodium 133.5 mg.

Jewish Mother's Tip: You can also add necks and giblets, but not chicken livers, to the soup.

Beef Soups: Savory Entrees from Small Amounts of Meat

In the Yemenite Jewish kitchen, beef soup is even more traditional than chicken soup on the Shabbat menu. Spiked with cumin and plenty of pepper and gaining a golden hue from turmeric, this soup has become popular with Israelis as a whole. Instead of matzo balls, it may contain rice, potatoes, or both and often is served as a main course rather than a starter. Jews of Moroccan and other Sephardic origins also celebrate the weekly holiday with hearty whole-meal meat and vegetable soups.

In the old days, when food was not plentiful in their native Yemen, people prized the fat in their meat soup. Today, many of the younger cooks in Israel and the United States skim off the fat for a more healthful soup.

Rachel's Yemenite Meat Soup

My mother-in-law's somewhat spicy soup becomes even hotter when served the Yemenite way — accompanied by fiery fresh hot pepper chutney called *zehug*, which is made of equal amounts of chilies and garlic. The soup's favorite partner is fresh-baked, good quality pita bread.

Once a secret of Yemenite kitchens, this type of soup has become well loved in Israel and is a favorite restaurant entree. I've even seen it featured proudly on Israeli restaurant menus in the United States. Traditionally, it's made with beef, but today many substitute chicken or turkey. In that case, two hours of simmering are enough.

Preparation time: *20 minutes*

Cooking time: *3½ hours*

Yield: *6 to 8 servings*

Keeping kosher: *Meat dish*

2 tablespoons ground cumin

2 teaspoons turmeric

½ teaspoon ground black pepper

1½ pounds beef chuck with bones or other cuts of beef for stewing

Salt to taste

1 large onion, peeled, left whole

2 ripe medium tomatoes, or 4 plum tomatoes, left whole

About 5 cups boiling water

6 small boiling potatoes

1 Mix cumin, turmeric, and black pepper. Put beef in a large heavy saucepan or Dutch oven. Sprinkle it with salt and with the spice mixture and heat it over low heat, turning the pieces occasionally, for about 5 minutes or until they are well coated with spices.

2 Add onion and tomatoes to the pan. Add enough boiling water to cover the meat. Bring to a boil. Skim foam from surface. Cover and cook over low heat for 2 hours.

3 Peel the potatoes and add to the soup. If necessary, add water to cover them. Cover and cook over low heat for 1 hour or until the meat and potatoes are very tender and the soup is well flavored. Taste and adjust seasoning. Remove onion and tomatoes. Serve hot, in shallow bowls with a few pieces of meat and a potato in each one.

Per serving: Calories 247.6; Protein 14.6 g; Carbohydrates 18.1 g; Dietary fiber 2.2 g; Total fat 12.7 g; Saturated fat 4.9 g; Cholesterol 47.1 mg; Sodium 108.2 mg.

Jewish Mother's Tip: *Some people like to thicken this soup with a slurry of flour and water. The technique is similar to the Chinese thickening of soups with cornstarch. To do this, mix 2 tablespoons flour with ¼ cup water in a small bowl until smooth. Slowly stir it into the finished soup. Return the soup to a simmer, stirring constantly to prevent lumps.*

Vegetable Soups: Plant Foods Become Supper

Observant families follow a custom of reserving chicken and meat for Shabbat and other holidays. The rest of the time, vegetables take center stage. Cooks from every Jewish community count vegetable soups among their most frequently prepared foods. After all, vegetable soups are versatile in their ingredient requirements, convenient to prepare in quantity, and easy to reheat when they are needed.

Bean and barley soups

Over the ages, Jews from Poland to India discovered that hearty soups of legumes and grains make filling, frugal ways to feed the family. Substantial split pea soups and barley soups with mushrooms or chicken have long been popular on Ashkenazic tables. Israeli cooks make delectable white bean soups flavored with tomato and garlic or spicy lentil soups scented with dill.

Another advantage of these soups is their broad appeal. Even when there's no time to cook, many choose these homey dishes when they eat at restaurants, whether in Tel Aviv or Los Angeles.

 Satisfying soups of beans or barley practically make the whole meal. Serve a light, fresh salad such as Israeli diced salad (Chapter 19) before the soup. You may also like to follow the popular custom of serving the soup with rye bread or other whole-grain bread.

Israeli Bean Soup

Home cooks in Israel enjoy making soothing soups by slowly simmering dried beans and keeping them on hand to feed the family. Often, they make them meatless, although the cooking liquid may be extra chicken broth left from the Shabbat meals. In most pots, tomatoes and tomato paste contribute taste as well as body to the soup. Small- or medium-sized white beans are the ones used most often. Bean soup is also a favorite at restaurants, where chefs frequently spice it with cumin and red pepper. I find it's an appealing appetizer or entree, and it's healthful, too!

Preparation time: *40 minutes*

Cooking time: *1½ hours*

Yield: *6 to 8 servings*

Keeping kosher: *Meat or pareve, depending on stock used*

1 pound dried white beans (about 2½ cups)	*2 thyme sprigs, or ½ teaspoon dried thyme*
2 tablespoon olive oil or vegetable oil	*A 28-ounce can diced tomatoes, drained*
3 medium onions, diced	*6 large garlic cloves, chopped*
1 small carrot, diced	*¼ teaspoon red pepper flakes, or cayenne pepper to taste*
2 celery stalks, sliced	
3 cups chicken, beef, or vegetable stock	*Salt and freshly ground pepper to taste*
3 to 5 cups water	*2 tablespoons tomato paste*
1 bay leaf	*⅓ cup chopped Italian parsley*

1 Sort beans in batches by spreading them on a large plate, discarding any broken ones and any stones. Rinse beans and drain.

2 Heat oil in large saucepan or a 2- to 3-quart dutch oven or stew pan, add onions, and sauté over medium heat, stirring often, about 15 minutes or until beginning to brown. Add carrot, celery, beans, stock, 3 cups water, bay leaf, and thyme. Bring to a boil. Cover and cook over low heat 1 hour.

3 Add tomatoes, garlic, pepper flakes, and salt. Mix tomato paste with 2 tablespoons water and stir into soup. If soup is too thick, add 1 or 2 cups water. Cover and cook for 30 minutes, or until beans are very tender.

4 Discard bay leaf and thyme sprigs. Season to taste with salt and pepper. Stir in parsley and serve.

Per serving: Calories 277.6; Protein 15.5 g; Carbohydrates 44.1 g; Dietary fiber 10.8 g; Total fat 5.6 g; Saturated fat 1.0 g; Cholesterol 1.9 mg; Sodium 627.6 mg.

Jewish Mother's Tip: *You can keep the soup in a covered container for three days in the refrigerator. If you prefer, freeze some of it for a busy week.*

Old Country Mushroom Barley Soup

Mushroom barley soup has become a standard on Jewish deli restaurant menus in both the United States and Israel, but it's even better when you cook it at home. Use either vegetable broth or chicken stock as the base for this soup, depending on your preference. It's doubly welcome to know that the pleasing pottage is also good for you because of the healthful fiber in the barley as well as the nutritional qualities of the mushrooms. If you prefer, remove the skin from the chicken pieces before making the soup to reduce the fat content. The soup thickens considerably on standing. If you make it ahead, add a little hot water when reheating, to bring it to the desired fluidity.

Preparation time: 30 minutes

Cooking time: 1¾ hours

Yield: 6 to 8 servings

Keeping kosher: Meat

1 ounce dried mushrooms, any kind	8 ounces fresh mushrooms, halved and sliced
1½ pounds chicken legs or thighs	Salt and freshly ground pepper to taste
12 ounces carrots, diced (6 small)	1 teaspoon sweet paprika
2 large onions, diced	¼ teaspoon hot paprika or cayenne pepper, or to taste
10 cups water	
⅔ cup pearl barley	3 tablespoons chopped parsley
5 stalks celery, diced	

1 Rinse dried mushrooms. Soak them for 20 minutes in 1 cup hot water. Remove mushrooms, reserving their soaking liquid. If using shiitake mushrooms, discard their stems, which are often tough. Dice any large mushrooms. Pour the soaking liquid into another bowl, leaving behind the last few tablespoons of liquid, which may be sandy; discard this liquid.

2 Meanwhile, in a large pot, combine chicken, carrots, onions, and 8 cups water and bring to boil. Skim foam from surface. Simmer for 15 minutes, skimming foam occasionally.

3 Add barley, celery, fresh and dried mushrooms, and reserved mushroom soaking water to the soup. Add salt, pepper, and sweet paprika. Cover and cook over low heat for 1¼ hours, or until chicken and barley are tender and soup is well flavored. From time to time, add a little more water if soup becomes too thick.

4 Remove chicken from soup and discard skin and bones. Return chicken meat to soup.

5 Skim off excess fat from soup. Add hot paprika. Taste and adjust seasoning. Serve sprinkled with parsley.

Per serving: Calories 190.0; Protein 14.2 g; Carbohydrates 26.4 g; Dietary fiber 6.0 g; Total fat 3.7 g; Saturated fat 1.0 g; Cholesterol 35.8 mg; Sodium 173.8 mg.

Two-way soups

Among families that keep kosher, the need to separate meat from dairy foods has often led to the development of two, or even three, versions of their favorite vegetable soup recipes. Depending on what other dishes will accompany the soups, cooks alter the liquids and fats used to make sure there are no conflicts with keeping kosher.

- ✔ **Meat:** A favorite way to lend a meaty flavor to vegetable soups is to simmer the vegetables in chicken or beef broth left from the festive Shabbat dinners. For kosher meals, these soups can be served only in dairy-free menus. To prepare carrot or broccoli soup, for example, you can sauté the vegetables in oil and simmer them in chicken broth.

- ✔ **Dairy:** For dairy dinners, observant Jewish cooks use vegetable broth or water to simmer the vegetables. To enrich a carrot or broccoli soup, they may sauté the vegetables in butter, finish the soup with milk or cream, or top it with sour cream.

- ✔ **Pareve:** Those who prefer to prepare a big pot of soup suitable for all sorts of meals, whether or not they contain meat or dairy, make them pareve. They opt for olive oil or vegetable oil for any sautéing and either vegetable broth or water as the soup's liquid. With judicious use of onions, garlic, herbs, and spices, these soups can still be delicious.

Keeping kosher means using different pots to cook meat and dairy soups.

Velvety Carrot Soup

Pureeing cooked carrots and rice gives this soup an appealing, velvety-smooth texture. It acquires a creamy consistency even if you make it without any cream.

Use this recipe as the basis for three soups. If you simmer the ingredients in vegetable broth and use vegetable oil for sautéing, the soup is pareve or neutral. This gives you the most flexibility in kosher cooking because you can serve the soup in a menu that includes any food. To make it for meat or poultry meals, use vegetable oil to sauté the vegetables and then simmer them in either chicken stock or vegetable broth.

For meals that include dairy products, make it with vegetable broth and sauté the ingredients in either butter or oil. If you like, enrich the soup with milk or cream for a more luscious taste.

Special tool: *Blender*

Preparation time: *20 minutes*

Cooking time: *40 minutes*

Yield: *6 servings*

Keeping kosher: *Pareve or dairy*

2 tablespoons vegetable oil or butter

1 large onion, chopped

1½ pounds carrots, peeled and diced

4 to 5 cups vegetable broth

3 tablespoons uncooked rice

Salt and freshly ground pepper to taste

2 thyme sprigs, or ½ teaspoon dried thyme

1 bay leaf

⅓ cup milk, light cream, or whipping cream (optional)

Pinch of sugar

1 Heat oil in a large heavy saucepan. Add onion and sauté over medium-low heat, stirring often, 7 minutes or until soft but not brown. Add carrots, 4 cups broth, rice, salt, pepper, thyme, and bay leaf. Stir and bring to a boil. Cover and cook over low heat for 30 to 40 minutes or until carrots and rice are very tender. Discard thyme sprigs and bay leaf.

2 Let soup cool 5 minutes. Pour soup into a blender and puree it until very smooth. Return it to the saucepan.

3 Bring the soup to a simmer over medium-low heat, stirring often. If soup is too thick, add about 1 cup broth, or enough to bring soup to desired consistency. Bring to a boil, stirring. Stir in milk or cream and heat gently. Season to taste with salt, pepper, and sugar.

Per serving: Calories 145.7; Protein 4.0 g; Carbohydrates 21.6 g; Dietary fiber 3.5 g; Total fat 5.8 g; Saturated fat 0.6 g; Cholesterol 1.8 mg; Sodium 829.3 mg.

Vegetable Stock

For dairy-free cooking, vegetable stock is an important asset in the kitchen. Use it to give good taste to soups, sauces, grains, and vegetable dishes. You can keep it up to three days in the refrigerator, or you can freeze it.

Save parsley stems and trimmings from carrots, celery, onions, squash, and mushrooms to make broths. French chefs treasure dark green leek tops for the fine flavor they add. You can use wilted green onions the same way. Avoid cabbage family vegetables unless you like the taste they impart.

Special tool: *Strainer*

Preparation time: *15 minutes*

Cooking time: *1 hour*

Yield: *About 6 cups*

Keeping kosher: *Pareve*

2 large onions, coarsely chopped

1 large carrot, diced

4 celery stalks with leaves, chopped

Dark green part of 2 leeks, rinsed thoroughly and sliced (optional)

2 quarts water

1 bay leaf

4 sprigs fresh thyme, or 1 teaspoon dried thyme

4 large garlic cloves, peeled and crushed

10 parsley stems (optional)

2 cups mushroom stems or sliced mushrooms (optional)

Pinch of salt (optional)

1 Combine all ingredients in a large saucepan. Bring to a boil. Cover and simmer over low heat for 1 hour.

2 Strain stock, pressing on ingredients in strainer; discard ingredients in strainer. Cool and refrigerate or freeze.

Per serving: *Calories 19.3; Protein 0.7 g; Carbohydrates 4.5 g; Dietary fiber 1.1 g; Total fat 0.1 g; Saturated fat 0 g; Cholesterol 0 mg; Sodium 27.7 mg.*

Part IV
The Heart of the Celebration

The 5th Wave   By Rich Tennant

"I'm using a slow cooker and all you have out is kosher meat. Should my slow cooker also be kosher?"

In this part . . .

This part covers the main event of the meal. Here I present delicious entrees for brunch, lunch, and dinner, both casual and elegant. You find main courses based on eggs, dairy foods, fish, meats, and poultry and see how to use them in kosher menus.

Chapter 13

Brunch Favorites

*1*n Jewish American homes, Sunday brunch is a treasured tradition. Its main quality is that it's fun. After all, brunch is composed of comfort foods. Brunch is a relaxed meal, enjoyed at a leisurely pace.

Each family has its favorites, and the menu may be simple or elaborate. Many brunch menus, however, share a few features. Generally, brunch fare is based on dairy foods, smoked fish, and eggs. Many of the home-cooked recipes have influenced the items on delicatessen menus.

If you've been wondering how to serve a Jewish-style brunch, you can find the answers in this chapter. You also discover how to easily make all those tasty egg dishes, scrumptious salads, and bagel sandwiches, plus some new ones.

Serving Bagels with Their Partners

For those of you who grew up in Jewish homes in America, a bagel with lox and cream cheese is the ultimate comfort food. More than any other food, bagel stands for brunch. You may add butter, too, but you have to have cream cheese. Purists insist on absolutely fresh bagels, and that's why Brooklyn has 24-hour bagel bakeries. Who knows, you may want brunch at midnight!

Bagel lovers do not toast their fresh bagels. They feel toasting's purpose is to improve bread that's no longer fresh. But brunch has no strict rules. Part of its charm is that everyone eats what he or she likes. Some do toast their bagels and then spread it with butter so that it melts into the toast, and then add cream cheese.

New bagel flavors seem to come out every week, but most traditionalists opt for the simple old-fashioned ones — plain, egg, poppy seed, or onion. And traditionalists have another good reason for their conservative choice. Most want to serve lox with their bagels, and these savory flavors go best with it. Bagels with sweet flavors like chocolate or blueberry do not.

Shmears

Cream cheese is bagel's mate. The cream cheese sold in tubs is easier to spread than the more solid kind sold in bars, although you can use it, too, if you let it soften at room temperature. In good Jewish markets, you can find freshly made cream cheese rather than the packaged kind. Today, some people opt for lowfat or fat-free cream cheese.

At delis and supermarkets, you can also buy flavored cream cheese, or you can make your own *shmears,* the Yiddish word for spreads. You simply mix plain cream cheese with the flavorings of your choice. Some common additions are hot pepper, snipped chives, chopped olives, grated lemon rind, or chopped lox. You just stir in a little sour cream or yogurt to soften the cream cheese. Then add any of the ingredients in Table 13-1 or combine several to your taste. Begin with small amounts. Then make up your own.

Table 13-1	Make Your Own Cream Cheese Spreads	
	Main Ingredient	*Good Partners*
Herbs	Fresh chives, parsley, dill, or thyme; dried dill, thyme, or oregano	Paprika, pepper, hot sauce
Hot and pungent stuff	Freshly ground pepper, cayenne, hot sauce, fresh or pickled jalapeno peppers, roasted chiles, garlic, olives	Herbs, vegetables

	Main Ingredient	*Good Partners*
Spice	Paprika, cumin, cinnamon	Vegetables
Cheese	Parmesan or other grating cheeses, crumbled feta, goat cheese	Herbs, pepper, cayenne, hot sauce, garlic
Fish	Lox or smoked salmon, smoked whitefish, other smoked fish	Chives, dill, parsley, lemon zest
Vegetables	Green onion, sun-dried tomato, diced bell pepper, tomato paste	Herbs, hot and pungent stuff
Fruit	Fresh or dried blueberries, raisins, dried cranberries, dried apricots	Cinnamon, nutmeg, lemon or orange zest

Fixings

Lox, or cured salmon, is the favorite match for bagels and cream cheese. Today, smoked salmon, which tends to be less salty than lox, is just about as popular. Third on the list of top fish fixings for bagels is smoked whitefish.

Many serve the bagels, lox, and cream cheese trio on its own and don't want anything else to interfere with its pure flavors. After all, they complement each other beautifully — chewy bagel, creamy cheese, and salty or smoky fish. Others prefer the bite of thin slices of onion to add interest. Tomato or cucumber slices and lettuce leaves also appear on many tables.

Bagels and Lox with — Don't Laugh! — Sun-Dried Tomatoes

Traditionalists will snicker, but sun-dried tomato shmear is on the menu of plenty of bagel bakeries. If someone at your table might never forgive you for this, make another spread for them of cream cheese with fresh chives or have some plain cream cheese.

For this sandwich, use the amount of lox you want, according to your taste and your budget. If you prefer, use just a little lox and stir it into the cream cheese along with the sun-dried tomatoes. Otherwise, use a slice of lox on each bagel instead of mixing it with the spread. You can make this with lowfat versions of cream cheese and sour cream if you like.

Preparation time: *15 minutes*

Cooking time: *None*

Yield: *4 to 6 servings*

Keeping kosher: *Dairy*

⅓ cup oil-packed sun-dried tomatoes, drained	*2 to 3 tablespoons sour cream (optional)*
8 ounces cream cheese (in tub), softened	*Freshly ground pepper to taste*
1 ounce lox or smoked salmon, finely chopped, or 4 thin slices, cut to fit bagels	*4 fresh, good quality bagels*
2 teaspoons chopped fresh chives	*4 thin slices ripe tomato*
	2 thin slices red onion, separated in rings

1 With scissors or food processor, finely snip or chop sun-dried tomatoes. In a small bowl, combine them with cream cheese, chopped lox, and chives. Stir until well blended. If spread is too stiff, stir in sour cream. Season to taste with pepper.

2 Cut bagels in half horizontally. Spread cream cheese mixture on both cut sides. Sandwich lox slices, if using, tomato slices, and a few onion rings between the two halves.

Per serving: Calories 423.5; Protein 13.4 g; Carbohydrates 44.5 g; Dietary fiber 2.7 g; Total fat 21.7 g; Saturated fat 13.6 g; Cholesterol 58.3 mg; Sodium 736.4 mg.

Choosing Companions for Eggs

Because eggs are allowed with dairy or meat meals, they have long been popular items on Jewish menus. With their non-aggressive flavor, they blend well with just about every other ingredient and are especially good with smoked meats and fish, vegetables, and cheese. Even *matzo*, a cracker-like yeast-free bread that replaces leavened bread during Passover (see Chapter 8), is matched with eggs, and indeed, the combination has become a classic.

Lox

Lox turns simple scrambled eggs into a luxurious dish. Although you may pay a pretty penny for it at a restaurant, you can make it economically at home by purchasing lox trimmings at a deli or good market. You don't need much to flavor the eggs.

Whether you're adding lox or smoked salmon to eggs, pasta salads, or fish chowders, you need to keep in mind two rules when you're cooking with lox:

- ✔ **Cut the lox into thin pieces.** Thick ones will taste too salty.

- ✔ **Add the lox to hot dishes at the last minute.** Add it when you take the dish off the burner so that it just warms from the retained heat of the dish. Overheated lox becomes dry and too salty.

Lox and Eggs

A popular pair at deli-restaurants serving Jewish-style cuisine, lox with scrambled eggs is ideal for preparing at home. It's very easy, takes no time, and costs much less when you make your own. Make it with either lox or smoked salmon.

Preparation time: 7 minutes

Cooking time: 5 minutes

Yield: 4 to 6 servings

Keeping kosher: Dairy

¾ cup thinly sliced green onions, white and green parts

10 large eggs

¼ teaspoon salt

Freshly ground pepper to taste

2 or 3 tablespoons butter

¾ cup thin strips of lox

1 Set aside 2 tablespoons green part of green onions for garnish. In a large bowl, whisk eggs with salt and pepper until blended.

2 Melt butter in a large skillet. Add remaining green onions and sauté over medium-low heat for 1 minute.

3 Add beaten eggs and scramble over low heat, stirring often, for 3 minutes, or until they are set to your taste. Remove from heat and gently stir in lox. Taste and adjust seasoning. Serve immediately, garnished with reserved green onions.

Per serving: Calories 272.3; Protein 20.8 g; Carbohydrates 2.5 g; Dietary fiber 0.3 g; Total fat 19.5 g; Saturated fat 7.7 g; Cholesterol 552.9 mg; Sodium 837.2 mg.

Salami

Although brunch is usually dairy, some people love salami scrambled with eggs so much that those who keep kosher forgo the dairy foods in order to enjoy this dish. Otherwise, they may make it for lunch or supper instead of brunch. Pastrami and eggs is another popular pair.

Vegetables

Jews have come up with dishes that match eggs with every vegetable, from artichokes to zucchini. The most often used vegetables are onions, leeks, mushrooms, peppers, and tomatoes. They're special favorites in scrambled eggs and flat omelets, but they also add color and interest to poached and baked eggs.

Here are two other popular vegetable combinations:

- ✔ **Ashkenazic onions and mushrooms:** Mushrooms sautéed with onions are especially popular in Eastern and Central European Jewish-style cooking for all sorts of egg dishes. This combination is an all-purpose flavoring for many other foods, too, from chicken stews to noodle kugels.

- ✔ **Sephardic tomatoes and peppers:** With their Mediterranean heritage, it's not surprising that Sephardic Jews love tomatoes and peppers in their scrambled eggs. They also cook tomatoes with peppers, often hot ones, to make a thick sauce and either bake or poach eggs directly in it, for a tasty brunch or lunch dish.

Eggs are pareve, and when cooked on their own or with vegetables, are suitable for meals with meat or with dairy, as in the following recipe.

Sephardic Scramble with Tomatoes and Zucchini

Eggs and vegetables are often on the Mediterranean Jewish menu for brunch or supper. Tomatoes top the typical list, with onion family members and sweet or hot peppers following closely behind. Whatever vegetables you have in the kitchen can be a candidate. Common choices are zucchini and other fast-cooking summer squash, potatoes, and cauliflower. Cayenne pepper often spices up the scramble, sometimes teamed up with cumin.

People use this all-purpose formula as a general way to enliven their egg dishes. Instead of scrambling the eggs, some let them set as a flat omelet. Those who want whole rather than beaten eggs may poach or bake the eggs directly in the hot vegetable mixture. Others opt to top their veggies with fried eggs.

The Sephardic style is to cook eggs thoroughly. A favorite way to serve this dish is to spoon it into a pocket cut in pita bread.

Preparation time: *15 minutes*

Cooking time: *12 minutes*

Yield: *2 servings*

Keeping kosher: *Pareve*

2 to 3 tablespoons vegetable oil or olive oil

1 small onion, chopped (about ½ cup)

½ bell pepper, any color, diced (about ½ cup) (optional)

2 small zucchini, diced (about 1½ cups)

1 garlic clove, minced

3 ripe, medium tomatoes, diced (total ¾ pound)

Salt and freshly ground pepper to taste

½ teaspoon ground cumin

¼ teaspoon cayenne pepper or hot sauce, or to taste

3 eggs, beaten, or 1 whole egg and 3 egg whites

2 tablespoons chopped cilantro or Italian parsley (optional)

1 Heat oil in a medium skillet. Add onion and pepper and sauté over medium heat for 3 minutes. Add zucchini and garlic and sauté for 2 minutes or until zucchini softens slightly. Stir in tomatoes, salt, pepper, cumin, and cayenne. Cook, stirring often, for 4 to 6 minutes.

2 Add beaten eggs and half the cilantro and scramble over low heat for 2 minutes, or until set. Taste and adjust seasoning. Serve immediately, topped with remaining cilantro.

Per serving: *Calories 315.3; Protein 13.1 g; Carbohydrates 19.1 g; Dietary fiber 4.9 g; Total fat 22.2 g; Saturated fat 3.4 g; Cholesterol 318.8 mg; Sodium 262.7 mg.*

Matzo

It may be hard to understand how Matzo brei, or fried matzo with eggs, became such a classic at deli restaurants. After all, it's made basically of two bland ingredients and doesn't have much seasoning either. But it's comfort food, like French toast. Undoubtedly, it began as a Passover dish, when people make everything out of matzo. In many homes, Matzo brei is a brunch standard throughout the year.

 In towns with large Jewish communities, matzo is easy to find in grocery stores, with the kosher ingredients. And, of course, matzo is also available in kosher specialty stores.

Matzo Brei

You can prepare this very easy dish in different ways. You can cut the matzo into small bits and blend it with beaten eggs, or you can use larger pieces embedded in an egg batter. Some people cook it like pancakes, others like an omelet, and then others like a scramble or a cross between several of these options. The time-honored ways to serve it are sprinkled with sugar or topped with jam or applesauce. But if you'd like to pour on maple syrup, why not?

I like to vary the basic recipe slightly by adding a little milk and using different matzo flavors, like whole wheat, onion, apple, or grape, instead of plain.

Preparation time: *10 minutes*

Cooking time: *5 minutes*

Yield: *3 to 4 servings*

Keeping kosher: *Dairy; Pareve if you omit the milk and use either pareve margarine or oil*

4 matzos	½ teaspoon salt
4 eggs, or 2 eggs and 3 egg whites	3 to 4 tablespoons butter, margarine, or vegetable oil
3 tablespoons milk (optional)	

1 Put matzos in a large shallow bowl and cover with cold water. Let them soak for 5 minutes. Drain off water. Break each into about 8 pieces and put in a medium bowl.

2 In a small bowl, beat the eggs with milk and salt. Pour mixture over matzos. Stir until matzo pieces are coated.

3 Melt butter in a heavy, medium or large skillet, preferably a nonstick one. Add matzo mixture. Cook it over medium-low heat, without stirring, until eggs begin to set, about 4 minutes. Then stir very lightly, turning the mixture over in pieces, so that it is lightly scrambled but remains in fairly large pieces. As soon as it is set to your taste, remove from heat and serve.

Per serving: *Calories 260.8; Protein 9.3 g; Carbohydrates 24.6 g; Dietary fiber 0 g; Total fat 13.6 g; Saturated fat 6.9 g; Cholesterol 235.8 mg; Sodium 354.9 mg.*

Making a Main Course out of Blintzes

Blintzes have a lot more to them than cheese. They are a popular brunch choice because they are so versatile. Instead of sweet cheese blintzes, some people prefer savory fillings when they want to make their brunch blintzes into an entree. Blintzes resemble thin pancakes and also taste good on their own, or with syrup. For more on blintzes, see Chapter 9.

Meat and chicken

Meat blintzes have long been popular for dairy-free brunches or lunches. Cooks make the filling from leftover braised brisket or poached beef from soup and flavor it with browned onions. If they don't have cooked beef, they sauté some ground beef instead. Today, many people opt for chicken blintzes instead.

Mushrooms and vegetables

Vegetables make great fillings for blintzes. The favorite way to prepare them is in a creamy sauce. Mushrooms of any kind are a tasty choice, on their own or combined with other vegetables, because they're so delicious in the luscious sauce and contribute a wonderful flavor to it (see following recipe). I also like spinach, asparagus, leeks, and zucchini.

Mushroom and Spinach Blintzes

One of my favorite treats at a late night out in Tel Aviv is a savory vegetable-filled blintz like this one. They are featured at the popular blintz restaurants, which resemble pancake eateries but with the focus on these thin-rolled filled pancakes.

At home I like to make them ahead, ready to reheat when I need them. If you like, serve the blintzes topped with a small dollop of sour cream and garnished with chives.

Preparation time: 50 minutes, plus time to prepare blintz wrappers

Cooking time: 45 minutes

Yield: 6 or 7 servings

Keeping kosher: Dairy

14 to 15 small blintz wrappers (see Chapter 9)	*4 tablespoons flour*
8 cups spinach leaves, rinsed well	*2½ cups milk*
10 tablespoons butter, plus a little more for buttering dish	*1 teaspoon freshly grated nutmeg, or more to taste*
1 pound small mushrooms, halved and sliced	*⅔ cup whipping cream, or ½ cup additional milk*
Salt and freshly ground pepper to taste	
1 teaspoon paprika	*Pinch of cayenne pepper*

1 Bring medium saucepan of salted water to a boil. Add spinach. Boil uncovered over high heat for 2 minutes or until wilted. Drain in a colander, rinse with cold water, and drain well.

2 Squeeze spinach by handfuls to remove as much liquid as possible. Chop spinach coarsely with a knife.

3 Melt 2 tablespoons butter in a large skillet. Add mushrooms, salt, pepper, and paprika and sauté over medium heat for 3 minutes or until tender. Add spinach and sauté, stirring often, for 2 minutes.

4 To make the sauce, melt 4 tablespoons butter in a heavy medium saucepan. Whisk in flour and cook over low heat, whisking constantly, for 1 minute, or until foaming but not brown. Remove from heat. Whisk in milk. Bring to a boil over medium-high heat, whisking. Add salt, pepper, and nutmeg. Cook over low heat, whisking occasionally, for 3 minutes. Whisk in cream and bring to boil. Cook over low heat, whisking often, for 5 minutes or until thick. Add cayenne.

5 Stir mushroom spinach mixture into sauce. Taste and adjust seasoning.

6 Preheat oven to 400°. Butter two 8-inch oval baking dishes or a large, shallow, 13- or 14-inch oval baking dish.

7 To fill blintz wrappers, spoon 3 tablespoons filling onto cooked side of each one, across lower third of wrapper. Fold sides inward so that each covers part of filling. Roll up in cigar shape, beginning at edge with filling. Arrange blintzes in single layer in buttered dish. Dot blintzes with small pieces of remaining butter.

8 Bake blintzes for 20 minutes, or until heated through and lightly browned. Serve hot.

Per serving: Calories 459.8; Protein 11.2 g; Carbohydrates 23.8 g; Dietary fiber 2.6 g; Total fat 36.6 g; Saturated fat 21.3 g; Cholesterol 187.7 mg; Sodium 324.2 mg.

Taste of Tradition: *To make these blintzes pareve, make the blintz wrappers with vegetable broth, soy milk, rice milk, or water instead of milk. In the filling, substitute soy milk or rice milk for the milk and cream, and pareve margarine or vegetable oil for the butter. If you're using vegetable oil, you can't dot the filled blintzes with oil; instead, brush or drizzle a little oil on each one.*

To make chicken-filled blintzes, do the preceding changes and omit the spinach. Add 1½ cups diced cooked chicken to the filling.

Getting ahead with filled blintzes

To save time, you can always prepare blintzes completely ahead, ready to bake in their baking dishes. Keep them covered up to 1 day in the refrigerator. To reheat them, take them out of the refrigerator while preheating the oven. Bake them as in the recipe.

Another option, if you like, is to prepare the blintz wrappers and the filling ahead and then refrigerate them separately up to 2 days. Or, to save time, you can use purchased crepes instead of making your own wrappers. Because crepes are large, you will probably need 4 to 6 of them to make 4 to 6 servings of one larger blintz each.

Preparing Deli Salads at Home

Deli standards — notably chicken salad, tuna salad, egg salad, potato salad, and cole slaw — started out as recipes from home kitchens. Most are made basically of the main ingredient mixed with a little mayonnaise. I grew up eating my mother's versions and had no idea that anyone thought of buying them. After all, they are so simple to prepare. And, of course, the ones made with chicken, tuna, and egg make scrumptious sandwiches.

Rarely do deli salads taste as good when you buy them as when you make your own because you can flavor them to your own taste. For example, I find that the egg salad, potato salad, and cole slaw at many delis have a thick sweet and sour dressing. To me, their sweetness is overpowering because I prefer the mayonnaise version. Sometimes, bought cole slaw seems to be a few strands of cabbage swimming in dressing, while I prefer barely enough dressing to moisten the cabbage.

Chicken salad became such a staple in the Jewish kitchen because it was a way to make use of the chicken cooked in Friday night's chicken soup. Poached chicken or turkey works well, but you can use poultry cooked by any technique. The salad is great for extra cooked turkey breast because it's a good way to serve it cold. Lean turkey breast tends to be dry when you reheat it.

You can make chicken or turkey salad just like tuna salad (see the following recipe). Of course, to keep it kosher, you would not put in any dairy products.

Tuna Salad with a Twist on Tradition

The old-fashioned formula is perfect for today's tuna, because so much of it is water-packed and needs a boost of creamy dressing. The tuna salad I grew up with had only mayonnaise, grated hard-boiled eggs, and a little diced celery. The grown-ups also had a little grated onion and vinegar in theirs. We made salads from canned salmon the same way. The tuna had to be white, and the salmon had to be red. If we were eating it on a sandwich, it was always on fresh rye bread with caraway seeds. As a salad, we served it on lettuce with a few tomato slices. (To make hard-boiled eggs an easy way, see Chapter 11.)

Today, I often stir mustard into the dressing, probably a habit from my culinary training in Paris, where we flavored our handmade mayonnaise with Dijon mustard. When I'm really straying from the straight path, I flavor the salad with orange juice and zest, cilantro, basil, or sweet and hot peppers. Sometimes I replace the mustard with another pungent preparation, such as _tapenade,_ or olive paste, which you can buy in a jar.

To reduce the calories and fat, I use half mayonnaise and half lowfat sour cream or yogurt. These dairy products, especially the yogurt, may clash with the vinegar, so I omit it if I'm adding them.

Preparation time: *15 minutes*

Cooking time: *None*

Yield: *6 to 8 servings*

Keeping kosher: *Pareve; Dairy if you add sour cream or yogurt*

Three 6-ounce cans white tuna in water or broth

⅓ cup grated onion

½ cup peeled, finely diced celery

1 to 2 teaspoons mild vinegar (5% acidity or lower), such as rice vinegar

¼ cup lowfat sour cream or plain yogurt (optional)

4 to 6 tablespoons mayonnaise, or more to taste

2 teaspoons Dijon mustard (optional)

1 or 2 hard-boiled eggs, grated or chopped

Salt and freshly ground pepper to taste

Green- or red-leaf or butter lettuce leaves (for serving)

Tomato wedges (for serving)

Cucumber slices (for serving)

Thin onion rings (for serving)

Black or green olives (for serving)

1 Drain tuna or leave some or all the liquid in, depending on how moist you want the salad. In a medium bowl, combine tuna with onion, and celery. If you're not using dairy products in the salad, add 1 teaspoon vinegar.

2 To make the dressing, spoon sour cream into a bowl and add 4 tablespoons mayonnaise. If you're not adding the dairy products, spoon in 6 tablespoons mayonnaise. Stir in mustard.

3 Add dressing to salad and mix until blended. Lightly stir in eggs. If you like, stir in more mayonnaise until the salad is as rich and as moist as you like it. Season to taste with salt and pepper and add more vinegar if you like. Refrigerate in a covered container for 1 hour or up to 2 days.

4 To serve, make a bed of lettuce leaves on each plate. Spoon each portion onto center of lettuce. Garnish with tomato wedges, cucumber slices, onion rings, and olives.

Per serving: Calories 215.0; Protein 17.4 g; Carbohydrates 8.0 g; Dietary fiber 1.9 g; Total fat 12.8 g; Saturated fat 2.0 g; Cholesterol 59.7 mg; Sodium 432.5 mg.

Jewish Mother's Tips: *At my neighborhood delis, when they make tuna or chicken salad sandwiches, they offer the option to add avocado slices or tomato slices to the sandwich. When they are ripe, both make tasty contributions.*

To peel celery, use a vegetable peeler and peel the length of the stalk to remove the stringy layer.

Chapter 14

Fish

*F*ish holds a place of pride on Jewish feast-day menus. On traditional tables, fish begins festive dinners as an appetizer or follows the starters as a separate course. Health-conscious, contemporary cooks frequently focus on fish as a holiday entree. In the kosher kitchen, fish plays an important part because it is permitted at dairy and meat meals. Here, you find tasty traditions from the Ashkenazic and Sephardic fish repertoires and easy ways to prepare them.

REMEMBER

Kosher fish have scales and fins (see Figure 14-1). Shellfish is not kosher.

Figure 14-1:
Kosher fish have scales and fins (see Chapter 1). Most commonly available fish are kosher.

SELECTION OF FISH

Famous — Or Infamous — Gefilte Fish

Gefilte fish, or poached fish dumplings, is the most familiar fish dish of the Jewish kitchen because of its wide availability in jars. Homemade gefilte fish is far superior and is a standard on many holiday tables. Most cooks serve it cold and top each portion with a dab of red horseradish, its preferred partner.

My brother is a fervent fan of gefilte fish, and I have always liked it, too. Those unfamiliar with the flavor of this Ashkenazic specialty sometimes find it an acquired taste.

Many Jews of Middle Eastern origin would not eat gefilte fish in the past. In an old Israeli film, a Sephardic man dining for the first time at his fiancée's parents' home surreptitiously fed his portion to the cat! Today, as a result of many marriages like the one in the movie, gefilte fish has become popular on most tables.

How to prepare the best gefilte fish is often a matter of heated discussion. There are numerous variations, both in the choice of fish and in the seasonings. With the dish's origins in central and eastern Europe, the traditional fish used are those of the fresh waters of the region — carp, whitefish, and pike. The flavor of the fish may be delicate, sweet, or somewhat peppery.

Originally, the dish was an entire fish cooked with a ground fish stuffing. *Gefilte* is a Yiddish word meaning filled or stuffed. Today, most people opt for an easier technique. Instead of preparing a whole fish, they make only the stuffing. Most often they shape it in spherical or oval pieces and poach them.

Gefilte fish baked as a loaf is another popular presentation. It's the fastest way to make use of the mixture because you simply spoon it into the pan.

My mother often divides her gefilte fish mixture into two parts. She poaches one part as balls for holiday dinners and bakes the rest as a loaf for serving warm at weekday suppers.

When I was a child, my mother labored for hours to make gefilte fish every week for Shabbat. She filleted the whole fish and chopped it in a wooden bowl with a round-bladed knife, sometimes with my grandfather's help. Today, a food processor makes short work of the job.

The market helps, too. You can buy fish fillets. At the best fish markets, you can buy a whole fish and ask them to fillet it. This way, you have the bones and heads for making the fish stock in which you poach the gefilte fish. If you don't have time to make fish stock, use vegetable stock.

To check for bones in your fish, run your fingers over the fillets. Using tweezers or small sharp knife, gently remove any bones you find, as shown in Figure 14-2.

Figure 14-2:
Removing
bones.

Easy Gefilte Fish

Serve the fish balls on a bed of lettuce with a garnish of cooked carrot slices. Be sure to provide red horseradish, made of horseradish root mixed with beets. Part of the charm of the dish is the contrast between the delicate dumplings and this sharp condiment. Purchase this condiment in the deli section of the market. If horseradish is new to you, go easy! People who are not used to it sometimes find it more potent than hot sauce. After you open the jar, the horseradish loses its heat.

Some people like sweet gefilte fish and season the fish mixture and the stock with a little sugar. This is not the way my family likes it and I continue our custom.

Preparation time: *45 minutes*

Cooking time: *1 hour*

Yield: *8 to 9 servings*

Keeping kosher: *Pareve*

1½ pounds whitefish fillets	*3 tablespoons matzo meal*
¾ pound cod or halibut fillets	*4 to 5 cups Fast Fish Stock (see recipe in this chapter)*
2 large eggs	*2 large carrots, peeled and sliced*
2 teaspoons salt	*Lettuce leaves, for serving*
½ teaspoon ground pepper	*1 jar horseradish prepared with beets, for serving*
2 onions, finely chopped	
½ small carrot, peeled and coarsely grated	

1 Remove any bones. Cut the fish in 2-inch chunks.

2 In a food processor, grind half the fish at a time until very fine. Leave half the fish in the processor. Add 1 egg, 1 teaspoon salt, ¼ teaspoon pepper, and half the chopped onions. Process until well blended. Transfer to a large bowl. Put the remaining fish, egg, 1 teaspoon salt, pepper, and onion in the processor and process until blended. Add this mixture to the first batch and mix with a wooden spoon. Stir in the grated carrot and matzo meal.

3 Bring the fish stock to a simmer in a large pot or deep saucepan. Add carrots. Season to taste with salt.

4 To shape the fish mixture, moisten your hands. Take ⅓ cup mixture and roll it in your palms to a smooth ball. Continue with the remaining mixture, moistening your hands each time.

5 Carefully drop the fish balls into the simmering stock. If they are not covered with liquid, carefully pour in enough hot water to barely cover them. (Pour it near the edge of the pan, not over the fish balls.) Return to a simmer, cover, and cook over low heat for 1 hour.

6 Cool the fish balls in their stock. With a slotted spoon, carefully transfer the fish balls to containers for refrigerating. Gently pour the stock with the carrots over the fish. Refrigerate for at least 4 hours.

7 Allow two fish balls per serving. Serve them on lettuce leaves and top each with a carrot slice from the stock. Serve the horseradish separately.

Per serving: Calories 190.1; Protein 23.7 g; Carbohydrates 9.4 g; Dietary fiber 2.1 g; Total fat 6.1 g; Saturated fat 1.1 g; Cholesterol 108.1 mg; Sodium 653.3 mg.

Jewish Mother's Tips: *If you are using frozen fish fillets, increase the matzo meal amount to 5 tablespoons. This adjustment prevents the gefilte fish mixture from being watery and helps ensure that the balls hold together during poaching.*

Do not allow the stock to come to a full boil once you have added the fish balls to it.

Fast Fish Stock

This savory stock enhances the taste of gefilte fish, soups, and sauces. Unlike meat stocks, it needs only 20 minutes of simmering. Use the heads, tails, and bones of any fresh- or salt-water fish except for oily fish with forceful flavors like tuna and mackerel. If you don't find fish bones and heads in the market's case, ask behind the counter. Often they will give them to you at little or no charge. You can also use fish pieces sold for soup or chowder.

Preparation time: *15 minutes*

Cooking time: *25 minutes*

Yield: *4½ to 5 cups*

Keeping kosher: *Pareve*

1 pound fish bones, heads and tails	*1 sprig fresh thyme*
1 onion, chopped	*6 parsley stems, leaves removed*
1 bay leaf	*6 cups water*

1 Put fish pieces in a large bowl in the sink and rinse them under cold running water for 3 minutes.

2 Place the fish pieces in a large saucepan. Add the onion, bay leaf, thyme, parsley, and water and bring to a boil, skimming off foam as it accumulates on the surface of the stock. Simmer uncovered over low heat, skimming occasionally, 20 minutes.

3 Strain into a bowl. Use right away or cool slightly and refrigerate.

Per serving: Calories 29.8; Protein 5.0 g; Carbohydrates 1.8 g; Dietary fiber 0.4 g; Total fat 0.2 g; Saturated fat 0 g; Cholesterol 9.8 mg; Sodium 23.2 mg.

Jewish Mother's Tip: *Be sure to refrigerate fish stock promptly, as it is perishable. You can keep it up to 2 days in the refrigerator. You can also freeze it.*

Cool Fish for Holiday Appetizers

Gefilte fish is not the only Jewish fish recipe. The Jewish repertoire is rich in delicacies from the sea, such as sweet and sour fish and spicy Sephardic fish. In their classic manuals, French chefs acknowledged this talent by giving one of these creations, shallot-scented carp, the name "carpe à la juive," or Jewish-style carp.

Many of these festive fish dishes are served as cold appetizers. This is a practical option for holiday entertaining, when there may be extra guests at the table because the fish is cooked ahead.

On Shabbat, the weekly holiday, observant Jews do no cooking. This partly explains why they have developed so many fish dishes designed to be enjoyed cold.

Hot Fish for Special Occasion Dinners and Weekday Suppers

For menus for festive occasions that do not entail cooking ahead, many Jewish families opt for a hot fish entree. There are several reasons for this. First and foremost, fish is popular in the Jewish kitchen. Second, fish is healthful. For those keeping kosher, focusing on fish as the main course means the meal is meatless, and everyone can enjoy butter on their bread as well as a creamy dessert.

Fried fish has long been a favorite among Jews of all origins and generally is served hot. Grilled or broiled fish is also best loved as a festive main course rather than a first course.

Sephardic Sea Bass in Saffron Tomato Sauce

Fish stewed in a savory sauce is one of the most versatile of dishes. Because it does not contain dairy products or starchy thickeners, it is good hot or cold. Pair this sensational sauce with any fish fillets or steaks you prefer. You can see a photo of this recipe in the color insert section.

Preparation time: *30 minutes*

Cooking time: *25 minutes*

Yield: *4 main-course or 6 appetizer servings*

Keeping kosher: *Pareve*

¼ teaspoon saffron threads

¼ cup hot water

1½ pounds sea bass steaks or fillets, about 1 inch thick

2 tablespoons extra virgin olive oil

4 large garlic cloves, chopped

1 pound ripe tomatoes, peeled, seeded, and chopped

3 sprigs fresh thyme, or ½ teaspoon dried

Salt and freshly ground pepper to taste

Pinch of cayenne pepper

¼ cup chopped Italian parsley

1 Slightly crush saffron with your fingers. Put in a small cup and add the hot water. Let stand for 15 minutes. Meanwhile, cut fish in 4 pieces to serve it as an entree or in 6 pieces to serve it as an appetizer.

2 Heat oil in a large, deep sauté pan or skillet. Add garlic and sauté over low heat, stirring, for 1 minute. Stir in tomatoes, thyme, and saffron mixture. Bring to a simmer over medium heat and cook the sauce for 10 minutes, or until it thickens slightly.

3 Add the fish to the pan in a single layer. Sprinkle it with salt and pepper. Return the sauce to a simmer over medium-high heat. Cover and cook the fish over medium-low heat for 5 minutes. Carefully turn the pieces over using two slotted spatulas. Cover and cook the fish for about 5 more minutes or until it is tender; when checked in thickest part with a small, sharp knife, its color should be opaque.

4 Discard thyme sprigs. Taste sauce, add cayenne, and adjust seasoning. Serve fish hot, warm, or cold, sprinkled with parsley.

Per serving: *Calories 231.5; Protein 28.3 g; Carbohydrates 6.6 g; Dietary fiber 1.5 g; Total fat 10.1 g; Saturated fat 1.7 g; Cholesterol 60.6 mg; Sodium 257.8 mg.*

Jewish Mother's Tip: *To save time or when you can't find ripe tomatoes, substitute a 28-ounce can of tomatoes for the fresh ones. Drain them of their juice, which you can save for other dishes, and chop them. In Step 2, simmer the sauce for only 5 minutes.*

Crunchy Spiced Sole

Kids love this crisp, golden sautéed fish entree, and so do I. My favorite way to season the fish is in my mother-in-law's Yemenite style with cumin, black pepper, and turmeric. You can garnish the fish with parsley sprigs and lemon wedges or, for even more spice, serve it with hot salsa the way our family does.

Preparation time: *15 minutes*

Cooking time: *5 minutes*

Yield: *4 servings*

Keeping kosher: *Pareve*

1 pound sole or flounder fillets

⅓ cup flour

¾ cup dry bread crumbs

½ teaspoon salt

½ teaspoon ground black pepper

1½ teaspoons ground cumin

½ teaspoon ground turmeric

2 eggs or 2 egg whites

⅓ cup vegetable oil

1 Remove any bones in the fillet. Cut each fillet in two pieces crosswise. Arrange them in one layer on plate.

2 Spread flour in a large plate. Put bread crumbs in a shallow bowl and add the salt, pepper, cumin, and turmeric. Mix evenly. Beat eggs in a shallow bowl.

3 Lightly coat a fish piece with flour on both sides. Tap and shake to remove excess flour. Dip piece in eggs. Last dip both sides in bread crumbs so that fish is completely coated. Pat and press lightly so crumbs adhere. Put coated fish on a large plate. Repeat with remaining fish. Set pieces side by side on the plate.

4 Set oven at 275° to keep fish warm. Heat oil in heavy large skillet over medium-high heat. Add enough fish pieces to make one layer, leaving room to turn them over. Sauté about 2 minutes per side or until golden brown on both sides. Turn carefully using two slotted spatulas. If oil begins to brown, reduce heat to medium. Set fish pieces side by side on a platter and keep them warm in oven while sautéing remaining fish. Serve hot.

Per serving: *Calories 408.1; Protein 25.7 g; Carbohydrates 23.3 g; Dietary fiber 1.0 g; Total fat 23.0 g; Saturated fat 2.6 g; Cholesterol 159.5 mg; Sodium 579.8 mg.*

Jewish Mother's Tips: *Try to use one hand for coating the fish in case the phone rings! Handle the coated fish as lightly as possible to avoid damaging the breading. After breading the fish, put it on a plate in a single layer so that its coating will not become gummy. At this stage, you can refrigerate the fish for a few hours before frying it.*

Moroccan Broiled Fish with Garlic and Cilantro

Moroccan-style flavors enhance this fish and keep it moist so that it needs no sauce. When you have time, marinate the fish after coating it with the spice mixture for 15 to 30 minutes. Instead of broiling the fish, you can cook it on a stovetop grill or on a barbecue.

For a festive meal, Sesame Spinach Salad with Barley (see Chapter 9) makes a terrific starter. Perfect partners for serving alongside this summery fish entree are green beans in tomato sauce and grilled sweet pepper salad (see Chapter 19).

Preparation time: *10 minutes*

Cooking time: *10 minutes*

Yield: *4 servings.*

Keeping kosher: *Pareve*

1½ pounds cod, sea bass, or salmon steaks, about 1 inch thick

2 tablespoons olive oil

2 large garlic cloves, minced

1 teaspoon ground cumin

½ teaspoon paprika

Pinch of cayenne pepper

3 tablespoons minced cilantro

Salt and freshly ground pepper to taste

Cilantro sprigs, for garnish

Lemon wedges, for serving

1 Put the fish steaks in a shallow bowl. Mix the olive oil, garlic, cumin, paprika, cayenne, and cilantro in a small bowl. Pour the mixture over the fish steaks and turn to coat both sides.

2 Set the broiler shelf about 4 inches from the heat source. Preheat the broiler. Lightly oil the broiler rack.

3 Sprinkle the fish with salt and pepper on both sides. Set the fish on the broiler rack and broil 4 minutes. Turn it over and broil 4 to 5 more minutes. To check whether fish is done, make a small cut with a sharp knife in thickest part of steak, or near bone if it's in the steak's center; color of flesh should have become opaque all the way through. Serve it hot, with cilantro sprigs and lemon wedges.

Per serving: Calories 150.8; Protein 18.8 g; Carbohydrates 1.0 g; Dietary fiber 0.4 g; Total fat 7.6 g; Saturated fat 1.1 g; Cholesterol 44.5 mg; Sodium 211.1 mg.

Jewish Mother's Tip: *For easy cleanup, line the broiler rack with foil. Oil the foil before putting the fish on it.*

Chapter 15

A Chicken in Every Pot — the 11th Commandment?

*I*n this chapter, you see why chicken has become so prominent on Jewish menus. You discover a variety of delicious ways to prepare poultry for holidays, weekends, and weekdays. Planning chicken and turkey dishes as a centerpiece for kosher meals is easy, and you also pick up tips on how to serve them for all sorts of occasions.

Roasting Chicken

Chicken is virtually synonymous with Jewish cooking. Shabbat chicken dinner is a standard on the tables of many Jews. In the American-Jewish kitchen, the chicken is often roasted for the Friday night and Saturday midday meals.

If you consider that Shabbat food cannot be served as soon as it is cooked, you may find the choice of roast chicken puzzling. After all, food experts tell you to serve roast chicken right away. Yet in observant homes, the chicken for Friday night must be kept warm, while that for Saturday is usually reheated. Jewish cooks have developed their own tricks for keeping the chicken juicy and appealing in spite of these constraints.

First, Jewish cooks roast the chicken at moderate heat instead of using the very high temperatures favored by chefs of fancy restaurants. Thus, the bird tends to remain moister when they have to wait for a while before serving it.

Why chicken is king of the kitchen

Chicken has enjoyed historic popularity for good reason. First, chickens are kosher. They are easier and faster to raise than animals, so they cost much less than meat and are accessible to many people. Chickens can adapt to most climates and thus appear on the menus of Jews from just about every country.

Second, if they're going to reheat the roast, Jewish cooks carve the bird before refrigerating it. If you try to warm a whole chicken, the meat will become dry before it is heated through. You reheat the chicken in a covered pan with a little of its roasting juices or a little chicken soup in the bottom of the pan. This technique helps maintain the bird's succulence.

If you want to save time roasting chickens and turkeys, remember that unstuffed birds roast faster.

To make sure that you're serving safe birds, follow these tips:

- ✔ Wash your hands, cutting board, and any utensils that came in contact with poultry before handling or using with other foods.
- ✔ Keep poultry refrigerated until you are ready to cook it.
- ✔ Never put cooked poultry on a plate that had raw poultry on it.

Keep in mind that kosher birds have already been salted during the koshering process. You don't need to sprinkle them with salt before cooking them by the dry-heat techniques — roasting, broiling, and grilling.

Easy Roast Chicken with Fresh Herbs

Some of my friends think roasting a chicken is complicated, but it's one of the simplest main courses to prepare. A quick way to enhance the flavor of a chicken as it roasts is to put a few sprigs of fresh herbs inside the bird. Sage, thyme, rosemary, or tarragon all work well.

Roast the chicken on its own or stuff it with Challah and Vegetable Stuffing with Corn and Toasted Walnuts (see next recipe) or with your family's favorite stuffing. If you're stuffing the chicken, put the herbs under the bird instead of in its cavity. You can see a photo of this recipe in the color insert section of this book.

Preparation time: *30 minutes, plus extra time if you're making stuffing*

Cooking time: *1½ hours*

Yield: *4 servings*

Keeping kosher: *Meat*

A 3- to 3½-pound chicken, giblets removed

4 to 6 fresh sprigs sage, thyme, rosemary, or tarragon, plus a few more for garnish

¼ teaspoon salt

¼ teaspoon ground pepper

½ teaspoon paprika

2 to 4 teaspoons vegetable oil

2 cups chicken stock

1 Preheat oven to 375°. Pull out fat from inside chicken cavity. Set chicken in a small roasting pan and put herb sprigs inside cavity (if you're not going to roast it with stuffing). Mix salt, pepper, paprika, and 2 teaspoons oil. Rub chicken all over with mixture.

2 To stuff chicken, spoon a cool stuffing mixture very lightly into chicken cavity. Do not pack it tightly. Fold skin over stuffing; truss or skewer closed, if desired. Tuck fresh herbs in pan under stuffed chicken.

3 If you have extra stuffing, grease a baking dish just large enough to contain it. Spoon stuffing into dish. Drizzle remaining 2 teaspoons oil over stuffing. Cover and refrigerate.

4 Roast chicken uncovered for 15 minutes. Pour 1 cup chicken stock carefully into roasting pan. Roast 30 more minutes.

5 After chicken has roasted for 45 minutes, add remaining chicken stock to roasting pan. Uncover dish of extra stuffing and put it in oven. Roast chicken and stuffing for 20 to 45 minutes, basting bird and stuffing occasionally with pan juices if you want. To check whether chicken is done, insert a skewer into thickest part of drumstick; it should be tender and juices that run from chicken should be clear. If juices are pink, roast chicken a few more minutes and check it again. Insert a skewer into stuffing inside chicken; it should be hot to the touch. If the chicken is done but the stuffing is not hot, remove the chicken from the oven, transfer the stuffing to a greased baking dish, and bake it for about 10 minutes or until it is hot.

6 Transfer chicken to a carving board or platter and remove any trussing strings or skewers. Spoon any stuffing into a serving dish or remove herbs from inside chicken.

7 If you like, serve roasting juices. Discard any herbs from pan, pour juices into a bowl, and skim off excess fat with a spoon. Reheat gently in a small saucepan.

8 Carve chicken and serve hot, with stuffing, roasting juices, and garnish of fresh herbs.

Per serving: *Calories 414.5; Protein 42.9 g; Carbohydrates 0.3 g; Dietary fiber 0.1 g; Total fat 25.7 g; Saturated fat 6.7 g; Cholesterol 168.0 mg; Sodium 272.4 mg.*

Challah stuffing

As in most homes in the United States, stuffing has always been a big favorite in our family for serving with roast birds. Yet ours was somewhat different from the typical American style bread stuffing. The bread was almost always *challah,* or Jewish egg bread, which contributes a lovely, rich taste.

We never added butter to our stuffings, as it would make the stuffing not kosher for serving with chicken or turkey. Following the usual custom, my mother sautéed onions and other vegetables in oil or margarine instead. Along with the well-browned onions and occasionally mushrooms when they were available, we loved our stuffing gently spiced with paprika or dill. The challah didn't need much dressing up to become a delectable stuffing.

This style of stuffing is most typical of Ashkenazic, or eastern European Jewish, cooking. Sephardic cooks tend to make stuffing less often. When they do, they might use rice, couscous, or bulgur wheat instead of bread.

Naturally, such nonkosher items as bacon or oysters, which appear frequently in American stuffings, are never used in the kitchens of observant Jews.

Keep these points in mind when you're making stuffing:

- ✔ About ½ cup stuffing per pound of poultry is enough to fill the bird. Because most people find that's not enough, plan ¾ to 1 cup stuffing for each pound of poultry. Bake any extra stuffing in a separate baking dish.

- ✔ When you bake the stuffing in a separate dish, if you want to add flavor from chicken or turkey roasting juices, baste the stuffing occasionally with the juices as it bakes.

- ✔ If you don't have dry or stale challah, set some slices out uncovered for a few hours or overnight to dry. For a faster way, bake the bread slices on a baking sheet in a 275° oven about 10 minutes per side or until dry.

TASTE OF TRADITION

Why use challah

Challah's light texture helps turn it into a moist stuffing, while its delicate taste makes it a good match for all styles of flavorings.

There is a practical reason, too, why Jewish cooks use challah. Challah is always around the house because most families buy at least two loaves for Shabbat. Today, people freeze the extra challah. Before freezers existed, cooks simply left the challah to dry.

The safest way to bake a stuffing is outside the bird. However, many people prefer the rich flavor that the bird's juices impart to the stuffing. Here are some tips to help you make safe stuffings:

- **Do not spoon hot or warm stuffing into a bird.** The stuffing should be cool or chilled.

- **Stuff the bird just before roasting it.** Never spoon the stuffing into the bird ahead of time.

- **Bake the stuffing until it is thoroughly done.** Check by inserting a skewer into stuffing inside chicken; it should be hot to the touch. Or insert an instant-read thermometer; the stuffing should reach 160°.

- **Remove all stuffing from the bird before carving it.**

- **Always refrigerate the baked stuffing in a container.** Never refrigerate stuffing inside the bird.

In our family, we love stuffing with plenty of vegetables for good flavor and moistness. Usually we sauté the onions and then add grated carrots and sometimes zucchini for good texture. I find corn kernels and toasted nuts delicious additions, too. Be sure to taste your walnuts to be sure that they are fresh.

Challah and Vegetable Stuffing with Corn and Toasted Walnuts

This stuffing is simple to make and fairly light. Baking it separately makes it easier to serve and gives it a light crust. Of course, if you bake the mixture in the chicken, it has the advantage of absorbing some of the tasty roasting juices. Sometimes we make a double batch of stuffing to have it both ways or to make enough for a small turkey.

The vegetables give this stuffing a light, crumbly texture. If you prefer a slightly denser stuffing, add 2 to 3 more tablespoons stock or oil to the mixture. You can see a photo of this recipe in the color insert section of this book.

Preparation time: *40 minutes*

Cooking time: *50 minutes*

Yield: *4 to 6 servings*

Keeping kosher: *Meat if made with chicken stock; otherwise Pareve*

⅓ to ½ cup walnuts	½ teaspoon dried thyme
4 to 5 ounces (6 to 8 slices) stale challah (egg bread)	¾ cup frozen corn kernels thawed, or canned kernels
3 tablespoons vegetable oil or olive oil, plus a little extra for greasing the baking dish	2 medium zucchini, coarsely grated
1 large onion, chopped	2 large carrots, coarsely grated
⅓ cup chopped celery	3 tablespoons minced parsley
2 large garlic cloves, minced	Salt and freshly ground pepper to taste
½ teaspoon paprika	1 large egg
	¼ cup chicken or vegetable stock (optional)

1 Preheat oven to 350°. Toast walnuts on a baking sheet in oven for 5 minutes or until light golden. Transfer to a plate.

2 Remove any dark crusts from challah if you like. Soak challah slices in a bowl of cold water for 5 minutes or until softened. Squeeze challah pieces to remove excess water. Transfer challah to a bowl and mash it with a fork.

3 Heat 2 tablespoons oil in a medium skillet. Add onion and celery and sauté over medium-low heat, stirring occasionally, about 7 minutes or until onion begins to turn brown. Add garlic, paprika, and thyme. Sauté for 10 seconds. Remove from heat.

4 Add sautéed vegetable mixture and corn kernels to challah and mix well. Let mixture cool for 5 minutes.

5 Add zucchini, carrots, parsley, and walnuts to stuffing mixture. Season to taste with salt and pepper. Add egg and mix well. Stuffing should be lightly moistened. If it seems dry, stir in enough stock, by tablespoons, to moisten it.

6 If you will use mixture to stuff a bird, refrigerate or cool it completely before spooning into the bird. Continue as in recipe, Easy Roast Chicken with Fresh Herbs.

7 To bake stuffing in a dish, preheat oven to 350° and grease a 9-inch square baking dish.

8 Spoon stuffing into dish. Drizzle with remaining tablespoon oil. Bake uncovered for about 40 minutes or until firm.

Per serving: Calories 212.6; Protein 5.4 g; Carbohydrates 21.6 g; Dietary fiber 3.4 g; Total fat 12.6 g; Saturated fat 1.4 g; Cholesterol 45.1 mg; Sodium 224.1 mg.

Turkey alternatives

Turkey is a big favorite on the Jewish menu and is used in a great variety of ways. American Jews share the beloved American Thanksgiving tradition of roast turkey with stuffing. In addition, many opt for a whole roast turkey as the main course for other important family get-togethers like Sukkot dinners or Passover Seders.

For Passover, stuffings are made with matzo, not bread. For an example, see Sephardic Spinach Stuffing in Chapter 8.

Rolled turkey breast roast is a frequent choice for Shabbat meals. Although it's called a roast, many prefer to pot roast it with a little liquid or to braise it rather than roast it so that the meat doesn't become dry.

Jewish cooks know that turkey also makes delicious soups. At huge family gatherings of my Yemenite in-laws in their village near Tel Aviv, the women make a big pot of spicy soup from a whole turkey. With it, they can easily feed everybody. Their seasonings are similar to those in Rachel's Yemenite Meat Soup (see recipe in Chapter 12).

Modern Jews have taken to the lean meat of chicken and turkey in a big way because of health awareness. They are busy turning many old-fashioned meat main courses into chicken specialties. Some examples are tzimmes, cholent, meat stuffings for vegetables, and meat balls.

In the following recipe, you use an instant-read thermometer (see Figure 15-2). This type of thermometer makes it easy for you to check whether thick pieces of chicken, meat, or other foods have cooked through. You simply pierce the rod of the thermometer into the food, wait a few seconds, and read the dial. Unlike with standard meat thermometers, you don't leave an instant-read thermometer in the food while it cooks. Most thermometers need to be inserted at least 2 inches into the food to register properly.

Roast Turkey with Orange Sauce and Dried Fruit

Turkey gravy doesn't need butter or cream to be delicious. Try this one, with a sauce made of gently spiced orange juice enhanced with dried cranberries, raisins, and orange segments. It needs few ingredients and is easy to make because it's made with cornstarch instead of a roux cooked with fat and flour. This substitution makes it lighter, too.

Roast the turkey on its own or fill it with a bread stuffing, such as Challah and Vegetable Stuffing with Corn and Toasted Walnuts (see previous recipe and make a double amount), or with the festive Rice Stuffing with Apricots, Almonds, and Cashews (see Chapter 18). With a stuffing, the roasting time will be somewhat longer.

Special tool: *Instant-read or meat thermometer (optional but useful)*

Preparation time: *1 hour*

Cooking time: *2 hours, 40 minutes*

Yield: *6 to 8 servings*

Keeping kosher: *Meat*

A 10- to 12-pound fresh or thawed frozen turkey, giblets removed	¼ cup dried cranberries
Salt and freshly ground pepper to taste	¼ cup golden raisins
3 to 4 tablespoons vegetable oil	1 tablespoon lemon juice
2 to 2¼ cups chicken stock	½ teaspoon grated orange zest
2 shallots, minced	Cayenne pepper to taste
½ teaspoon paprika	2 oranges, peeled and divided into segments
1 cup plus 3 tablespoons orange juice	Orange wedges, for garnish
4 teaspoons cornstarch dissolved in orange juice	

1 Preheat oven to 425° and remove top rack. Sprinkle inside of turkey with salt and pepper. Rub turkey with oil. Truss turkey if desired with skewers.

2 Set turkey on a rack in a large roasting pan. Pour 1 cup stock into pan. Roast turkey for 30 minutes.

3 Reduce oven temperature to 350°. Roast turkey for 1½ hours, basting with pan juices every 30 minutes. If pan becomes dry, add another ¼ cup stock.

4 Cover turkey with foil if it is brown enough. Continue roasting turkey about 20 to 30 more minutes, or until a meat or instant-read thermometer inserted into thickest part of thigh registers 180°, or until juices run clear when thickest part of thigh is pierced with a skewer. Transfer turkey carefully to platter or large board. Discard trussing skewers. Baste once with pan juices and cover turkey.

5 To make the sauce, skim excess fat from juices in pan. Add 1 cup stock and bring to a boil, stirring and scraping to dissolve any brown bits in pan. Strain into a medium saucepan. Skim fat again. Add shallots, paprika, and remaining stock to saucepan and bring to a boil. Simmer for 2 minutes.

6 Meanwhile, put cornstarch in a small cup and stir in 3 tablespoons orange juice. Add remaining 1 cup orange juice to sauce and bring to a simmer. Set heat at medium and gradually whisk in cornstarch mixture. Return sauce to a boil, whisking. Add cranberries, raisins, and lemon juice. Simmer sauce over low heat, stirring often, for 3 minutes, or until it is thick enough to lightly coat a spoon and dried fruit is tender. Add cayenne. Taste and adjust seasoning.

7 Carve turkey and arrange on platter. Garnish with orange wedges. Reheat sauce briefly. Add grated orange zest and orange segments and warm very gently. Spoon a little sauce with orange segments over turkey breast. Pour remaining sauce into a sauceboat and serve alongside turkey.

Per serving: Calories 799.1; Protein 92.0 g; Carbohydrates 17.9 g; Dietary fiber 1.6 g; Total fat 37.7 g; Saturated fat 9.8 g; Cholesterol 265.7 mg; Sodium 544.5 mg.

Jewish Mother's Tip: To keep the fresh flavor of orange and lemon juice, add them to sauces toward the end of the cooking time so that they do not boil for too long.

Figure 15-2:
An instant-read thermometer.

Simmering Stovetop Chicken Dishes

Stewing and braising rival roasting as top techniques for poultry preparation in the Jewish kitchen. They keep the chicken moist, taste even better when reheated, and best of all, produce a scrumptious sauce. Most cooks use the terms braising and stewing interchangeably, although technically *braising* refers to large cuts, such as a whole chicken or turkey breast, while *stewing* refers to chicken parts or other smaller pieces.

Jews of different origins like to stew chicken with fruit, especially dried fruit like apricots, prunes, and raisins. Ashkenazic Jews call this type of stew *tzimmes* and might accentuate the sweetness with honey. (For an example of a meat tzimmes, see Chapter 4.) Jews from Morocco call their poultry and fruit combinations *sweet tajines* and flavor them with onion and gentle spices like paprika or ground ginger. Among fresh fruit, some popular poultry partners are tart apples and *quinces,* an apple-like fall fruit that is always cooked, as well as lemon and orange juice.

Adding vegetables to chicken dishes is also a timeless tradition in every Jewish community. From aromatic vegetables like onions, carrots, and celery, to Mediterranean favorites like tomatoes, peppers, and eggplant to cold-climate staples like cabbage and potatoes, every vegetable may find its way into the stew pot at one season or another.

In the past, the reason was frugality, because a single chicken may need to feed the whole family for Shabbat, and families tended to be large. Today, people enjoy vegetables for the flavor, color, and nutrition they contribute to the meal.

For the following recipe, you need to cut the chicken into pieces, as shown in Figure 15-3.

Cutting up a chicken is easier than it looks! Just put the bird on a cutting board and get a sharp knife. Follow these steps, and you'll have that bird ready in a minute or two!

1. Turn the chicken on its side and pull the wing away from the body. Use the tip of a knife to cut around the joint attaching the wing to the breast... then do the other side !!

2. Turn the breast side up. While pulling the leg with one hand, use the tip of a knife to slice the skin between the drumstick and the breast.

3. With one hand holding the chicken, use the other hand to bend back the leg and pop out the joint that attaches the leg to the body. Cut around the joint to release the leg/thigh and then do the other side!

POP

4. Place leg/thigh, skin side down on cutting board. Use a knife to slice through fat line and locate joint. Cut through to separate the leg from thigh. Do it again on 2nd side!

5. Cut between bottom of rib cage and back of bird. The breast and back will be completely separated.

6. Starting at the tail end, cut along 1 side of the breastbone, when you hit wish-bone, cut along the other side and pop it out of the breast. Repeat on 2nd side of breastbone.

Don't forget to make a wish!

Figure 15-3: Cutting chicken in pieces.

Chicken with Green Beans, Mushrooms, and Olives

With its tomato, olive, and herb sauce, this savory stew is bursting with Mediterranean exuberance. My inspiration for the dish is from the style of the Jews of North Africa and southern France, who like to cook chicken with olives. I love it with couscous or with rice.

For a leaner dish, remove the chicken skin before cooking it and shorten the browning time to 1 to 2 minutes per side. If you prefer a rich sauce, leave the skin on the chicken.

Preparation time: *20 minutes*

Cooking time: *1 hour and 10 minutes*

Yield: *4 servings*

Keeping kosher: *Meat*

2 tablespoons olive oil

2½ pounds chicken pieces, patted dry

Salt and freshly ground pepper to taste

8 ounces mushrooms, quartered

4 large garlic cloves, minced

Two 28-ounce cans tomatoes, drained and chopped

½ cup chicken broth or water

¼ teaspoon hot pepper flakes

1 bay leaf

3 fresh thyme sprigs, or ½ teaspoon dried thyme

¾ pound green beans, ends removed, halved

½ cup pitted black or green olives

2 to 3 teaspoons lemon juice, or to taste

3 tablespoons chopped Italian parsley

1 In a large deep skillet or sauté pan, heat oil over medium-high heat. Sprinkle chicken with pepper on both sides and brown it, about 3 minutes per side, in batches in oil; transfer browned pieces to a plate. Discard all but 1 tablespoon fat from skillet. Add mushrooms, salt, and pepper and sauté over medium-high heat until lightly browned. Remove from skillet.

2 Add garlic to skillet and sauté a few seconds. Stir in tomatoes, broth, and pepper flakes and add bay leaf and thyme. Return chicken to skillet with juices on plate and bring to a boil. Cover and simmer over low heat about 35 minutes or until breast pieces are tender when pierced with a sharp knife. Transfer them to a plate. Cook remaining pieces about 10 minutes or until tender. Remove from pan. Skim fat from sauce.

3 Meanwhile, cook green beans uncovered in a medium saucepan containing enough boiling salted water to cover them generously. Boil them uncovered for 7 minutes or until just tender. Drain, rinse with cold water, and drain well.

4 Discard bay leaf and thyme sprigs. Add green beans to sauce and simmer uncovered for 3 minutes. Return chicken and mushrooms to sauce and add olives and lemon juice. Cover and warm over low heat 3 minutes. Add 2 tablespoons parsley. Taste and adjust seasoning. Serve hot, sprinkled with remaining parsley.

Per serving: *Calories 484.5; Protein 42.3 g; Carbohydrates 22.2 g; Dietary fiber 6.1 g; Total fat 26.3 g; Saturated fat 5.8 g; Cholesterol 49.2 mg; Sodium 912.5 mg.*

Jewish Mother's Tip: *To keep green beans green in a stew, keep in mind that boiling the beans separately and heating them briefly in the sauce keeps their color a brighter green. Plenty of Mediterranean cooks prefer to add the raw beans directly to the sauce, however, so it simmers slowly and absorbs more flavor, and are not concerned about the color. The choice is yours.*

Discovering Israeli Chicken Customs

In Israel, a variety of Jewish culinary customs mingle in close proximity. Cooks there have developed their own takes on regional poultry dishes.

Schnitzels in the skillet

The Austrian *schnitzel*, originally a breaded cutlet of veal, has been transformed into a chicken or turkey specialty. On Israeli tables, it appears more often than any other poultry dish. Children clamor for it for lunch, and mothers give in. Yet it's far from a plain, everyday dish. Restaurant chefs serve it frequently. Wedding and Bar-Mitzvah feasts feature chicken schnitzel as a popular main course. Everyone loves it.

Many people serve schnitzel for Shabbat meals also. I was surprised to learn this because fried dishes don't usually reheat very well. Apparently, the crunchy coating protects the meat from drying.

Tasty partners for turkey schnitzels are rice pilaf, Israeli salad, and Sautéed Zucchini in Tomato Dill Sauce (see Chapter 5). If you like, top the turkey with a spoonful of your favorite fresh salsa.

Spicy Turkey Schnitzel

Israeli schnitzel is, in fact, my favorite way to make fried chicken as well as turkey breasts. The crunchy breading helps protect the lean meat so that it is flavorful and juicy. Flour, egg, and bread crumbs are standard, but you can vary the coating by using whole-wheat flour and bread crumbs. You can also substitute matzo meal, corn meal, or cracker crumbs for the bread. If you prefer, use 2 egg whites instead of the egg. You can see a photo of this recipe in the color insert section of this book.

Preparation time: *20 minutes*

Cooking time: *20 minutes*

Yield: *4 servings*

Keeping kosher: *Meat*

1¼ pounds fresh turkey breast slices (4 to 8 slices), about ¼ inch thick

1 teaspoon ground coriander

1 teaspoon ground cumin

½ teaspoon paprika

¼ teaspoon salt

¼ teaspoon ground black pepper

¼ teaspoon cayenne pepper

⅓ cup flour

¾ cup unseasoned dry bread crumbs

1 or 2 eggs, or 2 to 4 egg whites

⅓ cup vegetable oil

Parsley sprigs and lemon wedges (for garnish)

1 If any of turkey slices is thicker than ¼ inch, pound it between 2 pieces of plastic wrap to even thickness of ¼ inch, using flat meat pounder or rolling pin (see Figure 15-4).

2 Arrange turkey in one layer on plate. Mix coriander, cumin, paprika, salt, black pepper, and cayenne in small bowl. Sprinkle 1½ teaspoons spice mixture as evenly as possible over one side of turkey pieces. Rub spices into each piece. Turn pieces over; sprinkle and rub second side with remaining spice mixture.

3 Spread flour in a plate. Spread bread crumbs in second plate. Beat 1 egg in a shallow bowl. Lightly coat a turkey slice with flour on both sides. Tap and shake to remove excess flour. Dip slice in egg. Last dip both sides in bread crumbs to coat turkey completely; pat and press lightly so crumbs adhere. Set turkey piece on a large plate. Repeat with remaining slices. If necessary, beat another egg. Handle turkey lightly so coating does not come off.

4 Heat oil in heavy large skillet. Add enough turkey to make one layer without crowding. Sauté over medium-high heat about 2 minutes per side, or until golden brown, turn pieces carefully using two wide spatulas. If oil begins to brown, reduce heat to medium.

5 Put sautéed turkey on paper towels. Arrange turkey slices side by side on a platter or baking sheet and keep them warm in a 275° oven. Serve garnished with parsley sprigs and lemon wedges.

Per serving: Calories 467.6; Protein 42.5 g; Carbohydrates 23.5 g; Dietary fiber 1.3 g; Total fat 21.6 g; Saturated fat 2.2 g; Cholesterol 155.5 mg; Sodium 401.3 mg.

Chicken Cutlets Pounded to an Even Thickness

Figure 15-4:
Pounding
cutlets.

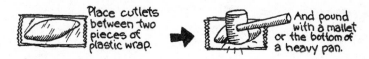

Place cutlets between two pieces of plastic wrap.

And pound with a mallet or the bottom of a heavy pan.

Birds on the grill

As a warm-climate country at the eastern end of the Mediterranean, Israelis have adopted the regional love for grilling poultry in a big way. Barbecue eateries abound, and people love to cook chicken outdoors on the grill for family get-togethers, especially in pieces or threaded on skewers as kabobs. To ensure tender meat, many marinate the chicken in a simple Mediterranean mixture of lemon juice, olive oil, garlic, and such herbs as thyme and oregano. Others go for a spicy rub of cumin, plenty of black pepper, and turmeric.

Even when you're cooking outdoors, don't forget the rules of good hygiene, including washing your hands after handling chicken. See the section "Roasting Chicken," earlier in this chapter.

Israeli Independence Day celebrations

For Israel's Independence Day, which takes place in late May or June, people love picnics like for the Fourth of July, featuring chicken on the barbecue. Here the resemblance ends. Typical accompaniments are Israeli salad, hummus, tahini, pita bread, and rice pilaf.

Sephardic Grilled Chicken

Chicken prepared this way appears on the barbecues of homes and restaurants throughout Israel. With its Mediterranean marinade of fresh garlic, olive oil, lemon juice, and herbs, the chicken becomes succulent and flavorful. All it needs before being put on the grill is a touch of cumin and plenty of pepper.

I like it with smoky eggplant salad, tahini sauce, grilled sweet peppers, refreshing Israeli vegetable salad, and fresh pita bread or rice pilaf. You can see a photo of this recipe in the color insert section of this book.

Special tool: *Barbecue/Grill*

Preparation time: *10 minutes, plus at least 4 hours for marinating chicken*

Cooking time: *40 minutes*

Yield: *4 servings*

Keeping kosher: *Meat*

¼ cup fresh lemon juice

¼ cup extra virgin olive oil

2 large garlic cloves, crushed

3 small sprigs fresh thyme, broken in pieces, or 1 teaspoon dried

1 teaspoon dried oregano

½ teaspoon ground black pepper

Pinch of cayenne pepper

2½ to 3 pounds chicken pieces

Salt (optional) and freshly ground black pepper to taste

2 teaspoons ground cumin, preferably freshly ground

1 To make the marinade, in a shallow baking dish large enough to hold chicken, mix lemon juice, oil, garlic, thyme, oregano, ½ teaspoon black pepper, and cayenne. Put chicken in dish and turn pieces over to coat all sides with marinade. Cover and marinate chicken in the refrigerator, turning it from time to time, for at least 4 hours or overnight.

2 Remove chicken from marinade, removing any pieces of thyme or garlic stuck to chicken; discard marinade. Sprinkle chicken with salt, freshly ground pepper, and cumin on both sides.

3 Prepare barbecue for indirect heat. Heat charcoal barbecue until the coals are glowing; or heat gas barbecue to medium. Set chicken on rack about 4 to 6 inches above heat source. Grill breast pieces for 20 minutes per side, and leg and thigh pieces for 30 minutes per side, or until thickest part of meat near bone is no longer pink; cut to check. Serve hot.

Per serving: *Calories 361.7; Protein 37.5 g; Carbohydrates 1.1 g; Dietary fiber 0.5 g; Total fat 22.1 g; Saturated fat 5.6 g; Cholesterol 148.6 mg; Sodium 111.9 mg.*

Warning: *Don't burn the bird on the barbecue. If the chicken browns too fast and begins to scorch, move it to a cooler part of the grill or reduce the heat.*

Chapter 16

Meat: Slow Cooking Is a Virtual Mandate

In This Chapter

▶ Creating meat main courses full of flavor

▶ Transforming inexpensive ground meat into family favorites

Recipes in This Chapter

▶ Cumin-Scented Lamb with Green Beans, Peppers, and Potatoes

▶ Sweet and Sour Beef and Butternut Squash Stew

▶ Veal Chops with Peas and Rosemary

▶ Zesty Beef Patties

▶ Meat-Stuffed Peppers with Tomatoes, Garlic, and Dill

🍴 🫘 🍲 🌶 🌿 🥬

Check out this chapter to find out why meat has long been at the center of celebrations on the Jewish menu. Discover the advantage, ease, and pleasure of the gentle, relaxed cooking methods for meat. You also find out the secrets behind frugal cooks' creative use of ground meat to make some of the best-loved main courses of all.

Turning Beef, Lamb, and Veal into Savory Entrees

Recently some food aficionados in the United States and Europe have discussed the virtues of returning to the slow food of times past as a relief from the fast food culture. But in Jewish homes, slow cooking is a way of life, not a memory of the past. Gentle cooking is the favorite way to prepare meat, especially for holidays. Perhaps the ultimate slow-cooked dish is the overnight Sabbath stew (see Chapter 10), but there are plenty of others. Jewish cooks are famous for these soothing simmered stews and braises.

Over the ages, Jewish cooks of all origins have become adept at stewing, braising, and poaching. The key to these techniques' appeal is the *flavor exchange principle*. As the meat, the sauce, and the vegetables cook together, they contribute good taste to each other. The flavor impact of the whole dish becomes more than a simple sum of its ingredients.

Although their duration on the heat can be long, these dishes do not demand a lot of effort because much of the cooking time is unattended. Once everything is in the pot, these dishes are often the easiest of all. Besides, these make-ahead dishes are ready in your refrigerator or freezer when you want them. They reheat beautifully and are even more delicious the second time.

The main reason for the prevalence of gently cooked dishes in Jewish cuisine is that they are perfect for many of the kosher cuts of meat. These cuts come from the forequarter of the animals and benefit from these moist-heat cooking methods to become tender and succulent.

Another important factor in opting for slow-cooked meats in observant households is the weekly necessity to cook the festive Shabbat food in advance (see Chapter 10). Meats cooked slowly in sauce or broth are most suitable for this style of menu.

To buy kosher meat, you need to go to a kosher butcher shop or kosher market. Unlike kosher chickens, which are easy to find at supermarkets in cities with substantial Jewish communities, kosher meat is not generally available. Often, the kosher butcher salts the meat himself to kosher it (see Chapter 1). Koshering it is impractical for typical supermarkets.

When preparing meat for stew, trim all visible fat from meat using a sharp knife. First trim the fat around the edge of the piece. As you cut the meat in cubes, you can also cut off any other pieces of fat you encounter in the center of the piece of meat (see Figure 16-1).

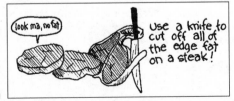

Figure 16-1:
Trimming
excess fat.

Here's another tip: Use a good quality pan for stewing meat or poultry. It should be heavy so that it will distribute the heat evenly and will enable the meat to brown and then to cook gently without burning. A two-handled, straight-sided pan is called a *rondeau* and is great for stewing (see Figure 16-2). Usually it is made of stainless steel. It should have a tight-fitting cover and a copper or aluminum core for efficient heat conduction. In addition, a heavy pan, such as a Dutch oven, is ideal for stewing and braising meat and poultry (see Figure 16-3). As a bonus, it's attractive, so you can serve the meat in its casserole at the table.

Figure 16-2:
Rondeau or two-handled stainless steel stew pan.

Figure 16-3:
Enameled cast-iron casserole or Dutch oven.

Spicy stews

Jews of Mediterranean and Middle Eastern origin are fond of highly seasoned stews. Beef is the meat of choice, and occasionally lamb or veal. They use spices and aromatics exuberantly and enjoy the way that slow cooking encourages these flavors to penetrate the meat as much as possible. Such favorites as garlic, cumin, turmeric, and hot peppers contribute to their stews' wonderful aroma and rich harmony of tastes. Frequently, cooks finish the stews with the fresh accents of dill, cilantro, and flat-leaf parsley.

Ashkenazic Jews usually prefer gentler seasonings, notably onions, carrots, bay leaves, paprika, fresh dill, and parsley, and perhaps a touch of cinnamon, nutmeg, or ginger. Depending on the place of origin of the community, some people enjoy the pungency of garlic, chilies, and hot paprika or use plenty of black pepper to spice up their simmered meats.

Vegetables are a major component of Jewish stews, often in generous amounts. Originally added for frugality, they now are popular because of their bright tastes and colors and for good nutrition. Depending on the season, almost any vegetable might find its way into the pot. In addition to the usual onions, carrots, peppers, and tomatoes, Jewish stews may include artichokes, eggplant, spinach, chard, and squashes of all types, both tender soft-shelled ones and firmer sweet ones like butternut.

Handling jalapeño peppers

Chilies add a lively flavor to many dishes. Take a few precautions when handling them because they can irritate your skin if you are sensitive to them. After preparing chilies, clean any utensils you used; otherwise, the heat of the chilies will affect these foods when the utensils come in contact with them.

✔ Wear latex gloves when handling jalapeño peppers and other chilies if you are sensitive.

✔ After handling jalapeño peppers and other chilies, wash the board, knife, and your hands.

✔ Remove the membranes and seeds for a taste that's less hot. Leave them in if you want the full heat of the chilies.

When handling meat, follow the same hygiene rules as for handling poultry (see Chapter 15).

Cumin-Scented Lamb with Green Beans, Peppers, and Potatoes

For meat and potatoes with a difference, try this bold-flavored meal in one pot. All you need to complement the spicy stew is a light refreshing Israeli salad or green salad, followed by some fresh fruit for dessert.

Jews from the Middle East love rice. Even though the entree contains potatoes, they may serve rice pilaf on the side to enjoy with the delicious sauce, or perhaps some fresh pita bread.

In the traditional Sephardic kitchen, the taste is for very tender vegetables. Cooks add the green beans along with the potatoes and simmer them in the stew for 30 minutes or longer so that they absorb the savory taste of the sauce. For this recipe, I cook them briefly in a separate pan instead to keep their texture al dente and their color brighter. Which way to do it is up to you. Cooks preparing this dish the old-fashioned way always peel their potatoes, but that's up to you.

You can keep the stew for two days in a covered container in the refrigerator. During that time, the stew becomes even better because the spices flavor the meat more deeply and the sauce gains depth of flavor from the beef.

Preparation time: *45 minutes*

Cooking time: *1 hour and 50 minutes*

Yield: *4 to 6 servings*

Keeping kosher: *Meat*

Shabbat: Easy Roast Chicken with Fresh Herbs (Chapter 15); Challah and Vegetable Stuffing with Corn and Toasted Walnuts (Chapter 15); and Rosemary Roasted Potatoes (Chapter 10).

Left page, Passover Seder: On Seder plate: Roasted lamb shank; Levy Family's Favorite Haroset (Chapter 8); three matzos; Asparagus and Carrots with Lemon Dressing (Chapter 8); and My Mother's Fluffy Matzo Balls (Chapter 8) in Grandma's Chicken Soup (Chapter 12).

Right page, Passover Seder: Garlic Roast Lamb with Potatoes (Chapter 8); Fruit and Wine Compote (Chapter 21); and Easy Almond Macaroons (Chapter 8).

Shavuot: Cheese Blintzes with blueberry preserves and Sesame Spinach Salad with Barley (both in Chapter 9).

Rosh Hashanah: Sweet Potato and Beef Tzimmes with Dried Apricots; Cinnamon Carrot Coins; and Sweet Beet Salad with Orange (all in Chapter 4).

Sukkot: Savory Drumsticks with Rice and Peppers (Chapter 5) and Green Beans in Garlicky Tomato Sauce (Chapter 19).

Hanukkah: Fast, Lowfat Corn Latkes; Spicy Vegetable Latkes; Pauline's Potato Pancakes; Homemade Cinnamon Applesauce (all in Chapter 6); and salsa.

Appetizers, on individual plate, clockwise from top: Falafel (Chapter 11); Feta-Filled Bourekas (Chapter 9); Israeli Salad, My Way (Chapter 19); Hummus (Chapter 11); and pita bread.

Fish for Feasts: Sephardic Sea Bass in Saffron Tomato Sauce (Chapter 14) and Mediterranean Lentils with Rice (Chapter 18).

Easy Menu: Spicy Turkey Schnitzel (Chapter 15); Couscous with Sweet Peppers, Pine Nuts, and Parsley (Chapter 18); and Sautéed Zucchini in Tomato-Dill Sauce (Chapter 5).

Summer Meal, the Israeli Way: Two-Way Eggplant Spread (Chapter 11) with pita; Sephardic Grilled Chicken (Chapter 15); and Grilled Sweet Pepper Salad (Chapter 19).

Casual Pareve Meal: Chickpea and Green Soybean Salad (Chapter 7) and Noodle Kugel with Asparagus and Mushrooms (Chapter 17).

Vegetables for Celebrating: Meat-Stuffed Peppers with Tomatoes, Garlic, and Dill (Chapter 16).

Purim Treats, in box, from left: Pecan-Chocolate-Raisin Rugelach (Chapter 20); Chocolate Almond Rum Balls (Chapter 7); and Hamantaschen with Poppy Seeds (Chapter 7).

Moist Cocoa Cake with Macadamia Nuts (Chapter 10).

My Mother's Creamy Cheesecake (Chapter 9).

1 or 2 tablespoons olive oil

2 medium onions, chopped

2 pounds lamb shoulder, excess fat removed, cut in 1-inch cubes

1 green bell pepper, cut in 1-inch dice

1 red bell pepper, cut into 1-inch dice

3 jalapeño peppers, chopped, or more for hotter taste

6 large garlic cloves, chopped

1 tablespoon ground cumin

1 teaspoon turmeric

Salt and freshly ground pepper to taste

¾ pound ripe tomatoes, chopped, or one 14-ounce can tomatoes, drained and chopped

1 cup water, more if needed

1 pound boiling potatoes

1¼ pounds green beans, ends removed, broken in half

1 tablespoon tomato paste

¼ cup chopped cilantro

1 Heat oil in a stew pan. Add onion and sauté over medium heat for 7 minutes, or until beginning to brown. Add lamb, bell peppers, jalapeño peppers, garlic, cumin, and turmeric. Sauté over medium-low heat for 7 minutes, stirring often to coat beef with spices.

2 Add salt, pepper, tomatoes, and water to pan. Stir and bring to a boil. Cover and cook over low heat for 1 hour.

3 Cut potatoes into 1-inch chunks. After stew has simmered for 1 hour, add potatoes. If stew appears dry, add ½ cup water. Cover and cook for 30 minutes, or until meat and potatoes are tender.

4 Meanwhile, cook beans uncovered in a saucepan of boiling salted water over high heat for 5 minutes, or until crisp-tender. Rinse with cold water and drain.

5 When meat and potatoes are tender, stir tomato paste into sauce. Add beans and 2 tablespoons cilantro and cook over low heat for 5 minutes. Taste and adjust seasoning. Serve sprinkled with remaining cilantro.

Per serving: Calories 384.2; Protein 36.0 g; Carbohydrates 30.6 g; Dietary fiber 6.3 g; Total fat 13.5 g; Saturated fat 4.3 g; Cholesterol 104.3 mg; Sodium 230.9 mg.

Sweet and sweet-sour selections

Fruit is a popular component of meat stews, notably among Ashkenazic Jews, but in some Sephardic homes as well. Favorites are dried fruits, which appear in both central European tzimmes (see Chapter 4 for a recipe) as well as in North African sweet stews known as *tajines.* Jews from Iran also enjoy meats cooked with fruit.

These fruit-and-meat combinations are especially popular for the Jewish New Year. You may find them surprising, but the resulting stews are not sugary-sweet. They are savory with an occasional sweet note. Cooks do not include so much fruit that it dominates the dish. In addition, they have all sorts of tricks for balancing the fruit flavor, by adding plenty of onions, other vegetables, ginger, cinnamon, or even saffron. Many fruits, such as dried apricots, have a touch of natural tartness, too.

In many Ashkenazic homes, sweet and sour braises and stews are often on the menu. Jews from Poland and Russia enjoy tender braised meats and winter vegetables like carrots, onions, and cabbage in tomato sauces enlivened with vinegar or lemon juice. To temper the sour taste, they add sugar or raisins.

Sweet and Sour Beef and Butternut Squash Stew

I find that chuck, or beef shoulder meat, makes a flavorful, appealing stew and acquires a wonderful, tender texture. You can also use brisket, a favorite cut of beef in the Jewish kitchen.

Other popular vegetables for Jewish sweet and sour stews are carrots, sweet potatoes, potatoes, cabbage, and beets. Often, the sauce is flavored with tomato in some form.

Old-fashioned recipes call for basic white vinegar, but you can use red or white wine vinegar if you prefer. Dried ginger is the custom in some versions, but I like to spice my stew with fresh ginger. Use either light or dark raisins or, for a new twist on tradition, try dried blueberries, cherries, or cranberries. Egg noodles make a good accompaniment for the savory beef and its tasty sauce.

Preparation time: 1 hour

Cooking time: 3½ hours

Yield: 6 servings

Keeping kosher: Meat

2 to 3 tablespoons vegetable oil

3½ pounds beef chuck or brisket, cut in 1¼-inch cubes, trimmed of excess fat, and patted dry

2 large onions, coarsely chopped

1½ tablespoons minced peeled gingerroot

1 quart water, or more if needed

Salt and freshly ground pepper to taste

2½ to 3 pounds butternut squash

2 tablespoons flour

¼ cup ketchup

¼ cup brown sugar, or more to taste

¼ cup white vinegar or wine vinegar, or more to taste

½ cup raisins

1 Heat 1 or 2 tablespoons oil in a stew pan. Add about ⅓ of beef and sauté it over medium heat until it browns on all sides. With a slotted spoon, remove beef from pan to a plate. Continue browning remaining beef in batches.

2 Add 1 tablespoon oil to stew pan and heat it. Add onions and sauté over medium-low heat about 10 minutes, or until deep brown. Add ginger and sauté for 1 minute.

3 Return meat and any juices from plate to pan. Add water, salt, and pepper. Bring to a boil, stirring a few times. Cover and simmer over low heat, stirring occasionally, about 2½ hours, or until beef is very tender. To check, lift a piece with a thin, sharp knife; beef should fall from knife.

4 Meanwhile, cut squash in half and scrape off any stringy parts from center of squash with spoon. Cut squash in large pieces, cut off peel from each one, and cut squash in 1-inch cubes.

5 When meat is tender, add squash and push it into liquid. Cover and simmer 10 minutes. Turn squash pieces over, cover, and simmer for 10 minutes, or until squash is tender.

6 In a small bowl, whisk flour with 2 tablespoons water. Using whisk, gradually stir in about 1 cup of sauce from stew. Return mixture to pan, stirring gently. Stir in ketchup, brown sugar, vinegar, and raisins. Bring to a simmer, stirring. Simmer, stirring occasionally, about 5 minutes, or until sauce thickens. If you prefer a thinner sauce, stir in a little water by tablespoons and return to a simmer. Taste, and add more salt, pepper, ketchup, brown sugar, or vinegar if you like. Serve hot.

Per serving: Calories 624.0; Protein 62.0 g; Carbohydrates 49.5 g; Dietary fiber 5.0 g; Total fat 19.8 g; Saturated fat 5.8 g; Cholesterol 181.8 mg; Sodium 356.4 mg.

Jewish Mother's Tip: Once the beef and butternut squash are tender, avoid vigorous stirring so that the pieces do not fall apart.

Beef-in-the-pot meals

A homey winter favorite, beef in the pot is so popular that family-style restaurants feature it frequently on their menus. The favorite cut is short ribs, but the pot may also contain a meaty chunk of chuck instead or in addition. Basically, it's beef poached slowly with aromatic vegetables, herbs, and spices until it becomes very tender and produces a richly flavored broth. Most cooks prefer that the beef be the star and highlight its taste with only a few flavorings — salt, peppercorns, bay leaves, onions, carrots, celery, and garlic. The magic happens during the long, gentle simmering.

In most kitchens, beef in the pot is a two-course meal, just like Chicken in the Pot with Leeks and Potatoes (see recipe in Chapter 4). First, you serve the broth, with noodles or matzo balls. Then the beef is the main course, along with extra carrots, potatoes, and other vegetables added to the pot when the beef has about an hour left to simmer.

Chops and steaks

When you want to prepare kosher meat on the grill, you can opt for chops and steaks. Beef and lamb rib chops are wonderful cooked this way, as well as in the broiler or in a skillet. Kosher butchers prepare steaks from a variety of cuts, but not from the loin or other hindquarter portions of the animal.

For roasting, you can buy a larger cut of beef chops or steaks. In the case of lamb, if the rib chops are left attached to each other, you have a rack. A rack of lamb makes a wonderfully festive roast.

Jewish cooks enjoy the versatility of veal chops and serve them in a great variety of ways. They're good braised, sautéed, breaded and fried, or baked in a sauce. If you want to grill them, marinate them first so that they will not be dry.

People who strictly observe the laws of keeping kosher cook their meat until well done. The reason is that blood is not kosher.

Veal Chops with Peas and Rosemary

A festive springtime dish of braised veal chops with bright green peas is always welcome. Veal chops are one of the fastest cuts to braise. By following this cooking technique, you will have veal chops that are succulent and delicious. The light, Mediterranean-style, herb-scented tomato sauce complements them beautifully.

Preparation time: *20 minutes (or about 50 minutes if shelling peas)*

Cooking time: *40 minutes*

Yield: *4 servings*

Keeping kosher: *Meat*

4 veal chops, about 8 ounces each, about ¾ to 1 inch thick, excess fat trimmed, patted dry

Salt and freshly ground pepper to taste

2 tablespoons olive oil or vegetable oil

1 onion, chopped

2 cloves garlic, chopped

1 pound ripe tomatoes, peeled, seeded, and chopped, or one 28-ounce can tomatoes, drained and chopped

⅓ cup dry white wine or chicken stock

2 thyme sprigs or ½ teaspoon dried

1 tablespoon fresh rosemary leaves, minced, or 1 teaspoon dried, chopped

3 pounds fresh peas, shelled, or 3 cups frozen peas

2 tablespoons chopped parsley

1 Sprinkle veal on both sides with pepper. Heat oil in heavy, large, deep sauté pan or skillet. Add 2 veal chops and sauté them over medium-high heat for 2 minutes per side, or until lightly browned. Transfer to a plate. Repeat with remaining chops.

2 Add onion to pan and sauté over medium heat for 5 minutes, or until soft but not brown. Add garlic and sauté for 30 seconds. Add tomatoes, wine, thyme, rosemary, salt, and pepper. Bring to a boil, stirring. Simmer uncovered over medium heat, stirring occasionally, until sauce thickens slightly, about 10 minutes.

3 Meanwhile, add peas to a large saucepan containing enough boiling salted water to cover them. Cook them uncovered over medium-high heat for 3 minutes. Drain well.

4 Add veal and peas to sauce and bring to a simmer. Cover and cook over low heat for 4 to 5 minutes per side, or until veal chops are tender and white inside when cut. Discard thyme sprigs. Taste sauce and adjust seasoning. Serve sprinkled with parsley.

Per serving: *Calories 399.1; Protein 39.7 g; Carbohydrates 22.5 g; Dietary fiber 6.9 g; Total fat 16.5 g; Saturated fat 3.5 g; Cholesterol 121.6 mg; Sodium 360.4 mg.*

Menu Maven Says: *Asparagus in vinaigrette dressing makes a tasty first course to celebrate the season. Simple steamed rice or new potatoes make a perfect accompaniment for the veal chops. For a light, springtime dessert for this menu, a fruit salad is perfect, like one of strawberries and pears. A refreshing dish of pears poached in red wine also makes a lovely close to the meal. For an additional treat for a kosher meal, accompany the fruit with sorbet or nondairy vanilla or fruit ice cream.*

Jewish Mother's Tip: *Although dried herbs are usually ready to use, dried rosemary is best chopped with a knife or coarsely ground in a spice grinder because its leaves can be sharp.*

Using Ground Meat to Your Best Advantage

Nearly everyone seems to make meat balls, meat loaf, burgers, and spaghetti sauce. Jewish cooks prepare these frugal entrees in creative ways.

Meat balls and patties

For meat balls in the Jewish kitchen, most people mix ground beef with bread crumbs or matzo meal and their preferred flavorings, whether spicy or subtle. Some add unusual ingredients, such as chickpea flour, a favorite of Iranian Jews.

Depending on the cook, they may sauté the meat balls first or skip this step. Then they simmer them in a tomato sauce that is either spicy, herb flavored, or sweet and sour. Unlike typical American meat balls, in Israeli homes, rice is a more frequent partner for meat balls than spaghetti. An alternative is to simmer the meat balls in a meat broth along with a little rice to make a soup.

In many kitchens, the same meat ball mixture may be turned into meat patties. Cooks just flatten the mixture, shape it in little cakes, and sauté them in a skillet. The patties make tasty suppers on their own, but many people them like to simmer them in tomato sauce for a more substantial dish.

Kosher meat has already been salted. If you are using kosher ground beef, you may not want to add any salt. For a way to check the mixture for seasoning, see Step 3 of the following recipe.

Zesty Beef Patties

Jewish cooks find meat patties versatile enough to play many roles, from a quick children's after-school lunch to a component of a holiday feast.

They prepare the patties by several methods. Some start with a potato or vegetable latke batter (see Chapter 6) and add ground beef and extra seasonings. Others begin with a hamburger type mixture and add eggs to make the cakes lighter and soaked bread or bread crumbs for a more tender texture.

Serve these beef patties Israeli style, in a pita bread with a quick salad of diced tomato, cucumber, and onion and your favorite relish or salsa. For entertaining, make them smaller and serve them as a first course with a dipping sauce such as tahini sauce or a fresh hot salsa. Another popular way to serve them at holiday meals is as an embellishment for a platter of couscous or rice.

Preparation time: *25 minutes*

Cooking time: *30 minutes*

Yield: *6 servings*

Keeping kosher: *Meat*

3 slices stale white bread	½ teaspoon salt, or more to taste (optional)
¾ pound lean ground beef	Pinch of freshly ground pepper
1 medium onion, minced	¼ teaspoon cayenne pepper
2 large garlic cloves, chopped	2 tablespoons chopped parsley
1 teaspoon ground cumin	1 large egg
1 teaspoon ground coriander	3 tablespoons vegetable oil, more if needed (for sautéing)
1 teaspoon dried thyme	

1 Break bread slices in a few pieces. Dip each piece in a bowl of water to moisten and soften it. Squeeze bread dry.

2 In a medium bowl, mix beef with moistened bread, onion, garlic, cumin, coriander, thyme, salt, pepper, cayenne pepper, and parsley. Add egg. Mix very well; the easiest way is to use your hands.

3 To taste the mixture for seasoning, put a teaspoonful on a piece of foil and broil it for 2 or 3 minutes on each side or until cooked through. Taste it and add more salt or pepper to the mixture if needed.

4 Shape mixture in patties, using ¼ to ⅓ cup mixture for each. Compact them between your hands. Flatten them.

5 Heat oil in a large heavy skillet. Add enough patties to make one layer. Sauté over medium-low heat for 5 minutes per side, or until cooked through and browned. Cut to check; beef should no longer be pink inside. Sauté remaining patties in same way, adding oil to pan if needed; heat oil before adding more patties. Drain patties on paper towels before serving.

Per serving: Calories 229.6; Protein 13.8 g; Carbohydrates 10.5 g; Dietary fiber 1.1 g; Total fat 14.5 g; Saturated fat 3.3 g; Cholesterol 73.7 mg; Sodium 125.3 mg.

Jewish Mother's Tips: *If onions are strong and you prefer a milder flavor in your patties, soak the minced onion in cold water to cover for 2 to 3 minutes and then drain well.*

Another way to soften the onion's taste is to sauté it for 3 to 4 minutes in 1 tablespoon oil. Let it cool before adding it to the mixture.

Stuffings

One of the most admired specialties of Jewish kitchens is tender vegetables with a savory meat stuffing. The stuffing lends such richness of flavor to the vegetables that these dishes, usually holiday first courses or entrees, never fail to impress. No matter what country Jews lived in, they produced some version of this type of dish, making use of whatever meats or vegetables they could find and accenting them with their favorite seasonings.

Ground beef is the most popular meat for the stuffing, often combined with rice and usually browned onions. Most typical are the sweet and sour stuffed cabbage of central Europe and the spicy stuffed eggplant of Mediterranean Jews. Nearly everyone seems to stuff peppers and squashes. Peppers are very easy to stuff. Once you remove their core and seeds, you'll see that the pepper has a natural cavity that seems to ask for stuffing! (See Figure 16-4.)

When you want a meat filling for blintzes and such pastries as knishes and bourekas, you can use a similar stuffing mixture. Usually, you would omit the rice, using just the ground beef, sautéed onions, and seasonings.

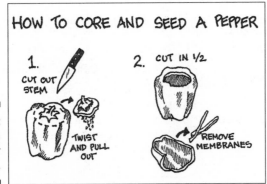

Figure 16-4: Preparing a pepper for stuffing.

Meat-Stuffed Peppers with Tomatoes, Garlic, and Dill

Jewish cuisine features countless ways to stuff peppers. Many are filled with meat mixtures, but some are pareve and have stuffings based on rice or vegetables. Some are braised, others are baked, while still others are fried and then simmered.

Peppers are simple to stuff. For this recipe, I cook them briefly in water to cut their baking time. I sauté the beef with the onions to develop a rich flavor and season it with the popular Israeli flavors of garlic, paprika, cumin, and dill. Adding tomatoes and tomato sauce to the stuffing keeps it exceptionally moist and luscious. You can see a photo of this recipe in the color insert section of this book.

Preparation time: 20 minutes

Cooking time: 55 minutes

Yield: 6 servings

Keeping kosher: Meat

4 large red or green bell peppers

2 tablespoons olive oil or vegetable oil, plus a little extra for oiling dish

2 medium onions, chopped

¾ pound lean ground beef

3 garlic cloves, minced

1 teaspoon ground cumin

1 teaspoon paprika

2 medium tomatoes, diced

½ cup chicken, beef, or vegetable stock

1½ cups tomato sauce

Salt and freshly ground pepper to taste

1 tablespoon chopped fresh dill, or 1 teaspoon dried

⅔ cup bread crumbs

1 Preheat oven to 375°. Halve 3 peppers lengthwise, discarding cores, seeds, and ribs (see Figure 16-4). Reserve pepper halves for stuffing. Dice the remaining pepper.

2 Cook pepper halves in a large saucepan of boiling water 3 minutes. Drain well. Lightly oil a shallow baking dish large enough to hold the peppers in a single layer. Set peppers, cut side up, in dish.

3 Heat oil in a large skillet. Add onions and diced pepper and sauté over medium heat, stirring occasionally, for 10 minutes, or until onion begins to turn golden. Add beef, garlic, cumin, and paprika and sauté, stirring to crumble meat, for 5 minutes, or until beef changes color. Add tomatoes, stock, ½ cup tomato sauce, salt, and pepper. Bring to boil and cook over medium heat for 10 minutes. Remove from heat. Stir in dill and bread crumbs. Taste and adjust seasoning.

4 Spoon stuffing into pepper halves, mounding it high. Mix remaining 1 cup tomato sauce with ½ cup water and pour into baking dish around peppers. Bake uncovered for 30 minutes, or until peppers are very tender. Serve peppers hot or warm, with sauce spooned over them.

Per serving: Calories 273.1; Protein 15.8 g; Carbohydrates 25.3 g; Dietary fiber 4.5 g; Total fat 12.9 g; Saturated fat 3.4 g; Cholesterol 41.1 mg; Sodium 686.8 mg.

Part V

Grains and Vegetables: Side Dishes and Pareve Entrees

The 5th Wave   By Rich Tennant

"You don't have to tell me the kitchen's a spiritual center of the house. God knows I pray for a good matzah kugel every Passover."

In this part . . .

This part explores kugel and other Jewish specialties made from pasta, grains, beans, and vegetables. Here I cover pareve foods and the special role these versatile, healthful foods play in kosher menus. The vegetables include salads suitable as appetizers as well as accompaniments.

Chapter 17

When It Comes to Kugel, Jewish Cooks Use More than Their Noodle

In this chapter, you find out about the incredible versatility of the *kugel,* or baked savory-or-sweet casserole of pasta or vegetables. You discover why the celebrated noodle version of this Jewish casserole has gained a place of honor on the table. You see how many roles kugels can play in meals and how to use them to enhance all sorts of menus, from casual brunches to grand dinners. Although noodle kugels are the best known, you find out how to make kugels out of just about any vegetable, too.

Noodle Kugels: My Childhood Favorites

Ever since I can remember, noodle kugel has been one of my best-loved comfort foods. I always looked forward to my mother's scrumptious kugels, whether she made them pareve for serving alongside meat, or dairy for including in *milchig,* or dairy, meals, whether they were gently spiced with salt and pepper or sweetened with apples and sugar. The melding together of the baked noodles with the other ingredients magically transformed them into something wonderful.

Later, when I wanted to make kugels in my own kitchen, I learned some good news — these delicious casseroles are also easy and convenient. In their most basic form, they consist of noodles mixed with flavorings and eggs and baked until golden. That's all! You can refrigerate the mixture in its baking dish, ready to bake, or bake the kugel ahead and reheat it later.

The custom of making kugels grew from the need to prepare foods that can be kept warm or reheated for Shabbat meals (see Chapter 10).

Savory kugels for brunch, lunch, or dinner

What you choose to mix with the noodles gives the kugel its character. Well-browned, sautéed onions are at the top of most lists, used as the sole flavoring (with salt and pepper, of course) or combined with almost any other ingredient, from mushrooms to spinach to meats to dairy foods. If you have cooked chicken or beef, you can shred some and stir it into an onion-flavored noodle kugel, or a noodle kugel of onions mixed with asparagus, spinach, or broccoli. In our house, the most popular kugel is mushroom onion noodle kugel. This kugel is a great accompaniment for roast chicken at a Friday night dinner.

Just about any kugel is good for lunch because it can be a complete main course of noodles, eggs, and vegetables and/or meat. For brunch, we like dairy versions of our kugels. We often stir cottage cheese and sour cream or yogurt into a kugel mixture flavored with sautéed onions, or onions and mushrooms. These dairy foods create richer, creamier kugels.

Although noodles (see Figure 17-1) are the time-honored choice, pasta of other shapes works fine. I've used the dairy formula with macaroni, cottage cheese, and sour cream and finished it with grated cheese. My kugel cousin of macaroni and cheese was so much easier than the American standard because no separate pot of white sauce was needed. I also like spirals, shells, diagonal-cut penne, and rice-shaped orzo.

Figure 17-1:
Use noodles
or other
pasta
shapes for
making
kugels.

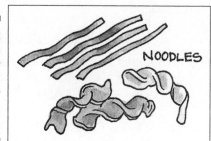

NOODLES

To make kugels to your taste, keep the following tips in mind:

- The ratio of noodles to flavorings, such as the sautéed onions and mushrooms, is up to you.

- You can vary the proportion of eggs, too. More eggs or extra egg yolks give a more custardy sort of kugel.

- Separating the eggs produces a souffle-like effect.

- You can substitute egg whites for part of the eggs if you like.

- Although the traditional noodles are egg noodles, you can replace them with yolk-free noodles.

- Kugels bake faster in shallow dishes than in deep ones.

Kugels can include chicken, meat, or cheese, but kosher kugels never combine meat products with dairy products.

Mushroom Asparagus Noodle Kugel

When asparagus is plentiful, I find it a delicious addition to our family favorite of noodle kugel with sautéed mushrooms and onions. Broccoli is a good alternative during other seasons. You can see a photo of this recipe in the color insert section of this book.

Preparation time: *20 minutes*

Cooking time: *1½ hours*

Yield: *8 to 10 servings*

Keeping kosher: *Pareve*

½ to ¾ pound asparagus, trimmed, peeled, and cut into 1- to 1½-inch pieces

1 pound wide egg noodles

5 to 7 tablespoons vegetable oil

2 large onions, chopped

8 to 12 ounces small mushrooms, sliced

Salt and freshly ground pepper to taste

1 teaspoon paprika

5 large eggs, beaten

1 Boil asparagus uncovered in a large pot of boiling salted water for 3 minutes, or until just tender. Remove asparagus with slotted spoon, rinse it with cold water, and drain it. Add noodles to the boiling water and boil them uncovered over high heat for 4 minutes, or until nearly tender but a little firmer than usual. Drain, rinse with cold water, and drain well. Transfer to a large bowl.

2 Preheat oven to 350°. Oil a 3½- to 4-quart baking dish or two 7- to 8-cup baking dishes.

3 In a large skillet, heat 2 to 4 tablespoons oil. Add onions and sauté over medium heat for 10 minutes, or until very tender. Add 2 tablespoons oil and heat. Add mushrooms, salt, pepper, and paprika. Sauté over medium heat for 10 minutes, or until mushrooms are tender and onions are browned. If mixture is watery, increase heat and cook, stirring often, about 5 minutes or until excess liquid evaporates. Remove from heat. Add asparagus and season mixture to taste with salt and pepper.

4 Add vegetable mixture to noodles and mix well. Taste and adjust seasoning. Add eggs and mix well. Transfer kugel mixture to prepared dishes. Sprinkle with remaining 1 tablespoon oil.

5 Bake kugel uncovered for 45 to 55 minutes, or until it is firm. Serve hot or warm from the baking dish.

Per serving: *Calories 268.8; Protein 10.1 g; Carbohydrates 32.6 g; Dietary fiber 2.4 g; Total fat 11.2 g; Saturated fat 1.6 g; Cholesterol 142.8 mg; Sodium 101.0 mg.*

Menu Maven Says: *Mushroom Asparagus Noodle Kugel is pareve and makes a terrific accompaniment for meat, chicken, or fish. If you would like a richer kugel for meat meals, you can use schmaltz (chicken fat) instead of the oil. For dairy meals, you can make the kugel with butter instead of oil and serve it topped with sour cream. You can also serve this kugel as a lunch or supper entree. Serve a green salad or diced vegetable salad on the side.*

Fruity kugels for accompaniment or dessert

Noodles scented with cinnamon, delicately sweetened with sugar, and accented with meltingly tender morsels of apple make one of the best kugels. No wonder everyone loves it so much! Some people can't wait until dessert to eat it, and this anticipation may explain why some families serve sweet kugels as side dishes for chicken or meat.

Serving a sweet side dish is not as unusual as it may sound at first. Americans like many sweet side dishes, such as applesauce and cranberry sauce. Besides, the amount of sugar in the kugel is up to you. For serving as an accompaniment, you can use less than you would in a dessert kugel.

You don't have to limit your sweet selection to apple and cinnamon. I also like kugels with pears, pineapple, and all sorts of dried fruits, from raisins to dried cherries to apricots, and flavorings of citrus juice and zest or vanilla. Chopped almonds, pecans, and other nuts are delicious additions, too.

Dairy dessert kugels may include cottage cheese, cream cheese, sour cream, yogurt, milk, heavy cream, or butter. A dessert kugel resembles bread pudding, but is made with noodles instead of bread, and just about any flavor you like in bread pudding is good in kugel, too.

As an alternative to noodles, some Jewish cooks make rice kugels, both savory and sweet. They simply mix the cooked rice with the other ingredients. For Passover, kugels are often made of matzo or matzo meal. See Apple and Matzo Kugel with Almonds in Chapter 8.

Noodle Kugel with Pears, Pecans, and Apricots

This irresistible sweet egg noodle pudding is flavored with cinnamon and lemon and studded with all sorts of good things. Dried apricots add a little color to each piece, but if you prefer to stay with the pear theme, use dried pears instead. If you like, serve each portion garnished with a few strawberries, raspberries, or pear slices. A dollop of sour cream is a traditional topping if the kugel is part of a dairy meal.

Preparation time: *45 minutes*

Cooking time: *1 hour*

Yield: *8 to 10 servings*

Keeping kosher: *Dairy if made with butter; pareve if made with pareve margarine*

14 ounces medium egg noodles	*1½ teaspoons ground cinnamon*
Pinch of salt	*1 teaspoon grated lemon zest*
1¼ pounds pears, ripe but firm	*½ cup diced dried apricots*
6 tablespoons butter or margarine, plus a little more for greasing the dish	*½ cup pecans, chopped*
6 tablespoons sugar	*4 eggs, separated*

1 Preheat oven to 350°. Grease a 13 x 9 x 2-inch baking dish. Cook noodles in a large pot of boiling salted water uncovered over high heat for 5 minutes, or until barely tender. Drain, rinse with cold water, and drain well. Transfer to a large bowl.

2 Meanwhile, peel, halve, core, and slice pears about ¼ inch thick. Heat 2 tablespoons butter in a large skillet. Add half of the pears and sauté over medium heat for 3 minutes, turning once. Remove with a slotted spoon. Add remaining pears to skillet and sauté them. Return all pears to skillet. Sprinkle with 2 tablespoons sugar and ¾ teaspoon cinnamon and sauté for 1 minute, turning pears gently to coat them. Transfer to a bowl. Add remaining butter to skillet and melt it over low heat.

3 Add lemon zest and 3 tablespoons melted butter to noodles and mix well. Stir in apricots and pecans.

4 In a large bowl, whip egg whites with electric mixer to soft peaks. Beat in remaining 4 tablespoons sugar and whip at high speed for 20 seconds, or until whites are stiff but not dry. Stir egg yolks into noodles. Stir in ¼ of whipped whites. Fold in remaining whites.

5 Add half of noodle mixture to greased baking dish. Top with pears in an even layer. Top pears with remaining noodle mixture and spread gently to cover pears. Sprinkle with ¾ teaspoon cinnamon and then with remaining 1 tablespoon melted butter. Cover kugel and bake for 30 minutes. Uncover and bake for 15 to 20 minutes, or until set. Serve hot or warm.

Per serving: Calories 339.7; Protein 8.2 g; Carbohydrates 45.5 g; Dietary fiber 3.8 g; Total fat 14.9 g; Saturated fat 5.6 g; Cholesterol 135.6 mg; Sodium 47.7 mg.

Jewish Mother's Tip: Separating the eggs gives a lighter textured kugel. When making this fruity noodle kugel, if you're pressed for time, you can simply beat the whole eggs with the remaining sugar and stir them into the mixture.

Potato Kugels: The Ongoing Controversy

Almost as cherished as the noodle kugel is the popular potato kugel. Family members often debate what is the best way to prepare it: Should you cook and mash the potatoes or bake a kugel from grated raw potatoes? Each technique produces different results in texture and in flavor. What you prefer is a matter of taste.

- ✔ **Mash the potatoes:** If you know how to make mashed potatoes, you've already mastered this kugel technique. You simply blend in some eggs and bake the mixture in a casserole. Like mashed potatoes, the kugel comes out smooth and creamy. To vary the taste, you can add other vegetables. I especially like this type of kugel with cooked pieces of asparagus, broccoli, or leeks stirred into the basic mixture.

- ✔ **Grate the potatoes:** In their composition, kugels made of grated potatoes resemble potato latkes, the pancakes everyone loves for Hanukkah (see Chapter 6), and contain mainly potato, eggs, and seasonings. Like latkes, these kugels are somewhat crisp and may have a crunchy crust.

Creamy Potato Kugel with Leeks

The French aren't the only ones who enjoy the combination of potatoes and leeks, which they use in a popular soup. I like the pair in a luscious kugel flavored, the French way, with plenty of freshly grated nutmeg.

Preparation time: *20 minutes*

Cooking time: *1 hour, 15 minutes*

Yield: *6 servings*

Keeping kosher: *Dairy*

2½ pounds boiling potatoes, unpeeled (about 10 potatoes)

Salt and freshly ground pepper to taste

1½ pounds leeks (2 large), split and cleaned

1 tablespoon vegetable oil

2 tablespoons butter, plus a little more for baking dish

½ cup warm milk

Freshly grated nutmeg to taste

About ¼ teaspoon paprika

2 eggs

1 Cut each potato in half. Put potatoes in a large saucepan with water to cover and a pinch of salt and bring to a boil. Cover and simmer over low heat for 25 minutes, or until very tender. Drain, rinse briefly, and leave until cool enough to handle but still warm.

2 Meanwhile, cut off dark green leaves of leeks. Reserve for making stocks or for other uses. Cut white and light green parts of leeks in thin slices. Rinse well. In a large sauté pan, heat 1 tablespoon oil and 1 tablespoon butter. Add leeks, salt, and pepper and sauté over medium heat for 5 minutes. Cover and cook over low heat, stirring often, for 5 minutes, or until leeks are tender.

3 Preheat oven to 350°. Peel potatoes, put in large bowl, and mash them. With a wooden spoon, beat in milk. Stir in leeks. Add nutmeg, ¾ teaspoon salt, and ½ teaspoon pepper, or to taste. Beat in eggs one by one, just until blended.

4 Butter an 8-cup baking dish and add potato mixture. Smooth top. Melt remaining butter, sprinkle it over top of kugel, and then sprinkle with paprika. Bake uncovered for 40 minutes, or until kugel is firm on top and light golden at its edges.

Per serving: Calories 246.2; Protein 5.9 g; Carbohydrates 37.3 g; Dietary fiber 3.4 g; Total fat 8.7 g; Saturated fat 3.5 g; Cholesterol 84.0 mg; Sodium 140.3 mg.

Menu Maven Says: *This rich potato kugel is a perfect accompaniment for fish dishes like Crunchy Spiced Sole (see Chapter 14) or for vegetarian entrees. If you would like to prepare a pareve version, replace the butter with pareve margarine or vegetable oil and use a nondairy milk such as soy milk, rice milk, or almond milk. For serving the kugel with chicken or meat, you also have the option of substituting chicken fat for the oil and butter, and chicken stock for the milk.*

Vegetable Kugels: From Artichokes to Zucchini

Although vegetables can be an element of noodle or even potato kugels, they can also stand on their own as a kugel's main component. Jewish mothers often find they are a great way to encourage their children to eat their veggies.

To realize the variety in kugel colors and textures, consider how many vegetable possibilities there are. The methods of making vegetable kugels resemble those for preparing potato kugels. You can mash or puree cooked vegetables or grate raw ones and then blend them with eggs and seasonings. With the cooked vegetables, you can also dice or slice them instead of mashing them.

You can make a kugel from a single vegetable or a medley of many. Carrot is a European classic, while sweet potato has become an American Jewish favorite. I also love spinach, cauliflower-mushroom, and a blend of grated summer squash, carrot, onion, and potato.

 Because some vegetables have a high water content, vegetable kugels may also contain a starch element to help hold it together, such as matzo pieces, matzo meal, bread, bread crumbs, or flour. Other options are a little potato, rice, or cooked pasta. For a richer kugel, you might make a cream sauce or, for a pareve version, a similar sauce with vegetable broth or soy milk.

Spice up those kugels!

Kugels of all types are very adaptable. Their neutral flavors go well with whatever herbs or spices you like. I've made zucchini and tomato kugel with an Italian accent of garlic and basil. Some of my Moroccan in-laws enliven their potato kugel with saffron, carrots, and peas.

My neighbor's family loves her curry-flavored potato kugel. You might like to try some traditional ones to get a feel for the basic kugel. Then, if you like, use your imagination and go wild!

Cauliflower Kugel with Corn

I often combine two or more vegetables in a kugel. I like to puree one vegetable and leave the other one in pieces for textural contrast. Instead of corn, you can use peas, lima beans, cut green beans, or diced carrots. You can even stir in ⅓ cup diced, oil-packed sun-dried tomatoes for a tasty surprise.

Special tool: *Food processor*

Preparation time: *30 minutes*

Cooking time: *45 minutes*

Yield: *4 to 6 servings*

Keeping kosher: *Pareve*

1 large cauliflower (about 2 pounds)

Salt and freshly ground pepper to taste

4 tablespoons vegetable oil

2 medium onions, chopped

½ teaspoon ground cumin (optional)

1¼ cups frozen corn kernels

4 tablespoons bread crumbs, plus more for baking dish

1 tablespoon chopped fresh dill, or 1 teaspoon dried

Cayenne pepper to taste (optional)

2 large eggs, lightly beaten

Margarine or a little more oil for greasing baking dish

½ teaspoon paprika

1 Preheat oven to 375°. Divide cauliflower in medium florets. Cut peel from large stalk and slice stalk. Boil cauliflower in a large saucepan of boiling salted water 8 to 10 minutes, or until stalks are very tender. Drain well. Rinse with cold water, drain well, and cool.

2 Meanwhile, in a large skillet, heat 3 tablespoons oil. Add onions and sauté over medium heat, stirring often, for 7 minutes, or until they are light brown. Add cumin and sauté for 1 minute.

3 Boil 1 cup water in saucepan and add corn. Bring to a boil. Simmer for 1 minute. Drain well.

4 Puree cauliflower in a food processor with a pulsing motion, leaving a few chunks. Transfer to a bowl.

5 Add corn to bowl of cauliflower. Lightly stir in onion mixture and any oil in pan. Stir in 2 tablespoons bread crumbs and dill. Season to taste with salt, pepper, and cayenne. Stir in eggs.

6 Grease a shallow 8-inch square baking dish. Coat sides and base with bread crumbs, as if flouring a cake pan. Add cauliflower mixture to dish. Sprinkle with remaining 2 tablespoons bread crumbs. Drizzle with remaining tablespoon oil and then sprinkle with paprika. Bake kugel for 30 minutes, or until it sets.

7 Serve hot or warm. Before serving, run a knife around edges of kugel. Cut carefully in squares and remove each one with a large spoon.

Per serving: Calories 205.7; Protein 7.0 g; Carbohydrates 20.5 g; Dietary fiber 4.5 g; Total fat 11.8 g; Saturated fat 1.4 g; Cholesterol 70.8 mg; Sodium 214.5 mg.

Jewish Mother's Tip: Margarine and butter work better than oil for greasing the baking pan for a kugel, before you"flour" the pan with bread crumbs, Margarine and butter help the bread crumbs adhere.

Menu Maven Says: This cauliflower and corn kugel is good with chicken, beef, or fish. For a dairy version, you can replace 2 tablespoons of the oil used to sauté the onions with butter, and use butter to grease the pan.

Spiced Vegetable Kugel

I like to flavor this kugel of shredded squash, carrots, and potatoes with a sauté of onions with coriander, hot pepper flakes, oregano, and paprika. As the onions brown with the spices, they gain an appetizing aroma and attractive reddish hue, which add interest to the kugel.

Special tool: *Food processor with shredding disk or hand grater*

Preparation time: *20 minutes*

Cooking time: *1½ hours*

Yield: *6 to 8 servings*

Keeping kosher: *Pareve*

4 tablespoons vegetable oil	2 large baking potatoes
2 large onions, cut in thin slices	1 to 1¼ teaspoons salt
¼ teaspoon hot pepper flakes, or to taste	¼ teaspoon ground pepper
1 teaspoon ground coriander	⅓ cup chopped parsley
1 teaspoon dried oregano	Cayenne pepper to taste (optional)
1 teaspoon paprika, plus more for sprinkling	3 eggs
¾ pound yellow squash or zucchini	¼ cup matzo meal
2 large carrots	

1 Preheat oven to 350°. Heat 2 tablespoons oil in a large skillet or sauté pan, preferably nonstick. Add onions and sauté over medium heat, stirring often, for 5 minutes. Add pepper flakes, coriander, and oregano. Cover and cook over medium-low heat, stirring often, for 10 minutes, or until tender; adding water by tablespoons if pan becomes dry. Increase heat to medium-high, add 1 teaspoon paprika, and sauté, stirring, for 2 minutes, or until onions brown lightly. Transfer to a large bowl.

2 Using shredding disk of food processor or large holes of a hand grater, coarsely grate squash and carrots. Put grated vegetables in a large strainer and squeeze out any excess liquid. Add to bowl of sautéed onion.

3 Peel potatoes. Coarsely grate them and squeeze out their liquid. Add to bowl of vegetables. Add salt, pepper, parsley, and cayenne. Mix in eggs and matzo meal.

4 Using 1 tablespoon oil, grease an 8-inch square cake pan or baking dish. Heat oiled pan in oven for 5 minutes. Quickly add vegetable mixture to pan. Sprinkle with remaining tablespoon oil and then with a little paprika. Bake for 1 hour, or until kugel is set and top is brown. Serve hot.

Per serving: Calories 164.6; Protein 4.5 g; Carbohydrates 17.4 g; Dietary fiber 2.9 g; Total fat 9.0 g; Saturated fat 1.1 g; Cholesterol 79.7 mg; Sodium 329.5 mg.

Warning: *Try not to peel or grate the potatoes ahead, because they may discolor.*

Chapter 18

The Pareve Plate

*I*n this chapter, you discover how versatile plant-based foods are and why they are pareve, or suitable for Jewish menus of all types. You find the secrets of Jews around the world for creatively using beans, grains, and pastas. Then you turn these varied ingredients into tasty appetizers, side dishes, and even desserts.

Protein-Rich Products of the Beanstalk

All plant foods, including legumes and grains, are pareve. *Pareve* means that they are neutral in the kosher kitchen, neither dairy nor meat. For this reason, pareve foods are appropriate for being combined with either dairy foods or meat foods in a dish or in a meal.

Old-world legumes with a legacy

Although many beans come from the Americas, certain key legumes come from Asia and play an important part on Jewish menus, both for holiday and everyday meals. Lentils and chickpeas have been familiar foods to the Jews from time immemorial (see Figure 18-1).

Fava beans, also called broad beans, both dried and fresh green ones in the pods, have been popular in the eastern Mediterranean for ages. In Middle Eastern grocery stores, you can find them dried, and, seasonally, fresh green fava beans in their large pods. Green ones are also available at farmers' markets.

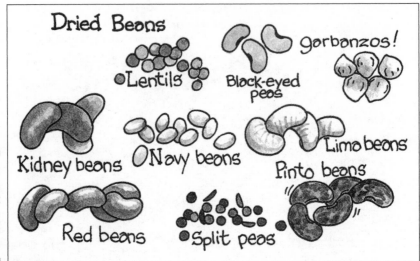

Figure 18-1:
Dried beans
are great
favorites in
Jewish
cooking.

Another old world bean, the soybean, does not play much of a role in old-fashioned menus, but has become a great favorite in modern pareve ones because of its chameleon-like ability to imitate meat and dairy.

Lentils and their biblical birthright

Lentils may be the most famous legume. Genesis recounts vividly how Esau sold his birthright to his younger brother Jacob for his lentil pottage. If only the Bible had given that recipe!

In Israel, lentils are loved to this day, especially as soups and stews, both at home and in restaurants. Often, they are made into a medley with rice and served as a savory side dish for meats and fish.

Lentils are widely available dried. In Israeli and Middle Eastern grocery stores and well-stocked supermarkets, you can also find them canned.

Chickpeas and their ancient origins

Chickpeas, also known as *garbanzo beans,* first came from southwest Asia, where they have been known since prehistoric times. With their nutty taste and somewhat meaty texture, they rival lentils as the best-liked legume in the Middle East. It's amazing that these humble beans can be turned into so many treats, from creamy *hummus* (chickpea spread) to crunchy falafel.

You can easily find chickpeas in cans, and their quality is usually good. You can also buy them dried and cook them yourself.

Mediterranean Lentils with Rice

A favorite among Sephardic Jews, especially those from eastern Mediterranean lands, this healthy, hearty entree has become widely popular in Israel, both for home cooking and in restaurants. It's a simple, natural-tasting dish of basically three ingredients — lentils, rice, and well-browned onions. You don't need to search out specialty lentils; the standard supermarket type is fine.

Serve it as a meatless entree with an Israeli diced salad of tomatoes and cucumbers, or one of yogurt, cucumbers, garlic, and mint. If you like, serve some hot sauce on the side. (You can see a photo of this recipe in the color insert section of this book.)

Preparation time: *15 minutes*

Cooking time: *50 minutes*

Yield: *4 to 6 servings*

Keeping kosher: *Pareve*

1 cup lentils	*Salt and freshly ground pepper to taste*
2 to 3 tablespoons olive oil or vegetable oil	*1¼ cups long-grain rice*
2 large onions, chopped	*Cayenne pepper to taste (optional)*
1 teaspoon ground cumin	

1 Sort lentils carefully, discarding any stones. Rinse and drain.

2 Combine lentils and 2 cups water in a medium saucepan. Bring to a boil. Cover and cook over medium heat about 20 minutes or until lentils are just tender. Drain the lentils, leaving them in their saucepan and reserving their cooking liquid in a measuring cup; add enough water to the liquid to make 2½ cups and reserve.

3 In a heavy skillet, heat oil over medium heat. Add onions and sauté, stirring occasionally, until they are well browned, about 15 minutes. Add cumin and sauté 30 seconds. Add mixture to pan of lentils.

4 Add lentil cooking liquid mixture to saucepan of lentils and bring to a boil. Add salt and rice and return to a boil. Cover and cook over low heat, without stirring, until rice is tender, about 15 minutes. Taste and adjust seasoning, adding cayenne and freshly ground pepper to taste. Serve hot.

Per serving: Calories 312.8; Protein 11.4 g; Carbohydrates 55.0 g; Dietary fiber 8.2 g; Total fat 5.3 g; Saturated fat 0.8 g; Cholesterol 0.0 mg; Sodium 102.0 mg.

New-world beans with multi-ethnic uses

White, red, and brown beans, which originated in the Americas, are well loved in Jewish homes, both Ashkenazic and Sephardic. They're great as side dishes, soups (like Israeli Bean Soup in Chapter 12), and, of course, in the quintessential Shabbat specialty, cholent (see Chapter 10).

In spite of their long history, beans have not been relegated to museums. In fact, many of the old-fashioned bean dishes have been revived in modern menus. Even chefs at fancy eateries use them often.

Beans and other legumes are powerhouses of nutrition. They're a good, virtually fat-free source of protein, iron, and folic acid and contain calcium and other nutrients. A wide selection of legumes is available at natural-foods stores.

When I'm cooking dried beans, I often double the following recipe. As long as you're simmering the beans for a while, you may as well cook enough for another meal. You can refrigerate them up to three days in their cooking liquid in a covered container. To keep them for several months, freeze them in all or part of their cooking liquid in a container. Reheat them gently in their liquid.

The big question: To soak or not to soak

Old-fashioned recipes always call for soaking dried beans, often overnight, before cooking them, and many traditional cooks follow this practice. Today, many cooks omit this step to save time and find that the beans are just as good this way. Skipping the soak may lengthen the cooking time slightly.

At the Parisian cooking school where I studied, the head chef explained that if beans are not old and overly dry, you don't need to soak them. If you buy them in bulk, choose a store that has good turnover. Packaged beans often are labeled with a date, so if they're not expired, you can safely skip the step.

Do whatever is convenient for you. Sometimes I do soak them the night before to shorten their simmering time. I also might do so if I'm cooking a bean I'm not familiar with for the first time and following a specific recipe. For instructions on preparing, soaking, and cooking beans, see Chapter 2.

Savory Beans in Coriander Tomato Sauce

Prepared in the Lebanese Jewish style, these beans are deliciously seasoned with ground coriander and cumin. You might like to add the coriander leaves also, which are sold in most stores as cilantro. If you like, spice up the beans with some hot sauce as well or serve your favorite salsa on the side.

This dish makes a tasty vegetarian main course. If you want it to seem meatier, you can heat some sliced vegetarian sausages in the beans for a few minutes. Of course, you can also add beef, chicken, or turkey sausages instead to make it into a meat entree. If you have family members of both persuasions, you can easily divide this dish and add a different kind of sausage to each half of the mixture.

Preparation time: *15 minutes*

Cooking time: *1¼ to 1¾ hours*

Yield: *4 servings*

Keeping kosher: *Pareve*

½ pound dried white beans, small or medium (about 1¼ cups), sorted and rinsed

Salt and freshly ground pepper to taste

1½ tablespoons tomato paste

1½ teaspoons ground coriander

1 teaspoon ground cumin

Cayenne pepper to taste (optional)

1 to 2 tablespoons olive oil

1 large onion, chopped

2 tablespoons chopped cilantro or Italian parsley

1 Bring 1 quart of water to a boil in a medium saucepan. Add beans and return to a boil. Cover and cook over low heat for 30 minutes. Add salt and continue cooking until beans are tender but not falling apart, about 30 to 60 more minutes; taste often to check. Drain beans, reserving their cooking liquid.

2 Return beans to pot. Mix tomato paste with ½ cup bean cooking liquid and add to pot. Add coriander, cumin, salt, pepper, and cayenne pepper.

3 In a heavy skillet, heat oil, add onion, and sauté over medium heat, stirring often, about 10 minutes or until well browned. Bring beans to a simmer. Add onion mixture. Cover and heat gently 5 minutes. Taste and adjust seasoning. Add cilantro and serve hot.

Per serving: *Calories 244.3; Protein 14.2 g; Carbohydrates 39.2 g; Dietary fiber 10.0 g; Total fat 4.2 g; Saturated fat 0.6 g; Cholesterol 0.0 mg; Sodium 160.4 mg.*

Jewish Mother's Tip: *When time is at a premium, skip the bean cooking step and use two 15-ounce cans of white beans instead of the dried ones. Simply drain them and continue with step 2, substituting water for the bean liquid called for in the recipe.*

Rice and Other Wholesome Grains

Grains are essential to Jewish menus. They are the classic complement for all sorts of foods, from legumes to vegetables to fish to meats. When a food has been braised or stewed, grains are especially welcome, as they absorb the savory sauce and make the dish much more enjoyable.

Many grain-based specialties developed from a cuisine of poverty; meat was often unavailable or not affordable. In modern days, these dishes have regained new favor because of their importance to health promoting diets.

As plant-based foods, grains can be combined with any other foods on kosher menus.

Familiar rice

Rice plays a major part in Jewish meals, especially among Sephardic Jews, many of whom eat rice every day, in pareve meals, with meat, and in soups.

As a simple accompaniment, Israeli cooks have three basic rice recipes: white rice, yellow rice, and red rice. White rice is plain, yellow rice is seasoned with turmeric or sometimes saffron, and red rice contains tomato in some form.

For a pareve meal, rice is perfect because it helps you turn any vegetable or legume dish into a meal. Simply choose such vegetable dishes as Spicy Eggplant (see Chapter 10) and spoon them over a bed of rice or serve rice on the side. The popular grain is also important in stuffings for vegetables and for chicken.

On traditional menus, white rice is king. Aromatic, long-grain Basmati rice is widely available in kosher markets. Once you've tried it, you'll cook it often. It is commonly available as white rice, but you can also find brown Basmati rice in natural-foods stores. In Israel's open-air markets, you see sacks of rice from many parts of the world, including Persian rice from Isfahan. Short-grain arborio rice, traditionally used for Italian risotto, is also great for a Jewish dessert favorite, rice pudding (see Figure 18-2).

Figure 18-2: Rice is a staple on the Jewish table.

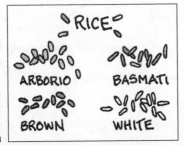

Nutritious brown rice is especially important in meatless, dairy-free meals. With the increasing interest among Jewish cooks in healthful cooking, many are using brown rice in all types of menus.

For holidays and other festive occasions, a favorite Jewish way to embellish rice is with a garnish of dried fruits and toasted nuts. Raisins and toasted almonds are the most traditional, but other dried fruits and nuts make festive variations. For an example, see the following recipe.

Lesser known carbs

Certain grains less familiar to most Americans are popular among certain Jewish cooks. The most prominent among these are kasha, bulgur wheat, and barley (see Figure 18-3).

Figure 18-3:
Bulgur, wheat berries, kasha (buckwheat), and barley are nutritious grains that are staples of Jewish cooking.

Kasha

Kasha, or buckwheat groats, is loved by Ashkenazic Jews, especially those of Russian or Polish extraction. They use it in many ways — as a partner for pasta, as a savory pastry filling, as a side dish to accompany meat, and even as a breakfast cereal. You can find kasha in the kosher foods section of many supermarkets.

Rice Pilaf with Apricots, Almonds, and Cashews

Rice garnished with nuts and fruit is a favorite special occasion dish, especially on the tables of Sephardic Jews. Delicious with vegetables in meatless meals, this lively, colorful dish accompanies chicken, turkey, and beef equally well. You can also make it into a stuffing for chicken or turkey.

Preparation time: *10 minutes*

Cooking time: *30 minutes, plus 10 minutes waiting time*

Yield: *6 servings*

Keeping kosher: *Pareve*

2 tablespoons vegetable oil

1 medium onion, minced

1½ cups long-grain rice

3 cups vegetable stock or water

Salt and freshly ground pepper to taste

⅓ cup diced dried apricots

3 tablespoons slivered almonds, lightly toasted

3 tablespoons cashews, lightly toasted

1 Heat oil in a large saucepan. Add onion and cook over low heat, stirring occasionally, about 7 minutes, or until soft but not brown. Add rice and sauté until its color changes to milky white, about 2 minutes.

2 Add stock, salt, and pepper. Bring to a boil. Stir once with a fork, add apricots, and cover. Cook over low heat, without stirring, until rice is tender and liquid is absorbed, about 18 minutes. Remove from heat and let stand, covered, for 10 minutes. Taste and adjust seasoning. Fluff it with a fork just before serving. Serve hot, garnished with toasted almonds and cashews.

Per serving: Calories 294.5; Protein 5.7 g; Carbohydrates 48.6 g; Dietary fiber 2.2 g; Total fat 8.7 g; Saturated fat 1.0 g; Cholesterol 0.0 mg; Sodium 128.6 mg.

Variation: *To prepare the pilaf as a stuffing for turkey, such as Roast Turkey with Orange Sauce (see Chapter 15), follow this recipe, but increase the quantities and cook the rice in a stew pan. For the cooking liquid, use chicken stock instead of vegetable stock. Use 3 tablespoons oil, 1 large onion, 2 cups rice, 4 cups chicken stock, ½ cup apricots, ¼ cup almonds, and ¼ cup cashews. Reduce the cooking time to 15 minutes because the rice will continue to soften inside the turkey. When stuffing the turkey, pack it lightly with the stuffing. Reheat any extra stuffing in a covered casserole in a 300° oven or in a microwave.*

Bulgur wheat and wheat berries

According to the Torah, wheat thrived in the land of Israel during biblical times. Wheat remains popular in Jewish cuisine not just as flour for making bread, but also as a grain. In its whole form, wheat berries, it enters the cholent pots in many homes.

Bulgur, or parboiled, cracked wheat, is much quicker to prepare than whole berries. You can simmer it briefly or simply soak it in water. Soaking is the traditional way to prepare bulgur for its best-known use, as *tabbouli,* for which the wheat is combined with lots of parsley as well as tomatoes, green onions, and mint. Sephardic Jews are fond of nutty-tasting bulgur wheat and also serve it like rice, as a partner for meats, fish, and vegetables.

In Middle Eastern groceries, you can find bulgur wheat of different sizes. For salads and side dishes, choose medium bulgur, which is the type available in well-stocked supermarkets.

Barley

Like wheat, barley also flourished in the ancient Israel. At delis, you often see mushroom barley soup on the menu. (See Old-Fashioned Mushroom Barley Soup in Chapter 12.) In Jewish homes, it's also popular in cholent and as a side dish. Pearl barley is the most widely available type, but you can find other forms of barley at Israeli and Middle Eastern stores.

For a fresh and light barley recipe, see Sesame Spinach Salad with Barley in Chapter 10.

Age-old fast food

Long ago people in the Near East discovered that wheat kernels could be parboiled, cracked, and dried. This method turned the cooked grain into easily portable quick-cooking nourishment.

Bulgur wheat needs only quick rehydrating in water to bring it back to its appetizing state of a fluffy grain.

Bulgur Wheat with Mushrooms, Tomatoes, and Green Onions

Like rice, bulgur wheat is good as a pilaf, made by sautéing the grain before liquid is added. This pilaf is then embellished with mushrooms, tomatoes, and both sautéed and fresh onions. It makes a tasty partner for a stew of beans, eggplant, squash, or other vegetables, as well as for meat dishes. If you would like to turn it into a vegetarian entree on its own, add cooked chickpeas, white beans, or fava beans.

Preparation time: *25 minutes*

Cooking time: *30 minutes*

Yield: *4 servings*

Keeping kosher: *Pareve*

3 tablespoons olive oil

1 onion, minced

4 ounces mushrooms, diced

Salt and freshly ground pepper to taste

Cayenne pepper to taste

3 large garlic cloves, minced

1 cup bulgur wheat

2 cups vegetable stock, or one 14½-ounce can broth mixed with ¼ cup water

4 plum tomatoes, diced

5 green onions, minced (about ½ cup)

1 Heat oil in heavy medium skillet over medium heat. Add onion and sauté, stirring often, about 5 minutes or until softened. Add mushrooms, salt, and cayenne and sauté 3 minutes. Add garlic and bulgur and sauté, stirring, 2 minutes. Add stock and pepper and bring to boil. Reduce heat to low, cover, and cook over low heat, until the bulgur is tender and liquid is absorbed, about 18 minutes.

2 Using a fork, gently stir in tomatoes. Cover and heat 2 minutes over low heat. Stir in green onions. Taste and adjust seasoning. Serve hot.

Per serving: *Calories 254.4; Protein 6.6 g; Carbohydrates 36.3 g; Dietary fiber 8.7 g; Total fat 11.0 g; Saturated fat 1.5 g; Cholesterol 0.0 mg; Sodium 174.9 mg.*

Pasta from Noodles to Couscous

If lukshen, kreplach, and couscous don't sound Italian to you, you're right. These are pastas of the Jewish kitchen. Jews adore pasta and use it in all sorts of ways, from soups to sweets. Of course, they love Italian pastas of all types, too, from fusilli to orzo to macaroni (see Figure 18-4).

Figure 18-4: Pasta of different shapes is a great contribution to the pareve pantry.

Special small pasta shapes, such as stars and letters of the alphabet, both English and Hebrew, are popular for soups (see Figure 18-5). Jewish mothers love them because they help entice the children to eat their soup!

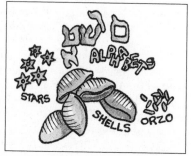

Figure 18-5: Small pastas are great in soup.

Ribbons, strings, and tubes

Noodles, or ribbon-shaped pasta, of varying widths are the most popular Jewish pasta. Called *lukshen* in Yiddish, the very fine ones are used in soups, and the medium-width noodles are loved in casserole-like noodle kugels, which can be savory or sweet. Another Jewish pasta is egg barley, which looks like chopped pasta and may be yellow or brown.

Kreplach

Kreplach are the Jewish equivalent of tortellini or ravioli. This Ashkenazic specialty is made of egg noodle dough with a savory filling. The most common fillings are made of mashed potatoes or chopped meats. Folded in half moons, squares, or tortellini-like shapes, kreplach are simmered and then usually served in chicken soup or with well-browned onions. In some specialty markets, you can buy them ready-made in the frozen foods section.

Couscous

Couscous is a Moroccan pasta so small that many think it's a grain. But it's made from semolina and is really a sort of chopped spaghetti. For Jews of North African origin, it is often the centerpiece of a feast, and its popularity has caught on with many other Jews, too.

Couscous makes a terrific accompaniment for all sorts of foods and is wonderful for soaking up flavorful sauces. For Shabbat, some cooks prepare couscous the old-fashioned way. They steam it at length above a simmering stew so that it absorbs the aromas and then serve it with the stew.

Today, many prefer the quick method of cooking couscous. They simply add it to a pan of boiling water and let it stand, and it's ready in five minutes. Because it doesn't need a big pot of water and has such a brief cooking time, it's the speediest form of pasta.

In some markets, you will find tapioca-size pearls of pasta labeled *Israeli couscous*. These pearls are much larger than the usual couscous and are cooked in boiling water and served like standard types of pasta. They should not be used in couscous recipes unless specifically called for, as their texture is different and they need a different amount of liquid.

Couscous with Sweet Pepper, Pine Nuts, and Parsley

Pine nuts are popular among Sephardic Jews and add a festive touch to this lively but very quick and easy side dish, which is delicious with vegetarian, fish, chicken, or meat entrees. If you don't have pine nuts, substitute slivered almonds. You can see a photo of this recipe in the color insert section of this book.

Preparation time: *10 minutes*

Cooking time: *10 minutes*

Yield: *4 servings*

Keeping kosher: *Pareve*

¼ cup pine nuts

1 to 2 tablespoons olive oil or vegetable oil

1 red bell pepper, diced

One 14½-ounce can vegetable broth (1 ¾ cups)

¼ cup water

One 10-ounce package couscous (1⅔ cups)

Salt and freshly ground pepper to taste

¼ cup chopped parsley

1 Preheat toaster oven or oven to 350°. Toast pine nuts in oven about 5 minutes or until lightly browned. Transfer to a plate.

2 Meanwhile, heat oil in a saucepan. Add pepper and sauté over medium heat until beginning to soften, about 3 minutes. Add broth and water and bring to a boil. Stir in couscous, and remove from heat. Cover and let stand until couscous is tender and absorbs the liquid, about 5 minutes.

3 Fluff with a fork. Season to taste with salt and pepper. Lightly stir in parsley. Serve hot, sprinkled with toasted pine nuts.

Per serving: *Calories 362.7; Protein 12.3 g; Carbohydrates 59.6 g; Dietary fiber 4.7 g; Total fat 8.7 g; Saturated fat 1.2 g; Cholesterol 0.0 mg; Sodium 593.3 mg.*

Chapter 19

Say L'chaim When You Eat Vegetables

In This Chapter

▶ Gaining knowledge about the many faces of tzimmes, a unique Jewish stew with sweet flavors

▶ Finding out about the fundamentals of using veggies in daily menus in Jewish homes

▶ Mastering the making of seasonal stews of several vegetables of differing textures and tastes

▶ Discovering secrets to enticing salads for every meal

Recipes in This Chapter

○ Sweet and White Potato Tzimmes with Orange Glaze

○ Ashkenazic Cabbage with Cranberries

○ Green Beans in Garlicky Tomato Sauce

○ Israeli Salad, My Way

○ Grilled Sweet Pepper Salad

*V*egetables play a primary role in the Jewish kitchen for many reasons. In this chapter, you find out why. You discover numerous tips for using vegetables and incorporating them into your own menus, for everyday cooking as well as special occasions. Whether cooked as intriguing stews or used raw as lively, appealing salads, you see how Jewish cooks use them simply and creatively to provide color and freshness to their families' meals.

L'chaim means "To Life!" and is the traditional toast with a glass of wine on happy occasions in Jewish households. I feel it also applies to vegetables; because they are wholesome, they definitely contribute to a good life. So you can also toast "L'chaim" with a cool glass of fresh carrot juice!

Like legumes and grains, vegetables are pareve, or suitable for any kosher meal, whether it contains meat or dairy products.

Certain vegetables are central to specific Jewish holidays, especially Rosh Hashanah, Passover, and Hanukkah, either through custom or symbolism. For a discussion of their significance, see Chapters 4, 6, and 8. Vegetables in general play a major part in the meals of Purim, Shavuot, and Sukkot for reasons of tradition. See Chapters 5, 7, and 9.

Sweet and Savory Tzimmes

A special stew from the Ashkenazic Jewish kitchen, *tzimmes* is unlike most other vegetable dishes in that it often includes fruit as well. This sweet component makes it especially popular for the Jewish New Year, to help express the wish for a good, sweet year.

Tzimmes fall into two basic categories. One type features meat. (See the discussion in Chapter 16 and the recipe for Sweet Potato and Beef Tzimmes with Dried Apricots in Chapter 4.) The second type of tzimmes is vegetarian and could be considered a glorious way to make glazed vegetables. In its simplest version, one or several types of veggies may be cooked with a little sugar or honey. Often, dried fruits are added and sometimes sweet spices like cinnamon or ginger. When apples or pears are in season, they, too, may find their way into tzimmes pots.

Generally, tzimmes is made of root vegetables. The quintessential tzimmes vegetable is carrots, but white and sweet potatoes are also popular. Sometimes rutabagas or turnips are used. I find that butternut and other hard-shelled squashes also make splendid tzimmes. Some people even make tzimmes from dried lima beans. And why not? Boston baked beans have a sweet element, too.

Sweet and White Potato Tzimmes with Orange Glaze

You can simmer vegetable and fruit stews called tzimmes on the stovetop or bake them, as in this recipe, to brown them slightly. You can serve this citrus-flavored tzimmes accented with cinnamon as a festive dish for holidays or other special occasions.

Preparation time: 20 minutes

Cooking time: 1 hour

Yield: 4 servings

Keeping kosher: Dairy or Pareve

¾ cup dried apples

¾ cup pitted prunes, preferably small ones

1½ pounds sweet potatoes

4 tablespoons butter, margarine, or vegetable oil

Salt and freshly ground pepper to taste

1 pound boiling potatoes

¼ cup brown sugar

½ cup fresh orange juice, strained

2 tablespoons fresh lemon juice, strained

½ teaspoon ground cinnamon

½ teaspoon ground ginger

1 Put apples and prunes in separate bowls and pour boiling water over each. Let soak for 10 to 15 minutes, or until nearly tender. Remove from liquid.

2 Meanwhile, peel sweet potato and cut in ¾-inch dice.

3 Preheat oven to 400°. Put 2 tablespoons butter into 2-quart baking dish. Heat briefly in oven to melt butter. Put the sweet potato in baking dish, add salt and pepper, and toss to coat them with butter. Bake, stirring occasionally, until barely tender, about 20 minutes.

4 Meanwhile, peel boiling potatoes and cut in ¾-inch dice. Put in medium saucepan with water to cover and pinch of salt. Bring to a boil. Cover and simmer over low heat until barely tender, about 10 minutes. Drain well.

5 To make glaze, combine brown sugar, remaining butter, orange juice, lemon juice, cinnamon, and ginger in small saucepan.

6 Drain apples and prunes and add to sweet potatoes in baking dish. Add boiling potatoes and mix very gently.

7 Heat glaze, stirring, until butter melts and mixture comes to simmer. Pour evenly over potato mixture. Bake uncovered for 15 minutes. Stir very gently. Bake, basting once or twice, until most of liquid is absorbed, about 10 minutes. Serve hot or warm.

Per serving: Calories 479.2; Protein 4.9 g; Carbohydrates 93.5 g; Dietary fiber 8.9 g; Total fat 12.0 g; Saturated fat 7.2 g; Cholesterol 31.1 mg; Sodium 183.5 mg.

Jewish Mother's Tip: *To reduce the cooking time and cut the fat in half, microwave the sweet potatoes instead of baking them with butter. Simply cut them in 3 or 4 pieces and microwave them at high power for 5 minutes or until barely tender and then dice them. Then you'll need only 2 tablespoons butter for the glaze.*

Veggie Standbys

Every Jewish community has its traditional ways to flavor vegetables. Naturally, people are always exchanging ideas on how to do so and develop numerous individual variations and family favorites. When I lived in Israel, my neighbor from Morocco prepared her green beans differently from another neighbor from Yemen, and these were altogether unlike the way my Polish-born mother prepares hers, yet all are aspects of Jewish cooking.

Old-fashioned recipes tend to focus on specific vegetables from their place of origin. However, good cooks make use of whatever is in season in their area, and many have expanded their repertoire after moving to the United States or Israel, for example.

Ashkenazic

Because traditional Ashkenazic recipes originated in the cold-climate regions of central and eastern Europe, the vegetables highlighted in these dishes come from that area. Potatoes are used extensively, in creamy salads, crisp pancakes, and substantial kugels. Asparagus, mushrooms, carrots, beets, cauliflower, and cabbage are popular, and so is sauerkraut. Favorite ways to enjoy vegetables are steamed and heated with sautéed onions, roasted in the oven, or stewed in sweet and sour sauce.

Sephardic

Sephardic cooks place great emphasis on vegetable dishes, as appetizer salads as well as side dishes. Naturally, they favor the Mediterranean vegetables, especially eggplant, zucchini, peppers, tomatoes, artichokes, and okra. A common way to prepare just about any vegetable is braised in tomato sauce. Stuffed vegetables are one of the choice holiday dishes.

For festive vegetable dishes, such as latkes and kugels, see Chapters 6 and 17.

Ashkenazic Cabbage with Cranberries

Originally from the Ashkenazic Jewish tradition of central Europe, sweet and sour cabbage remains a favorite. Apples provide a hint of sweetness as they melt into the cabbage during the simmering. To update the dish, I add dried cranberries instead of the usual raisins. If you like, you can combine golden raisins with the cranberries for a more colorful dish.

Although I follow custom in cooking the cabbage until it is tender, I do cut the usual cooking time by more than half so that the cabbage retains a slightly more chewy texture instead of being very soft. You can make it a day ahead. The dish will taste even better the next day.

This cabbage makes a tasty accompaniment for roast chicken or turkey, braised beef, or meat balls. To complete the meal, also serve steamed or mashed potatoes.

Preparation time: *20 minutes*

Cooking time: *30 minutes*

Yield: *6 to 8 servings*

Keeping kosher: *Pareve*

1 head green cabbage (about 2 pounds), cored and rinsed

2 or 3 tablespoons vegetable oil

1 large onion, chopped

2 tart green apples, such as Granny Smith, halved, cored, and diced

Salt and freshly ground pepper to taste

½ cup water

1 teaspoon sugar, or to taste

⅓ cup dried cranberries

2 to 3 teaspoons white wine vinegar or other vinegar, or to taste

1 Slice cabbage and cut it in strips.

2 Heat oil in a large stew pan or dutch oven. Add onion and cook over medium heat, stirring occasionally, for 7 minutes, or until soft and lightly browned. Add apples and sauté for 1 minute. Add cabbage, sprinkle with salt and pepper, and mix well. Add water and 1 teaspoon sugar; mix well. Bring to a boil, stirring often. Cover and cook over medium-low heat, stirring occasionally, about 15 minutes, or until cabbage is crisp-tender.

3 Add cranberries and cook uncovered over medium heat, stirring often, about 5 minutes to evaporate excess liquid from cabbage and soften cranberries slightly. Add vinegar and heat through. Add more salt, pepper, sugar, or vinegar to taste. Serve hot.

Per serving: *Calories 89.6; Protein 1.2 g; Carbohydrates 13.9 g; Dietary fiber 3.4 g; Total fat 3.8 g; Saturated fat 0.3 g; Cholesterol 0.0 mg; Sodium 80.7 mg.*

Jewish Mother's Tips: Use the whole cabbage to make this recipe. It may look like a lot when shredded, but it cooks down dramatically. If you need fewer portions, don't worry; it reheats beautifully.

Always flavor sweet and sour dishes like this according to your own palate. This is a delicate version. Some people prefer their cabbage much more sweet and sour. Simply add sugar and vinegar gradually until it suits your taste.

Green Beans in Garlicky Tomato Sauce

Among Israeli cooks, cooking in tomato sauce is one of the most popular ways to prepare vegetables. Many slowly stew the raw green beans in the sauce. They acquire a rich flavor, but their color becomes dull.

For this recipe, I use a shortcut by briefly blanching the beans before simmering them in the sauce. This method reduces their cooking time considerably. It also keeps their color better, although it's not as bright as beans that are simply cooked in water. The trade-off is the delicious taste they gain from their short sojourn in the sauce. You can see a photo of this recipe in the color insert section of this book.

Preparation time: *25 minutes*

Cooking time: *25 minutes*

Yield: *4 servings*

Keeping kosher: *Pareve*

2 to 3 tablespoons extra virgin olive oil

6 large cloves garlic, chopped

1½ pounds ripe tomatoes, peeled, seeded, and chopped, or one 28-ounce and one 14-ounce can whole plum tomatoes, drained and chopped

1 large sprig thyme or ½ teaspoon dried thyme

Salt and freshly ground pepper to taste

1½ pounds green beans, ends removed, broken in 2 pieces

Pinch of sugar (optional)

A few drops of lemon juice (optional)

1 Heat 2 tablespoons oil in a large sauté pan. Add garlic and sauté over medium-low heat for 30 seconds, stirring. Add tomatoes, thyme, salt, and pepper. Stir and bring to a boil. Cook uncovered over medium heat for 20 minutes, or until tomatoes soften and become a thick sauce but are not dry.

2 Meanwhile, add beans to a large saucepan of boiling salted water and boil about 5 minutes or until crisp-tender. Drain in a colander or strainer, rinse under cold running water until cool, and drain thoroughly.

3 Add beans to tomato sauce and sprinkle with salt and pepper. Cover and simmer over medium-low heat for 5 minutes. Discard thyme sprig. Taste sauce, adjust seasoning, and add sugar or lemon juice if you like. Serve hot or at room temperature. Just before serving, stir in remaining oil.

Per serving: *Calories 153.9; Protein 4.5 g; Carbohydrates 21.1 g; Dietary fiber 6.7 g; Total fat 7.8 g; Saturated fat 1.1 g; Cholesterol 0.0 mg; Sodium 165.9 mg.*

A Salad a Day: Myriad Uses of Vegetables for Every Occasion

When I lived in Israel, one of the most useful lessons in nutrition I learned was the importance of eating salads. People there feel that a menu is not complete without one. Whether raw or cooked, based on one vegetable or several, their lively freshness is essential to meals, even the simplest ones.

Serve them raw

When you think of typical American salads, big bowls of lettuce come immediately to mind. In the Jewish kitchen, other salads take priority.

Israeli chopped salads

In Israel, when someone is talking about salad, it's not lettuce, but a medley of diced tomatoes, cucumbers, and chopped onions. This salad is universally loved in Israel and is often known as Israeli salad. Some variation of this formula is a must for nearly every meal.

Usually served as an accompaniment for any food from omelets to roasts, this quick-to-make salad adds a lively note to any menu. The basic seasonings are simple — fresh lemon juice, olive or vegetable oil, salt, and sometimes pepper. The salad may also be flavored with flat-leaf parsley, green onions, or occasionally cilantro. Some cooks also add other vegetables, such as sweet peppers or a small amount of shredded romaine lettuce, shown in Figure 19-1. Other greens that taste good in the salad are spicy arugula and watercress, as well as iceberg lettuce or cabbage for a bit of crunch.

For their traditional salad, people from Israel like their vegetable dice to be tiny. They look beautiful in the bowl and taste delicious with the seasoning because each piece absorbs it more. In fact, Israelis often joke with Americans like me, saying that the longer the time since I've been to Israel, the bigger my vegetable pieces become!

Popular salad greens in the Jewish kitchen

Jewish cooks use all the common salad greens available at the market, but certain ones appear more often in traditional menus. Cabbage is among the most popular, both in salads and in cooking. Spinach is often used too, especially in Sephardic cooking. Other lettuces, such as Boston lettuce, leaf lettuce, romaine, and mixed baby lettuces, are liked as a bed for appetizers, such as chopped liver (see Chapter 11).

Figure 19-1:
Popular
salad
greens in
the Jewish
kitchen.

Israelis usually peel their cucumbers in salads. I peel those that are waxed. Otherwise, I leave the peel on for its color.

Grated vegetable salads

Depending on their texture, certain vegetables are good grated for salads. Carrots are a favorite. Israelis make them into a slightly sweet salad by tossing them with fresh orange juice and raisins — but in contrast to the typical American carrot salad, not usually with mayonnaise. Some carrot salads, notably those from Morocco, may be spiked with hot sauce or plenty of garlic.

Other vegetables popular for grating raw are cucumbers, radishes, and green and red cabbage. A less known vegetable to Americans is *kohlrabi,* a slightly sweet, globe-shaped member of the cabbage family, which tastes a bit like jicama. It is also popular grated in salads.

Israeli Salad, My Way

To the standard tomato-cucumber-onion trio, I love to add two other vegetables — sweet peppers and jicama. Although jicama is not available in Israel and is not part of Jewish tradition, it adds the perfect touch of delicate sweetness with a slightly crunchy texture. (You can see a photo of this recipe in the color insert section of this book.)

Try to use the best cucumbers and tomatoes you can find. I prefer the small, thin Middle Eastern cucumbers or the Japanese type. Hothouse cucumbers are also good. Choose tomatoes that are ripe but firm. When heirloom tomatoes are in season, enjoy them in this salad.

Like many cooks, I enjoy making many other variations of this salad. It changes with the seasons and with what I find in my herb garden. I might flavor it with chives or fresh oregano, or add radishes, celery, or even bok choy. When markets feature sweet onions, they are a welcome addition. Sometimes I follow my husband's aunt's custom and spice up the salad with chopped jalapeño peppers or a bit of Israeli-Yemenite chilie-garlic hot sauce.

Preparation time: *15 minutes*

Cooking time: *None*

Yield: *4 servings*

Keeping kosher: *Pareve*

½ hothouse cucumber, 1 medium cucumber, or 3 pickling cucumbers

8 ripe plum tomatoes or 4 medium tomatoes, cut in small dice

½ cup finely chopped red onion

1 small red, yellow, or green bell pepper, cut in small dice

½ cup finely diced jicama, or 4 diced radishes

3 to 4 tablespoons chopped Italian parsley

1 to 2 tablespoons extra-virgin olive oil

1 to 2 teaspoons strained fresh lemon juice

Salt and freshly ground pepper to taste

Peel cucumbers if you like. If they have a lot of seeds, cut the cucumbers in half and remove the seeds with a spoon. Cut cucumbers in small dice, no larger than ½ inch. Mix together diced cucumbers, tomato, onion, peppers, jicama, and parsley. Add oil, lemon juice, salt, and pepper to taste. Refrigerate until ready to serve.

Per serving: *Calories 82.2; Protein 1.9 g; Carbohydrates 11.7 g; Dietary fiber 3.4 g; Total fat 4.0 g; Saturated fat 0.6 g; Cholesterol 0.0 mg; Sodium 160.7 mg.*

Jewish Mother's Tip: *Although some people call this chopped salad, only the onions and herbs should be chopped. The rest of the vegetables should be cut in very small dice. Chopping the tomatoes and cucumbers would mash them too much.*

Salad for breakfast!

Even from a brief visit to Israel, the tourist learns the importance of salads on the menu, even for breakfast. Hotels often provide an impressive array of salads of every kind of vegetable, both raw and cooked, making for a memorable morning menu.

Use them cooked

In Jewish cuisine, salads of cooked vegetables are almost as common as those made of raw ones. The vegetables are not necessarily boiled or steamed. Instead, you might grill or sauté them. Often, a meal begins with marinated pepper salad or spicy cooked carrot salad.

Cooking several vegetables together makes for tasty salads. You might boil or steam winter vegetables, such as a mix of potatoes, carrots, and beets tossed with onions or diced pickles. More in the Mediterranean style are such favorites as chilie-spiked eggplant stewed with onions or sautéed pepper and tomato salad with garlic.

Potato salads are loved in all sorts of renditions. Many cooks like to flavor the potatoes simply with onions and parsley and dress the salad with mayonnaise. Lighter, tangy versions of potato salad, dressed with oil and either lemon juice or vinegar, also appear frequently on the menu.

Grilled Sweet Pepper Salad

Sephardic Jews love to serve this popular Mediterranean style appetizer. It is made of marinated sweet peppers of any color you like with extra virgin olive oil and garlic. Most people add a good squeeze of lemon juice or some fine quality wine vinegar.

Garnish the peppers with your favorite Middle Eastern or Mediterranean style olives. I like the oil-cured black olives often referred to as Niçoise style. For extra punch, you might like to sprinkle the peppers with a few capers just before serving them. You can see a photo of this recipe in the color insert section of this book.

Preparation time: *30 minutes*

Cooking time: *30 minutes (for grilling peppers)*

Yield: *4 to 6 servings*

Keeping kosher: *Pareve*

4 large bell peppers, any combination of red, green, and yellow, grilled and peeled (see Chapter 2)

3 large garlic cloves, peeled and halved

2 or 3 tablespoons extra virgin olive oil

2 tablespoons lemon juice or wine vinegar, or to taste

Salt and freshly ground pepper to taste

Cayenne pepper to taste (optional)

12 good quality olives, green, black, or 6 of each

Italian parsley sprigs

1 Remove pepper cores and seeds. Cut each pepper in 4 to 6 pieces lengthwise. Halve any long pieces. Put peppers in a shallow dish. Add garlic.

2 To make marinade, whisk 2 tablespoons oil with 1 tablespoon lemon juice, salt, pepper, and cayenne. Pour marinade over peppers and turn pieces to coat them. Let peppers stand at room temperature for 30 minutes or cover and refrigerate them overnight. Turn them over a few times in their marinade.

3 Before serving, remove garlic. Arrange peppers in a shallow serving dish. Add remaining oil and lemon juice to marinade and taste it for seasoning. Pour it over peppers. Garnish with olives and parsley sprigs. Serve at room temperature.

Per serving: Calories 85.8; Protein 1.1 g; Carbohydrates 8.4 g; Dietary fiber 2.2 g; Total fat 6.0 g; Saturated fat 0.7 g; Cholesterol 0.0 mg; Sodium 229.7 mg.

Jewish Mother's Tip: The first time I saw someone grilling and peeling peppers, it was my Moroccan next door neighbor in Israel. She simply set the peppers directly on the burner and turned them until their skin blackened all over. This works if you keep the flame low, but often the juices run so there's some cleaning up to do afterwards.

Part VI
Sweet Noshes

The 5th Wave By Rich Tennant

"QUIT MOPING—YOU WON FIRST PLACE IN THE MEAT LOAF CATEGORY, AND THAT'S GOOD. I'M THE ONLY ONE WHO KNOWS IT WAS A CARROT CAKE YOU ENTERED."

In this part . . .

Here you find cakes, dessert pastries, cookies, and other beloved sweets of the Jewish table, and you see how easy many of these scrumptious treats are to make. There are baked goods as well as comfort foods like puddings and fruit desserts, which have long been specialties of Jewish grandmothers everywhere.

Chapter 20

Mother's Baking Is Always Best

In This Chapter

▶ Finding out what kinds of cakes make Jewish home bakers so popular with their families

▶ Knowing how to bake bite-size scrumptious sweets

▶ Discovering the easiest ways to have homemade cookies ready when you want them

*W*ith such frequent feast days and other occasions to celebrate, no wonder Jewish cooks excel at baking tasty sweet treats. In this chapter, you find out their secrets to making cakes and cookies that are delicious and not difficult to prepare.

Cakes You Crave

Home baking is central to Jewish life. Throughout history, Jews have celebrated Shabbat as a weekly holiday that deserves a feast, and a sweet treat is a fitting finale. Over the ages, Jewish home bakers around the world have created many delightful cakes, cookies, and pastries.

Chocolate

In my family, chocolate has always been the No. 1 flavor for cakes. We all love it, and some of us even crave it. That's not just a family eccentricity. Chocolate cakes seem to be beloved by Jews around the world. When someone makes a new cake or pastry, a chocolate version soon follows.

From rich pound cakes to light sponge cakes, chocolate is king of the Jewish baker's kitchen. In this book, you find holiday chocolate cake recipes in Chapters 8 and 10.

Coffee

Coffee cakes rarely contain coffee as an ingredient. Rather, they are designed to be enjoyed with a cup of coffee, although they're just as good with a cup of tea or a glass of milk. The most popular ones among American Jews are made from a rich, sweet, sour cream batter with a cinnamon-nut filling marbled through it. Jews in Europe prefer a less sweet, yeast-risen cake usually baked in a fluted mold and studded with almonds.

Apple

More than any other fruit, apples appear in Jewish cakes and pastries, probably due to their versatility, their long season, and their availability in many regions of the world. Everyone seems to have his or her favorite version of apple cake. They may be light chiffon cakes layered with apple slices, dense loaf cakes studded with diced apples, or yeast cakes swirled with apple fillings. Most often, they are complemented by the apple's natural ally, cinnamon, but sometimes are enhanced by lemon, orange, vanilla, or a mixture of sweet spices.

Light cakes

Light cakes rise due to air beaten into eggs. Before baking powder was available, this cake category was the main one outside of the yeast cakes, which are more bread-like. Their airy texture and delicate taste makes them a favorite on Jewish tables throughout the year.

Sponge cakes are made from a simple batter of eggs, sugar, and flour. Usually, the eggs are separated so that the whites can be whipped on their own, providing maximum aeration and the lightest of cakes. To further ensure rising, they contain little or no butter or other added fats. Talented bakers give many of these cakes a luxurious taste and texture by folding in ground nuts or grated chocolate to create luscious tortes.

The role of sponge cakes is most prominent during Passover, when leavening by yeast and baking powder is not permitted (see Chapter 8).

Chiffon cakes are an enhanced form of sponge cake that contains baking powder in addition to the separately whipped eggs The combination of these two forms of leavening — baking powder and beaten eggs — enables them to rise high and become a more substantial cake, so that even the heaviness of such ingredients as oil or melted chocolate does not weigh them down. Perfect for serving at any meal, they tend to be pareve, because vegetable oil usually enriches them rather than butter.

Yeast-leavened cakes

Jewish bakers make all sorts of delectable cakes from yeast doughs. Some are simply embellished versions of challah, swirled perhaps with an apple, chocolate, or nut filling. When sweetened with sugar and enriched with more butter or oil, they become more cake-like and less bready. Depending on the way the dough is prepared, you can turn it into a cake or a sweet pastry.

Yeast-risen cakes are most often served as coffee cakes and breakfast sweet rolls rather than desserts at the end of a meal. Although waiting for the dough to rise requires time, you have plenty of flexibility because many of them can rise overnight in the refrigerator. The results are delicious, and the aroma is incomparable.

Baking cakes has an important place in the Jewish weekly schedule. When I was growing up, my mother baked at least one cake every week, for Shabbat, even when she worked full time. She continues this custom even now, living on her own. She knows there will always be someone who is happy to indulge, and besides, she wants to have cake for the weekly holiday, too.

Many cakes and pastries of the Jewish kitchen originated in Austria, Hungary, and other parts of eastern Europe. Light nut tortes, cheesecakes, strudel, and rugelach are influenced by that baking tradition. Jewish cooks adopted them as their own and adapted them to their lifestyle.

Jewish Apple Walnut Cake

Flavor this cake with cinnamon, orange, and vanilla, be sure to use fresh walnuts, and you will have a winner. In our family, this style of apple cake has long been popular. I find it's perfect for holiday dinners. The cake is pareve, as it contains no dairy products. Thus, you can serve it after any kosher meal.

The batter is easy to make because you don't need to beat any butter to soften it. Because the apples keep it moist and the cake is rich in taste, you don't need a frosting.

You can use either tart or sweet apples, according to your taste. Good tart ones are Pippin and Granny Smith. Golden Delicious is a readily available sweet apple that also works well in this cake.

Special tools: *Mixer, 8-inch square pan, cake tester*

Preparation time: *50 minutes*

Cooking time: *45 minutes*

Yield: *9 servings*

Keeping kosher: *Pareve*

1 teaspoon ground cinnamon	*1¼ teaspoons baking powder*
4 tablespoons brown sugar	*¼ teaspoon baking soda*
¾ pound apples, either tart or sweet (about 2 large apples)	*¼ teaspoon salt*
	¼ cup orange juice
2 large eggs	*1 teaspoon finely grated orange zest*
¾ cup granulated sugar	*1 teaspoon pure vanilla extract*
½ cup vegetable oil	*⅔ cup coarsely chopped walnuts*
1½ cups flour	

1 Preheat oven to 350°. Lightly oil an 8-inch square pan and flour pan lightly. Mix cinnamon with 2 tablespoons brown sugar. Pare apples and slice them slightly less than ¼ inch thick.

2 Beat eggs lightly in mixer. Add granulated sugar and remaining brown sugar and beat on medium speed until the eggs become pale in color. Add oil and beat to blend.

3 Sift flour, baking powder, baking soda, and salt. Add about half of flour mixture to batter. Blend it into batter at low speed, stopping to scrape it down a few times. Add orange juice, orange zest, and vanilla. Beat briefly to blend. Add remaining flour mixture and beat in at low speed. Last beat in walnuts at low speed.

4 Spoon ¼ of batter into prepared pan and spread evenly. Arrange ⅓ of apple slices on batter and sprinkle evenly with 1 heaping teaspoon of cinnamon mixture. Spoon another ¼ of the batter in dollops over apples and spread very gently; this is a small amount of batter, so don't worry. Repeat with 2 more layers of apples, cinnamon mixture, and batter, ending with batter. It's fine if top layer of apples is not completely covered with batter.

5 Bake for 40 to 45 minutes, or until a cake tester inserted in cake's center comes out dry. Cool cake in pan on a rack about 20 minutes. Run a metal spatula carefully around cake and turn out onto rack. Let cool.

Per serving: *Calories 368.7; Protein 5.0 g; Carbohydrates 45.6 g; Dietary fiber 1.9 g; Total fat 19.4 g; Saturated fat 1.8 g; Cholesterol 47.2 mg; Sodium 169.6 mg.*

Spice-Swirled Coffee Cake

Studded with pecans and accented with cinnamon, ginger, and nutmeg, this scrumptious sour cream cake is irresistible. In our family, we love coffee cakes like this one for Shabbat morning, when we enjoy a relaxed breakfast and often indulge in a special sweet treat.

Because the cake is rich, it keeps for two or three days at room temperature; in the refrigerator, it keeps slightly longer.

Special tools: *9½-inch bundt pan or fluted tube pan, cake rack*

Preparation time: *30 minutes*

Cooking time: *55 minutes*

Yield: *10 to 12 servings*

Keeping kosher: *Dairy*

½ cup unsalted butter, plus a little extra butter or nonstick cooking spray for greasing pan

¾ cup pecans, chopped

1½ teaspoons ground cinnamon

½ teaspoon ground ginger

¼ teaspoon freshly grated nutmeg

1 cup plus 3 tablespoons sugar

1¾ cups flour

1½ teaspoons baking powder

½ teaspoon baking soda

¼ teaspoon salt

3 large eggs

1½ cups sour cream

1½ teaspoons pure vanilla extract

1 Preheat oven to 350°. Cut butter into pieces and put them in bowl of electric mixer so that they soften while you prepare remaining ingredients. Generously butter a 9½-inch bundt pan or fluted tube pan, taking care to butter tube and each fluted section, or spray pan evenly with cooking spray.

2 In a small bowl, mix together pecans, cinnamon, ginger, nutmeg, and 3 tablespoons sugar.

3 Sift flour, baking powder, baking soda, and salt into another bowl.

4 Beat butter until smooth. Add remaining 1 cup sugar and beat until light and fluffy. Beat in eggs, one by one. At low speed of mixer, stir in flour mixture alternately with sour cream, each in two portions. Stop a few times to scrape mixture down sides of bowl with a rubber spatula. Stir in vanilla.

5 Pour slightly less than half the batter into prepared pan. Sprinkle with half the nut mixture. Gently spoon a little more batter over nut mixture, using just enough batter to cover it. Sprinkle with remaining nut mixture. Carefully spoon remaining batter in dollops over it. Spread lightly to cover nut mixture with batter.

6 Bake for 55 minutes, or until a cake tester inserted in cake comes out clean. Cool in pan for 10 minutes. Run a thin, flexible knife around tube of pan but not around its sides. Invert cake onto a rack and cool completely. Serve at room temperature.

Per serving: Calories 347.6; Protein 5.1 g; Carbohydrates 36.4 g; Dietary fiber 1.4 g; Total fat 20.8 g; Saturated fat 9.6 g; Cholesterol 87.5 mg; Sodium 181.2 mg.

Pastries You Make in Miniature

Depending on where they live, Jews often bake the pastries that people like in that area. You can find plenty of croissants and glazed fruit tartlets on the tables of the Jews of Paris and chocolate chip cookies and pumpkin pies baking in the ovens of American Jews.

Rugelach

One of the most popular Jewish pastries is the crescent-shaped rugelach. Many bake these tasty treats at home, as they are easy to make and delightful to eat. Most often they are made of a cream cheese dough wrapped around a cinnamon, fruit jam, or chocolate filling.

In recent years, rugelach have become increasingly popular in the United States, appearing in bakeries and supermarkets around the country. This crescent-shaped filled cookie of Ashkenazic origin used to be available mostly in Jewish bakeries.

You could describe rugelach as either a cookie or a pastry. Like croissants, it is made of a rich, flaky pastry. Yet it also resembles a filled cookie. However you define them, rugelach are scrumptious. Walnut and raisin filling is the most traditional flavor, but fillings of other nuts, chocolate, cheese, and fruit are becoming equally popular.

Rugelach are a pleasure to bake at home because the dough is easy to prepare and handles beautifully.

When baking rugelach for serving after meat meals, instead of using cream cheese pastry, many opt for pie dough made with nondairy margarine or vegetable shortening. Some bakers prefer to use an oil-based challah dough instead. These doughs make tasty rugelach variations.

Nut-filled fingers

The Sephardic baking tradition boasts delectable, flaky pastries made from filo dough. Filled with sweetened nuts and cinnamon and often moistened with syrup, they make wonderful holiday treats. They can be rolled into finger shapes like mini strudels or cut into diamonds, squares, or other forms.

Pecan Chocolate Raisin Rugelach

The most traditional rugelach are filled with nuts, raisins, and cinnamon. I find that adding chocolate makes them even more enticing. If you would like to make rugelach the old-fashioned way, you can omit the chocolate. You can see a photo of this recipe in the color insert section of this book.

Preparation time: *1 hour, 30 minutes, plus chilling time for dough and for shaped rugelach*

Cooking time: *22 minutes*

Yield: *4 dozen cookies*

Keeping kosher: *Dairy*

6 ounces bar-type cream cheese, cut in tablespoon-size pieces	*1 to 2 teaspoons orange juice or water (optional)*
2 cups flour	*½ cup sugar*
1 teaspoon grated orange zest	*1 tablespoon ground cinnamon*
¼ teaspoon salt	*1 cup pecans, finely chopped*
½ pound (1 cup) cold unsalted butter, cut in ½ tablespoon-size pieces, chilled, plus a little for the pan	*⅓ cup chopped semisweet chocolate*
	¼ cup raisins, chopped
⅓ cup sour cream	

1 Let cream cheese soften at room temperature. Keep butter pieces cold until ready to use.

2 To make dough, combine flour, grated orange zest, salt, and butter in food processor. Process with on/off turns until mixture resembles coarse meal. Scatter cream cheese pieces fairly evenly over mixture. Spoon sour cream over in dollops. Process mixture with on/off turns until dough just holds together. Add orange juice or water by teaspoons if dough is too dry.

3 Transfer dough to a piece of plastic wrap and press together to a ball. Flatten dough to a disk. Wrap and refrigerate for 4 hours or up to 2 days.

4 To make filling, mix sugar and cinnamon in a small bowl. Reserve 1 tablespoon of cinnamon sugar mixture for sprinkling on shaped cookies before baking. Mix pecans, chocolate, and raisins in another bowl.

5 Lightly butter 2 or 3 baking sheets. Divide dough in 4 pieces. Keep 3 pieces refrigerated. Press one piece of dough to a round and then flatten it. Roll it to a 9-inch circle about ⅛ inch thick. Sprinkle 2 tablespoons sugar-cinnamon mixture evenly over circle; then sprinkle ¼ of nut-chocolate-raisin mixture near outer edge of circle. Press with rolling pin so that nut mixture sticks to dough.

6 With a heavy knife, cut circle in 12 wedges, making each cut with a sharp movement of heel of knife. Roll up each wedge tightly from wide end to point. Take care to enclose filling, to make sure that raisins don't burn from exposure to heat. Put cookies on baking sheets, with points of triangles facing down, spacing them 1 inch apart. If you like, curve each to a crescent. Refrigerate while shaping more cookies. Refrigerate cookies at least 20 minutes before baking.

7 Preheat oven to 350°. Sprinkle cookies lightly with reserved tablespoon cinnamon sugar mixture. Bake cookies for 22 minutes, or until they are light golden. Cool on racks.

Per serving: Calories 102.3; Protein 1.2 g; Carbohydrates 8.1 g; Dietary fiber 0.6 g; Total fat 7.6 g; Saturated fat 3.7 g; Cholesterol 14.9 mg; Sodium 24.2 mg.

Jewish Mother's Tip: *You can get ahead in many ways when you're preparing rugelach. You can make the dough 2 days ahead and keep it well wrapped in the refrigerator. You can freeze the shaped cookies, ready to bake. Once you've baked the cookies, you can keep them in airtight containers at room temperature up to 4 days.*

Small Cookie Bites You Love

Frequent visits from friends, neighbors, and relatives during holidays means that coffee, tea, and sweet treats are often on the table. Many find cookies convenient because they keep well, ready when you need them, although sometimes you need to hide them from the family so that they won't immediately disappear!

Double-crisp mandelbrot

Similar to Italian biscotti, *mandelbrot* is a special kind of cookie that is baked twice. First, the sweet cookie dough is shaped in a rough log and baked. Then it is sliced and each slice is baked again until it becomes lightly toasted and crisp. Italians dunk their biscotti in wine, while Jews dip theirs in tea to soften them a bit before biting into them.

Mandelbrot means almond bread in Yiddish because almonds are the original flavor for these cookies. Today, cooks often stud them with other nuts and even with chocolate chips.

Mandelbrot is another example of an old-fashioned Jewish cookie made with oil so that it will be pareve.

Chocolate chip cookies

A favorite among American Jewish bakers, this treat has migrated to Israel and in recent years has become well liked there as well. Now, Israeli chocolate companies make chocolate chips. When I lived there in the early 1970s, I had to chop my chocolate. To make their cookies pareve, Jewish cooks generally use nondairy margarine and semisweet chocolate, which is usually dairy-free.

Seed-topped cookies

Cookies topped with poppy seed or sesame seed are loved in the Jewish kitchen. They are easy to make from any cookie dough or sweet pastry dough. When you make filled cookies or pastries, such as hamantaschen for Purim (see Chapter 7), often you have extra dough. You roll it out, cut circles with a cutter, and sprinkle them with the seeds before baking them.

Macadamia Mandelbrot

Although almonds are the most traditional in mandelbrot, or Jewish biscotti, and I sometimes make this recipe with blanched almonds. I also like to vary the nuts. I especially love the delicate richness of macadamia nuts in these double-baked cookies, with a hint of orange and lemon zest to complement their flavor. These cookies keep well in a cookie tin for about 2 weeks. Serve them with tea, coffee, or milk for dunking.

Preparation time: *1 hour*

Cooking time: *45 minutes*

Yield: *About 3 dozen cookies*

Keeping kosher: *Pareve*

3 eggs

1¼ cups plus 1 tablespoon sugar

¾ cup plus 2 tablespoons vegetable oil

1 teaspoon grated lemon zest

1 teaspoon grated orange zest

1 teaspoon pure vanilla extract

4 cups flour

1½ teaspoons baking powder

¼ teaspoon salt

1 cup macadamia nuts, chopped

1 teaspoon ground cinnamon

1 Preheat oven to 350°. Oil a baking sheet. In mixer bowl, beat eggs with 1¼ cups sugar and oil until blended. Add lemon and orange zest and vanilla and beat briefly.

2 Sift flour with baking powder and salt. Add to egg mixture. Stir on low speed of mixer, scraping mixture down several times, just until blended. Stir in macadamia nuts on low speed.

3 Dough will be sticky. Shape it in 4 log-shaped rolls of about 2-inch diameter. Do not worry if their shape is not even. Place logs of dough on baking sheet. Refrigerate 30 minutes. Dough will spread slightly.

4 With rubber spatula, smooth dough and reshape into a smoother log shape. Mix cinnamon with remaining tablespoon sugar. Sprinkle top with sugar and cinnamon and pat to make it adhere to sides of log as well.

5 Bake logs for 30 minutes or until lightly browned and set. Transfer carefully to a board and let stand until cool enough to handle. Leave oven on. Clean baking sheet to use for toasting the cookies. Have ready another 1 or 2 baking sheets.

6 With a sharp knife, carefully cut in diagonal slices about ½ inch thick; dough will be slightly soft inside. Put slices side by side on baking sheets.

7 Bake cookies for 7 minutes on each side, or until lightly toasted to a beige color dotted with golden brown spots. First check side of cookie touching baking sheet; it will brown first. Watch carefully; do not brown cookies throughout or they will taste bitter. Cool cookies on a rack. Keep them in airtight containers.

Per serving: Calories 159.0; Protein 2.3 g; Carbohydrates 18.5 g; Dietary fiber 0.7 g; Total fat 8.7 g; Saturated fat 1.0 g; Cholesterol 17.7 mg; Sodium 37.8 mg.

Sweets You Cut in Squares

Brownies and other bar cookies are the easiest bite-size sweets to make because you don't need to shape each one. You simply bake them in a square pan like a cake and cut them. Their charm lies in their richness and intense flavor. For practical bakers, their advantage over cakes is that they tend to keep longer.

Brownies

Of all American sweets, brownies may be the most popular ones of all made in the Jewish kitchen because chocolate is such a beloved flavor. With the dominant taste of chocolate, brownies are delicious also when made pareve, with margarine or vegetable oil substituted for the butter. Flavor them with chocolate throughout or stud them with chocolate chips and nuts to create blond brownies, a sort of chocolate chip cookie in brownie form.

For such good taste, brownies are also one of the easiest treats to bake. When I began baking, I tried a brownie recipe first, and I was very pleased with the results.

Crumble-topped squares

Square or oblong cookies with a delicate crumble topping known as a streusel are a Jewish specialty that originated in the European kitchen. To prepare it, you top a layer of cookie dough with filling — either jam, fruit filling, cheese, or chocolate. Then you sprinkle a crumbly sweet mixture over that and bake it. Before serving, you cut the cookies into squares for a wonderful sweet bite.

Apricot Almond Streusel Squares

I learned to make these tasty sweets when I lived in Israel. They consist of a rich, sweet cookie dough base, an apricot jam filling, and a crumbly almond streusel topping.

These cookies are pretty easy to shape. For the base, you pat the dough in the pan. You don't need to use a rolling pin. Then you make the topping from the same dough mixture as the base of the cookies. By handling the dough differently, you get a different texture. Apricot preserves give a delicious result, but you can use other preserves if you like.

Preparation time: 45 minutes, plus time for chilling dough

Cooking time: 30 minutes

Yield: 24 to 28 bars

Keeping kosher: Dairy

1¼ cups blanched almonds	*2 teaspoons grated lemon zest*
3 large egg yolks	*1 cup unsalted butter, cut in 16 cubes, cold*
½ cup plus 2 tablespoons sugar	*2 cups flour*
¼ teaspoon salt	*½ cup apricot preserves*
2 teaspoons pure vanilla extract	

1 Set aside ¼ cup almonds for topping. Chop remaining almonds fairly fine in food processor. Transfer to a bowl.

2 Combine egg yolks, ½ cup sugar, salt, vanilla, lemon zest, and butter in processor. Mix using 10 on/off turns; then process for 5 seconds until nearly blended. Add finely chopped almonds and 1¾ cups of the flour. Process for 2 seconds. Scrape down and process about 3 seconds, or until dough begins to form sticky crumbs but does not come together in a ball. Wrap dough, press together, and shape in a rectangle. Refrigerate for 1 hour.

3 Preheat oven to 350°. Have ready an ungreased 13 x 9 x 2-inch baking pan. Clean and dry food processor work bowl.

4 Coarsely chop reserved ¼ cup almonds. Reserve ¼ of dough in refrigerator for topping. Pat out remaining dough in pan to make an even layer on pan's base. Gently spread preserves over dough, leaving a ½-inch border.

5 For crumble topping, cut reserved dough in 10 pieces and put in food processor. Add remaining 2 tablespoons sugar and ¼ cup flour. Process with a few on/off turns until sugar and flour are blended in but dough is still very crumbly. Crumble dough quickly between your fingers to separate any lumps. Sprinkle crumbs evenly over preserves. Sprinkle with chopped almonds.

6 Bake for 30 minutes, or until crumbs are firm and light brown. Cool in pan on a rack until lukewarm. Cut in bars of about 1½ x 2 inches in pan.

Per serving: Calories 166.4; Protein 2.8 g; Carbohydrates 16.3 g; Dietary fiber 1.0 g; Total fat 10.5 g; Saturated fat 4.5 g; Cholesterol 40.5 mg; Sodium 26.8 mg.

Menu Maven Says: *To serve these cookies after a meat meal, make the dough using nondairy margarine instead of butter.*

Jewish Mother's Tip: *You can store these cookies up to 3 days in an airtight container at cool room temperature.*

Chapter 21

Jewish Grandmothers' Specials

In This Chapter

▶ Finding out why homey fruit desserts are so loved today

▶ Exploring the joys of sweet specialties from the Old World

Recipes in This Chapter

↺ Fruit and Wine Compote

↺ The Rebbetzin's Strawberry Nectarine Pie

↺ Citrus-Scented Rice Pudding with Treats

↺ Challah Pecan Pudding with Fruit and Chocolate Chips

↺ Vanilla Whipped Cream

*W*ith the amount of experience that tradition-loving Jewish grandmothers acquire in the kitchen, it's no wonder they make such good desserts. After all, they pay close attention to what their family likes to be sure to please everyone. Discover easy ways to prepare the delightful sweet finales to meals that people expect at their Jewish grandma's house.

With so many new alternatives to milk, you can achieve new, nondairy flavor variations of many puddings and other desserts. Experiment with soy, multigrain, and rice beverages, plain or in vanilla or chocolate flavors, to come up with new sweet creations.

Old-Country Fruit Is Back in Fashion

Even chefs of fancy restaurants are returning to the desserts that home cooks have always made. From simple fruit compotes to seasonal pies, everyone appreciates their pure tastes.

In Jewish homes, these kinds of desserts have never gone out of style. Part of the reason lies in traditional cooks' desire to keep meals kosher. Jewish mothers and grandmothers are always looking for good desserts that are pareve so that they can serve them at festive dinners that feature a meat or poultry main course. Over the centuries, they have developed numerous dairy-free desserts. Many of them are composed of fruit. Jewish cooks creatively make use of fruit in all its forms — fresh, dry, and preserved.

Like vegetables, all fruit is pareve, and can be enjoyed at any kosher meal, as a healthy sweet finale to the meal on its own, or as a component of a dessert. See Figure 21-1 for some ideas.

Sephardic Jews usually end a meal with fruit. Ashkenazic Jews often prefer to turn the fruit into desserts, especially for festive dinners.

Figure 21-1: Fruit desserts appear often in festive Jewish meals.

Baked and stewed

Baking apples for holiday meals is a standard in many homes. When I was growing up, I thought it was practically a commandment from above! Pears, peaches, nectarines, plums, pineapple, and bananas are other favorites for baking. You can bake them whole or sliced, sweetened with sugar or honey, and sometimes moistened with orange or apple juice or wine.

Stewed fruit, sometimes called *compote,* is a centuries-old holiday sweet. You can stew any fresh fruit. In preparing this simple type of dessert, you achieve a flavor exchange between the fruit and its syrup of sugar and water that results in a taste experience completely different from eating the fruit fresh.

The technique has long been popular for dried fruit as well. Russian grandmothers gently simmer dried plums and other fruits in tea. Others enhance the fruit's flavor by poaching it in sweet wine instead of making a syrup. Select the fruit according to what's best in the market and what you have at hand. You can stew one type of fruit on its own or mix and match several as a medley.

Good cooks know that baked or stewed fruit are tasty as desserts on their own, but they also make wonderful building blocks for other sweets. Wrap these fruits in blintzes, spoon them into pie shells, or ladle them over ice cream or plain cakes. You will discover countless ways to enjoy them.

Here are some tips for adding interest and variety to your stewed and baked fruits:

✔ In addition to the time-honored choices of wine, water, tea, or orange juice, you might like to try poaching fruit in other juices. Try cranberry apple juice or apricot, peach, or mango nectar.

✔ Do not use wine labeled cooking wine; it has salt in it.

✔ When poaching fresh fruit, try my mother's trick: Add several plums to the syrup. They help to impart an appetizing pink hue to the syrup, as well as a good taste.

✔ Good home cooks — whether or not they are grandmothers! — are practical. When you stew apples, for example, turn some of them into applesauce. For a recipe for Homemade Cinnamon Applesauce, see Chapter 6.

✔ When poaching prunes, you can use prunes with pits if you like. Either remove the pits after soaking the fruit or leave the pits in and let your guests know they are there. If you poach the prunes with their pits, they may take a few extra minutes to become tender.

✔ To make prunes sound more appealing, call them dried plums! It's perfectly okay!

One reason the custom of cooking fruit arose was the necessity to preserve nature's bounty. Stewed fruit keeps much longer than fresh fruit does.

Fruit and Wine Compote

This easy, tasty dessert has long been a favorite on Jewish tables. It is basically fruit poached in liquid with sugar, which form a syrup. The dessert is perfect for making ahead and tastes even better after it has been refrigerated for a day or two. (You can see a photo of this recipe in the color insert section of this book.)

Vary the compote according to the seasons and to your taste. You can make it with firm, fresh fruit, such as apples, pears, peaches, plums, or cherries. For a completely different effect, try dried fruit, such as prunes, pears, apricots, apples, or figs. Mixing fresh and dried fruit also makes for interesting sweets. I like to poach apples together with prunes, apricots, dried cranberries, or a mixture of dried fruit.

Preparing compote is also a good "rescue recipe" for dried fruit that got too hard. It softens beautifully as it gently poaches in the syrup.

Wine is my favorite liquid for making compote, and many other cooks agree. You can use dry white, red, or rose. Sweet wine is fine, too; if you use it, start with half the sugar specified, then add more to taste when the fruit is nearly tender. If you'd rather not use wine, substitute light tea.

The wine syrup and fruit create a flavorful dessert on their own, but for an extra accent, cinnamon sticks are a popular choice. You can also add cloves, vanilla beans, strips of lemon or orange zest, or all of the preceding. Serve the dessert cold in small bowls or spoon it warm over ice cream or pancakes.

Special tool: *Vegetable peeler, preferably one with a swivel blade*

Preparation time: *20 minutes, plus 30 minutes soaking time*

Cooking time: *25 minutes*

Yield: *4 to 6 servings*

Keeping kosher: *Pareve*

¼ pound pitted prunes	*Zest of 1 lemon*
¼ pound dried apricots or pears	*2 cinnamon sticks*
3 cups dry white, rose, or red wine	*½ cup sugar, or more if needed*
1½ pounds Granny Smith, Pippin, or other tart apples	*About 2 cups water*
	1 tablespoon lemon juice (optional)

1 Combine prunes, apricots, and wine in a glass bowl. Cover with a plate that fits inside the bowl to help keep fruit submerged. Let soak at room temperature for 30 minutes or for 2 or 3 hours in refrigerator. Drain wine into a large saucepan.

2 Peel and core apples and cut them in thick slices. Put them in the saucepan of wine. Pare lemon zest in thin strips with flexible vegetable peeler. Add to pan. Add cinnamon sticks and sugar. Heat for 2 minutes, stirring gently to dissolve sugar.

3 Add dried fruit to saucepan and enough water to barely cover fruit. Bring to a boil. Simmer uncovered for about 15 minutes, or until apples, apricots, and prunes are tender when pierced with the point of a knife. Taste syrup and add lemon juice or more sugar if needed. If adding sugar, stir very gently to dissolve it, without breaking up fruit. Pour compote into a glass bowl and let cool.

4 Remove strips of lemon zest. You can leave cinnamon sticks in compote if you like. Serve cold in bowls or either warm or cold over ice cream.

Per serving: Calories 220.8; Protein 1.8 g; Carbohydrates 58.2 g; Dietary fiber 5.8 g; Total fat 0.2 g; Saturated fat 0.0 g; Cholesterol 0.0 mg; Sodium 4.6 mg.

Wrapped in blintzes

Fruit-filled blintzes are nearly as popular as those made with cheese. Apple tops the list of favorite fillings. Blueberry blintzes are beloved as well. Creative cooks use almost any fruit, taking advantage of whatever produce is at hand. Some use raw fruit so that it bakes inside the blintzes, whereas others prefer to poach or stew their fruit before using it to fill the blintz wrappers. For a recipe for blintz wrappers, see Chapter 9.

Enclosed in pies

Pies may be the best-loved fruit desserts on the Jewish menu, as on the standard American one. They are a perfect finale for special occasion meals, no matter what the main course.

Around the world Jewish cooks adapt popular pies from the region's culinary traditions to suit the requirements of kosher cooking. French Jewish grandmothers prepare strawberry, peach, or other fruit tarts with a sparkling fruit jelly glaze. Those in America opt for pies, especially with apple filling spiced with cinnamon. In Israel, many prefer an Ashkenazic version of single-crust fruit pies. They prepare a sweet cookie dough, spoon a fruit filling over it, and bake it with a tasty crumble topping similar to the streusel used on cookies and cakes (see Chapter 20).

The Rebbetzin's Strawberry Nectarine Pie

This fresh fruit pie is inspired by a recipe from my mother's friend, Betty Solomon, a rebbetzin (rabbi's wife) who has long enjoyed a reputation in Jerusalem for her entertaining. She bakes a pie shell and fills it with a creamy strawberry filling.

To simplify the pie, I begin with a prepared pie pastry shell or a graham cracker crust. Next I spoon in a tasty, no-cook creamy vanilla filling and top it with fresh seasonal fruit and a shiny glaze. If you'd like to use peaches instead of nectarines, peel them. The pie is easy to prepare, pretty, and festive. If you have any left over, keep it uncovered in the refrigerator up to 2 days.

Preparation time: *25 minutes*

Cooking time: *3 minutes*

Yield: *6 servings*

Keeping kosher: *Dairy*

One 8-ounce package cream cheese, softened

6 tablespoons sugar

¼ cup sour cream

1 teaspoon pure vanilla extract

1 teaspoon lemon juice

½ teaspoon finely grated lemon zest

9-inch pie crust, baked according to package directions, or a 9-inch graham cracker crust

2 cups small or medium strawberries

1½ cups nectarine slices

6 tablespoons red currant jelly

2 teaspoons water

2 teaspoons fruit brandy (optional)

1 In a mixing bowl, beat cream cheese with an electric beater until smooth. Beat in sugar, followed by sour cream, vanilla, lemon juice, and lemon zest. Pour into crust. Refrigerate, uncovered, while preparing fruit.

2 Rinse and hull strawberries. Pat dry. Halve them lengthwise. Arrange nectarine slices on top of cream cheese filling, at outer edge of pie. Cover center with strawberry halves, cut side down.

3 In a small saucepan, melt jelly with 2 teaspoons water over low heat, stirring often. Off heat, stir in fruit brandy. Cool slightly. Brush or spoon jelly over fruit pieces and then in spaces between them. Refrigerate uncovered about 30 minutes or until ready to serve.

Per serving: *Calories 441.5; Protein 3.8 g; Carbohydrates 51.5 g; Dietary fiber 1.7 g; Total fat 24.7 g; Saturated fat 13.5 g; Cholesterol 52.3 mg; Sodium 258.7 mg.*

Jewish Mother's Tip: *For a pareve alternative, you can prepare the filling using tofu cream cheese and nondairy sour cream. To make the pie low in fat, use Neufchatel or lowfat cream cheese and lowfat sour cream. Slice nectarines a short time before using them. Slice the fruit inward towards pit.*

Old-Fashioned Comfort Food Never Goes Out of Vogue

Comfort food desserts from home like sweet kugels and puddings seem to be what everyone craves, no matter how many sophisticated restaurants he or she may have visited. Even after the delights of living in Paris for years, I always love my mother's noodle and rice puddings no less than her grandchildren do.

For many Jewish cooks, adapting desserts to kosher cooking becomes almost second nature. When preparing puddings for serving at the end of meal meals, they opt for fruit juice instead of milk and substitute vegetable oil or nondairy margarine for butter. Sometimes, the interesting taste variations they come up with this way are so good that their family asks them to stick with these, even for dinners when dairy is permitted.

Rice puddings

You can often find creamy rice pudding at Jewish delis. With its luscious texture and wonderful taste, it's no wonder it's one of the ultimate comfort foods.

You may find it surprising that rice pudding can be one of the easiest desserts to make at home. Accented with raisins or other dried fruit and sprinkled lightly with cinnamon, this lovely dessert is welcome at any season, served warm or chilled.

Citrus-Scented Rice Pudding with Treats

I love to prepare rice pudding this way — it's creamy, luscious, and much quicker and easier than other methods. First, I cook the rice briefly so that it is partially tender. Next it produces the pudding through gentle simmering in milk, which is thickened by the rice. Flavor the pudding with sugar or substitute honey if you like. You can also give your dessert extra depth of flavor by adding orange and lemon zest, as in this recipe, or a vanilla bean, which will infuse the pudding with its flavor as it cooks.

The fun part is choosing the treats to add. Raisins, the most common one, can be dark or golden, but why stop there? Try dried cranberries, cherries, blueberries, diced dried apricots, apples, pears, or good quality dates. In specialty shops, you can even find dried mangoes. For contrasting texture, you might like to garnish each serving with a few banana chips.

Some people love to add punch to their pudding with chopped candied fruits, too; if you're adding these, be sure that they are of good quality. Candied ginger is a favorite of mine, but it's spicy as well as sweet — add it in small quantities and taste before adding more. Finish it with a sprinkling of cinnamon and, if you like, some chopped fresh nuts. Walnuts are the usual, but for an exotic touch, try chopped unsalted pistachios. Grandma would be so proud!

Preparation time: *5 minutes*

Cooking time: *30 minutes*

Yield: *7 to 8 servings*

Keeping kosher: *Dairy*

1½ cups arborio or other short-grained rice	*Grated zest of ½ orange*
6 cups milk	*½ cup raisins, dried cherries, dried cranberries, or other chopped dried fruit*
1 vanilla bean	*Cinnamon for sprinkling*
Pinch of salt	*¼ cup finely chopped walnuts, pecans, or unsalted pistachios (optional)*
½ cup plus 1 tablespoon sugar	
Grated zest of ½ lemon	

1 Choose a large, heavy saucepan or deep stew pan so the milk will not boil over or scorch. Bring 6 cups of water to a boil in the saucepan and add rice. Boil uncovered 7 minutes; drain well.

2 Bring milk and vanilla bean to a boil in same saucepan over medium-high heat, stirring occasionally. Add rice and salt. Cook uncovered over medium-low heat, stirring often, about 20 minutes or until rice is very soft and absorbs most of milk. Rice should look creamy, not soupy and not dry.

3 Remove vanilla bean. Stir in sugar, grated lemon and orange zests, and dried fruit. Cook for 2 minutes, stirring. Serve warm or cool in small bowls, sprinkled with cinnamon and chopped nuts.

Per serving: *Calories 356.9; Protein 9.3 g; Carbohydrates 64.7 g; Dietary fiber 1.6 g; Total fat 6.2 g; Saturated fat 3.8 g; Cholesterol 24.9 mg; Sodium 110.2 mg.*

Jewish Mother's Tips: *Arborio, also known as risotto rice, is available at many super-markets, as well as at Italian groceries and gourmet markets.*

Rinse lemons and oranges before grating their zest and pat them dry. Use the fine holes of a sharp grater.

For this rice pudding, use any kind of milk you choose — whole milk, lowfat, or skim. For pareve meals, you can substitute nondairy soy milk, rice milk, or coconut milk.

Challah puddings

Like rice puddings and sweet noodle kugels (see Chapter 17), challah pud-dings were created for reasons of economy. In the case of challah pudding, you have a basic food — leftover bread — that you have to use up. Thus, it may be the most frugal dessert of all.

Yet, as all bread pudding lovers know, challah can make the pudding absolutely delicious, and for this reason, some of the most famous chefs are proud of these puddings. By making the leftover challah into a sweet batter and enhancing it with fresh or dried fruit, nuts, or chopped chocolate, Jewish grandmas transform dry, uninspiring bread into tasty treats.

To make this pudding lower in fat, you can use lowfat or skim milk.

For a pareve challah pudding to serve at a meal that includes meat or poul-try, substitute soy milk, rice milk, or apple juice for the milk, and nondairy margarine for the butter.

Challah Pecan Pudding with Fruit and Chocolate Chips

Jewish grandmothers know that challah, or egg bread, can be put to good use even when it's dry. This dessert is a cold-weather favorite that started out as a way to use up stale challah left from the weekend. To make it, you briefly soak the bread in milk and then mix it with sugar, eggs, and treats — in this case, apples, raisins, nuts, and chocolate chips. You can add any treats that you like.

Serve the dessert warm, accompanied by warm applesauce or fruit compote and, if you like, with sour cream or Vanilla Whipped Cream (see next recipe).

Preparation time: *30 minutes*

Cooking time: *45 minutes*

Yield: *6 servings*

Keeping kosher: *Dairy*

4 ounces (4 thick slices) stale challah (egg bread), crust removed

1¼ cups milk

7 tablespoons sugar

1½ teaspoons ground cinnamon

½ pound apples, tart or sweet

1 teaspoon finely grated orange zest

2 eggs, separated

¼ cup dark raisins, rinsed with hot water

½ cup chopped pecans

⅓ cup semisweet chocolate chips

2 tablespoons butter, cut in small pieces, plus a little extra for baking dish

1 Preheat oven to 400°. Grease a 5-cup baking dish.

2 Cut bread in cubes and put them in a medium bowl. Bring milk to a simmer in a small saucepan. Pour hot milk over bread. Let stand a few minutes so that the bread absorbs milk. Meanwhile, in a small bowl, mix 1 tablespoon sugar with ½ teaspoon cinnamon.

3 Peel and core apples. Quarter them and slice very thin.

4 Mash bread with a fork. Stir in 4 tablespoons sugar. Add orange zest, 1 teaspoon cinnamon, egg yolks, apples, raisins, pecans, and chocolate chips. Mix well.

5 Beat egg whites to soft peaks. Beat in remaining 2 tablespoons sugar and whip until stiff and shiny. Fold whites, in two portions, into bread mixture. Transfer to baking dish. Sprinkle with reserved cinnamon-sugar mixture. Scatter butter pieces on top.

6 Bake pudding for 40 to 50 minutes, or until a toothpick inserted in center comes out dry. Serve hot or warm.

Per serving: *Calories 411.2; Protein 6.9 g; Carbohydrates 56.9 g; Dietary fiber 5.3 g; Total fat 19.3 g; Saturated fat 6.7 g; Cholesterol 99.5 mg; Sodium 141.7 mg.*

Vanilla Whipped Cream

For dairy meals, many people enjoy whipped cream to accompany a variety of desserts, especially when they're made of chocolate or apples. Somehow, the luscious yet light texture of whipped cream complements them perfectly.

Serve a spoonful of whipped cream to accompany pear strudel (see Chapter 5) or chocolate cakes (see Chapters 8 and 10). A dollop is also welcome with warm sweet kugels and puddings, such as Challah Pecan Pudding with Fruit and Chocolate Chips (see preceding recipe). Do remember, though, to serve whipped cream sparingly — a little goes a long way!

Preparation time: *2 minutes, plus 15 to 30 minutes for chilling bowl*

Cooking time: *None*

Yield: *8 servings*

Keeping kosher: *Dairy*

1 cup whipping cream, well chilled

2 teaspoons sugar

1 teaspoon pure vanilla extract or vanilla sugar

Chill a large mixer bowl and beaters for whipping cream for 15 to 30 minutes. A short time before serving, with an electric mixer or hand beater, whip cream with sugar and vanilla in chilled bowl. Begin at high speed, then reduce speed as cream begins to thicken. For dessert toppings, whip it until it forms soft peaks. To use for frosting, whip it until it is stiff. Do not overbeat, or the cream may curdle and turn to butter. Serve as soon as possible.

Per serving: *Calories 107.8; Protein 0.6 g; Carbohydrates 1.9 g; Dietary fiber 0.0 g; Total fat 11.0 g; Saturated fat 6.9 g; Cholesterol 40.8 mg; Sodium 11.2 mg.*

Part VII

The Part of Tens

The 5th Wave — By Rich Tennant

"Why don't you start with some falafel and I'll finish smoking the salmon."

In this part . . .

In this part, you find kosher menus for celebrating the holidays and for everyday cooking. Here also are useful Web sites for further exploration of Jewish culture and cuisine, as well as tips for success in the kitchen.

Chapter 22

Ten Kosher Menus for Holidays and Everyday

- -

In This Chapter

▶ Designing delicious dinners for the Jewish holidays

▶ Using simpler combinations for everyday meals

- -

*P*lanning Jewish meals uses common-sense guidelines for good eating:
Choose foods that you and your family love and go for ingredients that
are seasonal and fresh.

What's special about meal planning in traditional Jewish homes is that the
menus are kosher. Using the kosher principles is part of everyday life. In this
chapter, you see some examples of how they are put into practice for delicious dinners for festive occasions as well as for everyday suppers. You see
how easy it is to plan kosher meals, and you'll enjoy creating your own.

Making It Easy

Not all menus in this chapter are fast, but preparing them should be enjoyable. Follow a few hints to make it easy and have fun with your family and
friends.

> ✔ **Cook ahead as much as possible.** Many Jewish specialties taste even
>   better when prepared in advance.
>
> ✔ **Share the cooking.** Suggest that your friends and relatives bring some
>   of the food. They'll be happy to participate, and their contributions add
>   interest to the menu.

- ✔ **Buy some prepared foods.** At the markets, you can find plenty of tasty foods to add to your meal so that you can cook as much or as little as you like.

- ✔ **Add produce for good taste, cheerful color, and balanced nutrition.** Remember that produce is pareve, and fruit and vegetables can go with any meal. Feel free to supplement these menus with your favorite seasonal salads and steamed vegetables

- ✔ **If you want to keep kosher, purchase any prepared foods at kosher markets or in the kosher sections of supermarkets.** That way, you're certain that any prepared foods you buy are kosher.

Rosh Hashanah: The Jewish New Year

Include plenty of sweet foods in your menu to give the year a sweet start. Serving this dinner is also a wonderful way to introduce your friends and family to the savory and sweet taste of traditional Jewish cooking. The dishes listed in Table 22-1 appeal to everyone, even finicky eaters!

Table 22-1	Meat Menu for Rosh Hashanah
Recipe Title	*Chapter*
Apples dipped in honey	None
Round challah	None
Pretend Chopped Liver	Chapter 11
Golden Baked Fish with Sautéed Peppers	Chapter 10
Sweet Potato and Beef Tzimmes with Dried Apricots	Chapter 4
Cinnamon Carrot Coins	Chapter 4
Orange Hazelnut Honey Cake	Chapter 4

Sukkot: Supper in a Sukkah

Enjoy these portable foods in a picnic-like atmosphere for this holiday. Sukkot is perfect for potluck so ask your friends to prepare some of the dishes listed in Table 22-2 or to bring their own Sukkot specialties.

Table 22-2	Meat Menu for Sukkot
Recipe Title	**Chapter**
Almost Old-Fashioned Chopped Liver	Chapter 11
Savory Drumsticks with Rice and Peppers	Chapter 5
Sautéed Zucchini in Tomato Dill Sauce	Chapter 5
Jewish Apple Walnut Cake	Chapter 20

Hanukkah: Let's Party

Celebrate the Feast of Lights with the traditional potato latkes and some New World latkes, too. Before the latkes, I like to serve an easy, delectable salad that's pareve and packed with protein. To turn the meal into a complete dinner, I love to include a tasty fish entree enhanced with sweet peppers. Give the children Hanukkah chocolate coins and bake some rugelach and a rich coffee cake for all to enjoy. See Table 22-3 for a menu.

Table 22-3	Dairy Menu for Hanukkah
Recipe Title	**Chapter**
Chickpea and Green Soybean Salad	Chapter 7
Trout with Sweet Peppers	Chapter 4
Pauline's Potato Pancakes, with sour cream	Chapter 6
Fast, Lowfat Corn Latkes	Chapter 6
Homemade Cinnamon Applesauce	Chapter 6
Pecan Chocolate Raisin Rugelach	Chapter 20
Spice-Swirled Coffee Cake	Chapter 20

Passover: A Scrumptious Seder

A Seder is a banquet with many courses (see Table 22-4). Cook them in advance and then relax and enjoy them. Be sure to honor the festival of springtime with plenty of fresh vegetables.

Table 22-4	Meat Menu for Passover
Recipe Title	*Chapter*
The Levy Family's Favorite Haroset	Chapter 8
My Mother's Fluffy Matzo Balls	Chapter 8
Chicken soup (see Grandma's Chicken Soup with Noodles; omit the noodles)	Chapter 12
Garlic Roast Lamb with Potatoes	Chapter 8
Asparagus and Carrots with Lemon Dressing	Chapter 8
Apple and Matzo Kugel with Almonds	Chapter 8
Passover Pecan Chocolate Cake	Chapter 8

Shavuot: Celebrating with Dairy Foods

Will it be blintzes or cheesecake? Well, you could prepare both! Better yet, for this two-day holiday make cheesecake on one day and cheese blintzes on another. See Table 22-5 for some more Shavuot ideas.

Table 22-5	Dairy Menu for Shavuot
Recipe Title	*Chapter*
Feta-Filled Bourekas	Chapter 9
Crunchy Spiced Sole	Chapter 14
Sesame Spinach Salad with Barley	Chapter 9
My Mother's Creamy Cheesecake	Chapter 9

Shabbat: Enjoying the Taste of Tradition

Celebrate the wonderful custom of serving a holiday meal with your family every week. You'll find it such a joy. Try time-honored specialties or vary them with your own favorites. Buy your challah from a good bakery. But once in a while, take the time to bake your own! See 22-6 for a sample Shabbat menu.

Table 22-6	Meat Menu for Shabbat
Recipe Title	*Chapter*
Challah	Chapter 10
Easy Gefilte Fish	Chapter 14
Grandma's Chicken Soup with Noodles	Chapter 12
Easy Roast Chicken with Fresh Herbs	Chapter 15
Challah and Vegetable Stuffing with Corn and Toasted Walnuts	Chapter 15
Green Beans in Garlicky Tomato Sauce	Chapter 19
Moist Cocoa Cake with Macadamia Nuts	Chapter 10

Come Over for a Pareve Lunch

Pareve or vegetarian — call it what you like. Everyone will enjoy this satisfying, delectable, meat-free dairy-free menu and won't miss either one. See Table 22-7 for a wonderful pareve menu.

Table 22-7	Pareve Menu for Lunch
Recipe Title	*Chapter*
Spicy Vegetable Latkes	Chapter 6
Mushroom Asparagus Noodle Kugel	Chapter 17
Spicy Eggplant	Chapter 10
Chocolate Almond Rum Balls	Chapter 7

Supper that Kids Love

This menu disproves the notion that you can't get children to enjoy nutritious food. Kids adore these recipes, including the nutrient-rich hummus and Israeli salad. Adults will like the crunchy turkey main course, too. When you pair it with couscous and finish the meal with sweet and crisp apricot almond cookies (see Table 22-8), everyone will love you!

Table 22-8	Meat Menu for Supper
Recipe Title	*Chapter*
Hummus — Chickpea or Garbanzo Bean Dip	Chapter 11
Israeli Salad, My Way	Chapter 19
Spicy Turkey Schnitzel	Chapter 15
Couscous with Sweet Pepper, Pine Nuts, and Parsley	Chapter 18
Apricot Almond Streusel Squares	Chapter 20

Fast and Festive Summertime Feast

Combine dishes from several Jewish culinary traditions to create a meal that's fun to serve and to cook (see Table 22-9). Begin with two Mediterranean specialties — a salad of grilled peppers and a sesame dip. You can make both ahead and serve them at your convenience. Continue in the Sephardic theme, with the savory entree and its delectably different accompaniment that pairs rice with a legume. Finish with a colorful pie inspired by the Ashkenazic style but made easy, the modern American way!

Table 22-9	Festive Dairy Menu
Recipe Title	*Chapter*
Grilled Sweet Pepper Salad	Chapter 19
Tahini Sauce — Sesame Sauce, with fresh pita bread	Chapter 11
Sephardic Sea Bass in Saffron Tomato Sauce	Chapter 14
Mediterranean Lentils with Rice	Chapter 18
The Rebbetzin's Strawberry Nectarine Pie	Chapter 21

Homey and Hearty Supper

Prepared in the Ashkenazic tradition, this menu features the kind of comfort food that nobody can resist. Offer this warm, welcoming meal (see Table 22-10) to your family or friends during the cold-weather months, for holidays or simply for the pleasure of each other's company.

Table 22-10	Meat Menu for Supper
Recipe Title	*Chapter*
Old-Fashioned Potato Salad	Chapter 5
Old Country Mushroom Barley Soup	Chapter 12
Meat-Stuffed Peppers with Tomatoes, Garlic, and Dill	Chapter 16
Macadamia Mandelbrot	Chapter 20
Fruit and Wine Compote	Chapter 21

Chapter 23

Ten Commandments of Jewish Cooking

In This Chapter

▶ Getting familiar with rules and suggestions for making cooking easy and fun

True, these principles are not biblical commandments brought down by Moses from Mount Sinai! But you'll find that following the guidelines in this chapter will make cooking, shopping, and all aspects of food preparation better and more enjoyable. Keep them in mind when you're planning meals.

Enjoy the Cycle of Celebration

The Jewish holidays illustrate beautifully how central Jewish cooking is to Jewish culture. The festivals revolve around the table. Follow the custom of looking for tasty foods and planning special treats for holidays.

Having plenty of festivals to look forward to, even one every week, gives a sense of optimism and can really help put you in a good mood.

Feast with Family and Friends

After you have taken the time to cook, you'll find it so much more enjoyable to share the fruits of your kitchen. Most families make a point of getting together for as many holidays as possible. In addition, Jewish cooks find plenty of personal festive occasions, such as Bar and Bat Mitzvahs, birthdays, and weddings.

Follow one of my family's customs and share not just the feasting, but the cooking. Planning potluck dinners is fun and divides the time needed for shopping and cooking. This way, one person doesn't do it all.

Take advantage of another benefit of cooking together — potluck meals are interesting. You get an opportunity to sample other people's home cooking, to experience new flavors, and to discover new dishes.

Use Both Fresh Ingredients and Time-Savers

I grew up eating few packaged foods. Few kosher soup powders and cake mixes were available. Anyway, my mother has always felt that fresh is better. The more you cook, the more you'll agree that the wholesome flavor of freshly cooked foods is wonderful.

Get to know your fresh vegetables and fruit and their seasons. When you buy them at their peak, you have the optimum freshness. Shopping at farmers' markets and fine produce markets will help you to find the best and to familiarize yourself with the best ways to use them.

Still, since time is often at a premium, get to know what shortcuts you can use when you need them. Enjoy the taste of tradition without the toil. Make use of your food processor and other time saving equipment to cut the preparation time of vegetables and many other foods. You can even buy packaged chopped vegetables at the market.

Complement your fresh ingredients with time-saving foods. These foods are not simply modern shortcuts, but time-honored enhancers to the meal, like Mediterranean olives, kosher dill pickles, and marinated vegetables.

Even when time is very short, you can still enjoy a feast at home with your family and friends. Cook as many dishes as you like. Then round out your menu with such treats as fine pastry appetizers from a Jewish deli or tasty sweets from a good bakery.

Remember the Healthful Aspects of Jewish Cooking

Try the exuberant flavors of Sephardic cuisine. As you discover this whole new world of tastes, you're likely to find the spicing invigorating and exciting.

Once you get to know Sephardic cooking, you'll probably recognize it as the Jewish branch of the healthful Mediterranean diet. Based on tomatoes, garlic, a judicious amount of olive oil, and a lavish use of vegetables in the menu, it is wholesome, good for you, and delicious.

The Ashkenazic style offers plenty of healthful choices, too. Lighten up your kugels and other dishes when you like. Often, I give a range of oil amounts so that you can use more if you prefer the taste, less if you want to opt for a leaner result. If you have good, nonstick pans, you can often reduce the fat further.

In planning kosher menus, you see that built-in brakes inhibit gluttony! After all, you can't serve cheesecake after an entree of beef stew.

Find Out How Easy Kosher Menus Are to Devise

If the principles of keeping kosher are new to you, you might like to incorporate them into your cooking gradually. You'll find them easy to get used to.

Follow the *Keeping kosher* line in each recipe to see whether a dish is dairy, meat, or pareve. Put together your menus by choosing dishes that are all in one category or that combine pareve dishes with either of the other. After a while, you'll be able to tell, from just a glance at a recipe, which category it belongs to.

Find out about the versatility of pareve dishes by exploring the many options at natural-foods stores. Cooking with beans and grains will enhance your kosher menus as well as your sense of wellbeing.

See Shopping as a Chance to Expand Your Knowledge

Turn food shopping into a valuable learning experience. Exchange ideas and insights with the vendors and the other shoppers. Make friends with the kosher butcher so that you'll find out how to get the best cuts of meat. Get to know the produce person, the baker, and the lox expert at the deli to find out when the best of their foods comes in.

Discover the Wonderful Flavor and Convenience of Long-Simmered Dishes

When you're trying to save time in the kitchen, think beyond looking for recipes with brief cooking times. Like many Jewish cooks, you'll find that slow-cooked dishes may be the most suitable for busy schedules. Often, these types of dishes simmer unattended. They have another benefit, too — most taste even better the next day. Make them ahead and refrigerate or freeze them, and they'll be ready when you need them.

Remember the wonderful tastes you can achieve by preparing stews, soups, and braised dishes. Take into account the flavor exchange that takes place, in which each ingredient contributes flavor to the others as they remain in contact for a long time. Besides, you'll love the way they make kosher cuts of meat so tender and succulent.

Be Frugal

Many traditional Jewish dishes are economical, too. Some of the best came about when cooks simply took advantage of the ingredients at hand. The wonderful meat and bean casserole called cholent uses beans and potatoes to stretch the meat. Many of the best-loved soups, like mushroom barley soup, were also created this way. Take advantage of all the flavor in ingredients. Use vegetable trimmings in vegetable stock, freeze fish bones for fish stock, and turn extra bread into delectable challah puddings.

Be economical with your time, too. Follow the custom in many households of planning to have leftovers. Extra roast chicken and cooked noodles come in very handy for making casseroles or quick pasta dishes. Leftover chicken soup has multiple uses for making new soups, flavoring rice dishes, and braising vegetables. Scrumptious chocolate almond rum balls can be your choice sweet when you simply want to use up leftover cookie crumbs.

Try New Flavors and Cook to Your Taste

No traditional food is set in time like a commandment from the scriptures. Throughout the ages, cooks have tried new ingredients when they could find them. The advantage today is that a much greater wealth of foods in incredible variety is available. Try new tastes whenever the mood strikes you. If a seasoning is new to you, add just a little, and then taste to see its effect. Then add more. If it's a spice you know you love, you can add it more generously.

Consider amounts of spices, herbs, and flavorings in recipes as a guide. Each person likes more or less of them according to his or her background.

With the same recipe, an Ashkenazic Jewish cook may add a few tablespoons of Italian parsley, while a Moroccan one making the dish may throw in several handfuls and then add a bunch of cilantro for good measure.

Even if you're crazy about hot food, be considerate of those who prefer theirs less peppery. Generally, I use hot flavors in moderation in my recipes, following the custom of many cooks. I put hot sauce or salsa on the table for those who want extra heat. You'll probably find this a practical solution, too.

Have Fun and Be Confident

If you're new to cooking, approach it without hesitation. Don't worry about how much or how little experience you have.

As you cook, enjoy the aromas and flavors. Taste as you go along to see how each ingredient affects the final dish. You will learn through your sense of taste, and you'll know more the next time. This is how you gain familiarity with your food.

Many people say to me, "I can't cook." I always respond, "If you cook with love, your food will be good."

Chapter 24

Ten Useful Web Sites

In This Chapter

▶ Finding some resources on Jewish food, cooking, and ingredient sources

▶ Reading more about Jewish culture

*I*n this chapter, you can find sources for both general and in-depth knowledge about all aspects of Jewish cooking. You find out where to buy good ingredients and equipment. You also see how to chat with others about their experiences with Jewish cooking. If you would like to read more about Jewish customs and holidays, you can find this information, too.

Jewish Community Online

A great site for an introduction to Jewish culture, at www.jewish.com, you find brief articles on a variety of subjects, such as the basics of Judaism, Jewish holidays, and Jewish centers in other cities and other countries. You also get news about issues of Jewish interest, advice on buying Jewish gifts and holiday items like challah covers and Seder plates, and a feature called "Ask a Rabbi."

Shamash: The Jewish Network

At shamash.org, which is hosted by the Hebrew College of Brookline, you find information on kosher restaurants, subjects of Jewish interest, and an extensive guide to links to other Jewish sites. The organization states that it strives to be the highest quality central point of Jewish information and discussion on the Internet.

The Orthodox Union

This is the site of the most important kosher food certification organization. If you go to www.ou.org/kosher, you see such features as an in-depth kosher primer, lists of newly certified kosher products, a kosher restaurant directory, and questions and answers about keeping kosher.

Kosher Mall

If your local market doesn't carry enough kosher foods, at www.koshermall.com, you can shop for many of them. This site features a large selection of kosher foods, over 4,000 items including dairy products, poultry, meat, deli foods, condiments, baked goods, frozen foods, specialty items, and Passover products.

High Holy Days on the Net

To read more about celebrating Rosh Hashanah and Yom Kippur, check out www.holidays.net/highholydays. You find information about traditions, the lore behind the holidays, links to other Jewish holidays, and recipes.

Virtual Jerusalem

At www.virtualjerusalem.com, you find a great variety of information of Jewish interest. The subjects featured on the site range from Jewish cooking, keeping kosher, and celebrating holidays to history, articles on Jewish issues, and travel tips for visiting Israel.

Kosher Express Kitchen

At www.koshercooking.com, you find recipes sent in by readers, questions and answers about keeping kosher, and articles on kosher cooking. You also get links to a variety of Web sites of Jewish interest including lists of kosher restaurants, shopping for kosher foods, and information about Jewish holidays.

Jewish Vegetarians of North America

If you're interested in vegetarian cooking, check out www.orbyss.com/jvna.htm. The stated purpose of the Jewish Vegetarians of North America is to promote the practice of vegetarianism within the Judaic tradition. The site includes articles on the relationship between Judaism and vegetarianism and features vegetarian recipes.

Epicurious

Epicurious.com features recipes from *Gourmet* and *Bon Appétit* magazines. From my experience writing for both these magazines, their recipes are well tested. Go to the site when you want an extensive general recipe database. You can find plenty of Jewish recipes as well, from chopped liver to rugelach, which you can easily locate by searching. You also find a dictionary of cooking terms and articles on farmers' markets, food travel, and cookbooks.

Food TV

At Foodtv.com, you can find all sorts of recipes prepared on the TV Food Network in the searchable database. This includes such American Jewish favorites as kugel and cheesecake. You also find information on ingredient substitutions, wine tips, gadgets, food products, and events.

Metric Conversion Guide

• •

*N*ote: The recipes in this cookbook were not developed or tested using metric measures. There may be some variation in quality when converting to metric units.

Common Abbreviations

Abbreviation(s)	What It Stands For
C, c	cup
g	gram
kg	kilogram
L, l	liter
lb	pound
mL, ml	milliliter
oz	ounce
pt	pint
t, tsp	teaspoon
T, TB, Tbl, Tbsp	tablespoon

Volume

U.S. Units	Canadian Metric	Australian Metric
¼ teaspoon	1 mL	1 ml
½ teaspoon	2 mL	2 ml
1 teaspoon	5 mL	5 ml

(continued)

Volume *(continued)*

U.S. Units	Canadian Metric	Australian Metric
1 tablespoon	15 mL	20 ml
¼ cup	50 mL	60 ml
⅓ cup	75 mL	80 ml
½ cup	125 mL	125 ml
⅔ cup	150 mL	170 ml
¾ cup	175 mL	190 ml
1 cup	250 mL	250 ml
1 quart	1 liter	1 liter
1½ quarts	1.5 liters	1.5 liters
2 quarts	2 liters	2 liters
2½ quarts	2.5 liters	2.5 liters
3 quarts	3 liters	3 liters
4 quarts	4 liters	4 liters

Weight

U.S. Units	Canadian Metric	Australian Metric
1 ounce	30 grams	30 grams
2 ounces	55 grams	60 grams
3 ounces	85 grams	90 grams
4 ounces (¼ pound)	115 grams	125 grams
8 ounces (½ pound)	225 grams	225 grams
16 ounces (1 pound)	455 grams	500 grams
1 pound	455 grams	1/2 kilogram

Measurements

Inches	Centimeters
½	1.5
1	2.5
2	5.0
3	7.5
4	10.0
5	12.5
6	15.0
7	17.5
8	20.5
9	23.0
10	25.5
11	28.0
12	30.5
13	33.0

Temperature (Degrees)

Fahrenheit	Celsius
32	0
212	100
250	120
275	140
300	150
325	160

(continued)

Temperature (Degrees) *(continued)*

Fahrenheit	Celsius
350	180
375	190
400	200
425	220
450	230
475	240
500	260

Index

• C •

Notes

Notes